The Crea

The Creative Tree

Active Participation in the Arts for People who are Disadvantaged

Edited by Gina Levete

Michael Russell

First published in Great Britain 1987
by Michael Russell (Publishing) Ltd
The Chantry, Wilton, Salisbury, Wiltshire
Typeset by Arrow Typesetting, Bournemouth
Printed and bound in Great Britain
by Biddles Ltd, Guildford and King's Lynn

Interlink
114 Gloucester Terrace, London W2 6HP

ISBN 0 85955 139 3

For a human heart

Contents

Acknowledgements

As Director of the Interlink Trust, I should like to acknowledge the support of the Leverhulme Trust, the Royal Jubilee Trusts, the World Association of Christian Churches and Günther Dahl. This book was made possible by their generosity. The Trustees would also like to thank John Hale, the Lady Hoare Trust, and Occidental International Oil for their contributions. I must record my personal thanks to the Trustees of Interlink, and to Charlotte Coudrille and Michael Russell for helping to produce the book; and also to all those individuals and organisations who have supported Interlink over the years – in particular Fondation de France, Duncan Lawrie Ltd., the Leverhulme Trust, a Swiss Foundation which wishes to remain anonymous, and the Overseas Administration.

GINA LEVETE

Foreword

Active involvement in the visual arts, in poetry, dance, drama or music, is still confined to a small minority, and while appreciation of these arts has spread widely, participation occupies only a small part of the daily concerns of most people. Maybe the complexity of daily living and the materialism of our society are inimical to the development of a wider role for these activities; or, possibly, when it comes to developing a deeper appreciation or acquiring the skills necessary for participation, human nature is just disinclined to accept the disciplines involved. As a result the majority is not significantly interested.

In our society, the less successfully competitive need not suffer the physical deprivation they would have faced a hundred years ago. However, expectations have risen while family and community bonds have weakened, so that there are still people living both in isolation and in deplorable conditions; and isolation by its very nature discourages contact with artistic activity, the very experience that can engender enthusiasm, companionship and a counter-measure to despair. Prominent among the socially deprived are people with severe physical handicaps who are too often not fortunate enough to get the best help (at least in theory) that can be offered. The same applies to those with mental handicap or emotional problems, or a combination of these.

My own involvement in the arts has been unexceptional, but I was particularly fortunate to meet a dancer working with severely physically disabled children at the hospital to which I was appointed as a consultant paediatrician in 1969. I had rapidly become aware of the isolation affecting many handicapped children and their families, and of the practical difficulties they faced in experiencing many things which most people take for granted. This resulted in an impoverishment of their life experience, sometimes so extreme as to lead to apathy and resistance to attempts to help their independence by special training in a specialised centre. It became apparent that the introduction of drama, imaginative play and story participation, symbolic movement, and many other activities involving the arts, exerted a restorative effect on some children, elevating mood, improving the effectiveness of treatment and, seemingly, their enjoyment of life.

In retrospect this seems quite basic, it could hardly be otherwise; yet much professional and some personal resistance had to be overcome. Many people may still regard the arts as an optional extra in life and begrudge any resources spent on them for the handicapped: I can only assure them of the folly of that view. A breakdown of isolation and expansion of experience of life increases the motivation to use whatever independence is possible; and without such motivation, conventional treatment may lose much of its value. I feel sad that this may still be worth saying some thirty-five centuries of human experience after the creation of the beautiful frescoes of Mycenae and Thera. If there were such ancient communities able to delight in creative art, could we not hope to advance, before the end of this century, to the point where this delight could be shared by everyone?

Creativity is a curious thing. There is probably not enough of it around, and preoccupation with material needs discourages its development or expression. Yet experience suggests that, given the right opportunity or stimulus, many people can be artistically creative. That is what this book is about. It is challenging, in that the readers who feel in tune with the pioneers in this field are unlikely to make their lives easier and may well face a lonely battle against ignorance, prejudice and indifference. Their reward will be in knowing the benefit to those who are helped to find something enriching that they might otherwise never have experienced.

CLAUS NEWMAN

Claus Newman, MB, FRCP, DCH, *Consultant Paediatrician for the Westminster Hospital Group and Queen Mary's Hospital, Roehampton (Leon Gillis Unit), has been encouraging and supporting the use of arts since 1969. His help and involvement have done much to spread the activities described in* The Creative Tree *throughout the United Kingdom.*

The History of Interlink

Gina Levete, a dancer, has worked for a number of years in the field of establishing arts opportunities for disabled and disadvantaged people. Between 1964 and 1972 she worked freelance in the United Kingdom using dance movement with the disabled, including thalidomide children, and her subsequent research uncovered a gap in the arts provision and a need for creative activities amongst the disabled, ill and disadvantaged. In 1976 she decided to create a free link service, which would offer the performing and participatory arts to any area of social disadvantage, while at the same time encouraging similar regional schemes outside London. She founded Shape in 1976 which has now developed into a very successful United Kingdom national network.

During 1979 it became apparent to her that there was a gap in communication between countries in the exchange of information about this kind of work. She therefore decided to establish an international communications exchange network and, with the active support of the trustees, left Shape in 1980. From 1980 to 1981 she undertook initial research to establish that there was a need for such a service. Interlink became operative in January 1982, with small grants from UNESCO Fund for the Promotion of Culture, Fondation de France, and the Manpower Services Commission, United Kingdom.

THE SERVICES PROVIDED BY INTERLINK

1 The international service gathered together and provided information on the creative activities that existed within nations.

2 Issued an international newsletter, *Positif*, that enabled people from different countries to write about their work or needs.

3 Offered a free arts advisory service that helped set up arts projects in other countries. The service could be used by large or small organisations.

4 Arranged short creative arts courses and 'Ideas' training sessions. A team of visiting artists with various skills gave participatory workshops to staff of local artists and disabled students.

Interlink Arts Advisory Service has worked in many countries to help set up local independent arts services. The Trustees of Interlink decided that an important project for Interlink should be the writing of *The Creative Tree*, which would leave a form of the Arts Advisory Service in print for many new initiatives to be introduced.

ORGANISATIONS AND PROJECTS SET UP THROUGH INTERLINK

India Interlink, Calcutta (established 1984): a link service between artists and areas of poverty, illness and disability.

'Utsah' (1985): a puppet project working in Amedabad.

'People of This World' (1986): performing group puppets made with disabilities.

Okhla Centre, Delhi (school for mentally disabled children): an extensive arts programme (1984).

Interlink, **Sri Lanka** (1984): link service.

'ZITA', **Zimbabwe** (1985): Zimbabwe Integration Through Arts, Harare, Bulawayo: two link services.

'Tose Sonke' (1985): educational theatre group of amateur actors with and without physical disabilities.

Interlink Hermosilla, **Mexico** (1986): link service.

As a direct result of Interlink Arts Advisory Service new arts programmes have been introduced in France, Poland, New Zealand, Hong Kong and Colombia (1983-86).

Introduction

This book is for anyone interested in setting up an arts project or programme anywhere in the world. It is particularly directed towards those who are working with people isolated by their disadvantaged circumstances, but it is applicable, too, to general community or educational work. *The Creative Tree* is written to provide Interlink's Arts Advisory Service in print. We hope to inspire professional staff, therapists, nurses, doctors, psychiatrists and consultants to introduce new creative programmes into their work environments. We hope that it will encourage artists or art organisations to take the initiative and introduce themselves to pockets of the community where creativity is neglected. The book is to be an answer to what we imagine could be your queries and to lay a foundation from which you can begin. It is written by people working in the arts who have been sharing their skills with people who are disadvantaged. Their interaction with these important groups of a community are beginning to fill in creative gaps. They and their students are now becoming part of the 'creative tree'. Enjoyment, integration, self-expression, a sense of purpose, a feeling of belonging, a realisation of independence, discovery and achievement, are but a few of the leaves that stem from the tree.

The book first sets out how to begin and what can be done. The chapters do not describe a technique but ways in which different art forms can be applied and introduced. We write about how to set up an activity; the value and magic of the art form; cost, materials required, where to find a tutor if readers do not feel able to undertake the activity themselves. There are more general chapters on fund-raising, training, a section on link services which can put artists in touch with new groups of people.'Integration' gives examples of projects which have enlisted the involvement of one group to help another. How theatre performances by actors with disabilities can develop public awareness and understanding. Another chapter describes the work with people who have a terminal illness. The second part of the book is an International Directory of Ideas, with addresses and brief analyses of projects world wide, together with appendices on therapy training courses and markets for craft products.

EXPLANATION OF TERMINOLOGY

1 We ask readers to be patient with the terminology describing a disability or situation. What is acceptable in one country may not be elsewhere. Therefore our thought has been to specify any group or individual first and foremost by themselves and subsequently affix the disability, e.g., 'student with a physical handicap'.

2 Arts: the arts include activities which fall under the heading dance, drama, puppetry, poetry, creative writing, music, visual art, video photography, crafts, flower arranging, garden design.

3 Artists – when referring to artists or crafts people we obviously include those of us who are disabled.

4 Artistic therapy: this book does not discuss artistic therapy separately, i.e. art, dance, drama or music therapists. Such people have had a specialised art training and then continued with a training in therapy. The Directory lists a number of these therapy training courses.

5 Therapists: some occupational or physiotherapists do arrange or undertake arts activities themselves; they are indeed creative people. However, it is partly because of their requests to Interlink for guidance and help that this handbook has come into being.

6 'Workshop' is a word often used instead of 'session' or 'class'. For the purpose of this book a workshop is a regular weekly activity lasting one or more hours in which students (of any age) can participate.

WHO NEEDS AN ARTS PROGRAMME?

Is active creative participation something that we feel is enriching for special minority groups of people throughout the world? Do the arts have a role to play in the lives of those who are ill? If so, what is this role? Is it to aid recovery, or as a diversion, a stimulus, an outlet for communication, an opportunity for self-expression? Is it essential to provide creative stimulus for elderly people? Should arts programmes be a serious part of rehabilitative programmes? Does it help to make a creative environment within prisons? Can young unemployed people be stimulated and given an incentive by involving themselves in arts activities? Should we ensure that the worlds of culture and entertainment open their doors to special groups and thus encourage such people to mix in a new environment?

If the answer to these questions is in the affirmative – and it is – then why is it that most countries still do not regard this aspect of self-development as any more serious than dimly benign, usually provided only if someone else pays? Why is there so little centralised information on a country's involvement in these areas and aspects of the arts? Why has there been no serious attempt until the emergence of Interlink to gather this data internationally? I think the fault is partly our own. The artists and administrators who work creatively in this field tend to talk to the converted, rather than to those who make the cultural, educational and social welfare policies of a nation. Our energies have not been sufficiently applied to lobbying the policy-makers – to make them take notice and see for themselves the healing and wider potentialities of the arts. Because we have not done this as an international body we have suffered from a gap in communication. Therefore much of the valuable work done in this area is fragmented and loses the impact of cohesive effort.

At present most of this work is dependent on voluntary financial support. In many countries where it is successfully practised its growth is restricted by lack of funding. In other countries it has hardly begun, not only for financial reasons but because until Interlink came into being there was no central network through which to communicate. Which is why this book affords a bridge between learning and sharing.

Every human being is creative in some way. Many people wish to be creative through channels that do not involve the arts. Certainly artists do not have the monopoly on creativity – indeed there is a view that the most creative act is to be quite still and empty of thought. Nevertheless here we focus on the role art can play in freeing the creative energy, even for those whose lives are lived with illness, disability or abject poverty, and whose priorities are nourishment, shelter and health care. It has the capacity to 'foster' the spirit; by providing ways to be creative we can help it succeed.

ART IN TERMINAL ILLNESS

We have learned to alleviate physical pain and physical symptoms but we have not found ways to ease the grief of parting, or to come fully to terms with physical weakness and immobility. Art activities can be used in a terminal structure to provide stimulus and improve communication, and as a way of developing creativity for its own sake. Such therapy programmes can help people deal with the inner turmoil that frequently attends terminal illness – and can help the patient's family too, if they become involved as well.

ART IN MENTAL ILLNESS

Psychiatric hospitals are all too often the Cinderellas of a society. Interlink has visited them in many parts of the world. In some instances there have been only two desperately overworked occupational therapists endeavouring to provide some kind of stimulus and diversion for over two thousand patients. Here is an area where artists or arts organisations really can play a healing role and do have a responsibility to introduce themselves. There are those hospitals which have lively arts programmes and clearly believe in them; indeed under the umbrella of the arts some hospitals now explore the potential of many forms of Eastern movement, relaxation and meditation. Holland in particular is using meditation practice to help heal some psychiatric patients. If any of these activities can assist in reducing the need for tranquillising drugs and medication, it can only be good.

It is essential that when introducing an arts activity or programme the consultant psychiatrists and hospital administration are made aware of and in some way involved in the programme from the outset. Too often it is left to the therapists to organise these activities alone and perhaps too the doctors may have reservations because the effects cannot be scientifically measured. What is possible is an intuitive assessment or evaluation of the patient's response; which is why the staff's own participation is important, so that they can see for themselves.

ART IN ADDICTION AND REHABILITATION

For people who have an illness of dependency, art is a communication outlet. Dance or drama therapy have enabled people to look at themselves from the outside, poetry and writing provide a release for pain, visual art discovery. In such situations the tutor needs to work closely with the rest of a medical team. Finding the right person is important.

For the artist the work can have its lighter moments. A mime artist working with two boys who were weaned from hard drugs had one of his students so eager to attend the workshop that he always arrived early. The tutor enquired what he liked about mime. His reply was: 'I reckon if I get really good at playing another part, when I next come up against a judge and he asks me if I'll behave, your classes will help me convince him.'

ART IN PRISON

Art in a prison environment provides a link with normality. There are a number of interesting and effective programmes in many countries, but too few. The reason for this is often the attitude of the prison staff. The governor of an establishment may welcome a number of different arts activities, but some staff feel it will involve them in extra work, or that it is a security risk, or that prison treatment is meant to be punitive, and creativity is a luxury. Once an activity is under way these fears are usually allayed because the inmates respond so positively. However, it should be said that there are projects which have failed because the visiting tutors became too emotionally involved with the situations of their students. Here again it is essential to find the right person with an objective view who is primarily interested in communicating his or her skill to a new group of people.

ART AND DISABILITY

Providing a wide range of opportunities to participate in the arts gives people who have a mental disability a new way to break through and integrate into a community by developing independence, confidence and dignity. It is now being recognised that such students' creative ability and potential has been frequently under-assessed.

The reasons for providing creative opportunities for people with physical disabilities are the same reasons as for the rest of us, but there are practical distinctions. Often the facilities which make it possible to participate are not provided. There are a number of reasons for this, and with determination all of them can be overcome. If students want to work creatively in public places, transport and access are needed. Access is the severest problem and planning departments must face up to the situation. Volunteer helpers should be organised for people with severe physical limitations. We must arrange for activities to be taken into institutions or centres if students are unable to work outside.

A wide choice of art forms should be available and care must be taken not to decide for students what you feel they are capable of or what is suitable for them. For example if a student who is limbless wishes to take a creative movement class, or a student who is deaf chooses to make music, he or she should be able to so so. Challenging the disability and improvising can be stimulating in itself.

The arts world needs to recognise the ability and talent of some of these students. It is difficult enough for any artists to make a start, but it is much more difficult if you are disabled. Modifications to the teaching syllabus might be introduced so that disabled people could pursue a professional training alongside able-bodied young artists. Happily the situation is changing for the better in some countries, with many performing groups who have disabilities making an impact for their ability rather than because of their disability.

ELDERLY PEOPLE: A NEW DIMENSION

The weakening of the family unit in the West means that many older people are abandoned at the time when they most need family support. In other parts of the world to be old is to be respected, and it is a welcome relief to see this applied – particularly after visiting some of the old people's homes in the United Kingdom. Encouraging older people to be actively creative through art, perhaps to see them discover a hidden talent which they had no time to develop during their working lives, is a real pleasure for those of us who work with them.

The United States is an example to us all in its imaginative arts provision for the elderly. Very often older people take matters into their own hands and organise their own projects. A reader can pick up many ideas from the Directory on projects for the elderly. The older generations are very definitely the roots to the creative tree, and there are many skills which the older person can pass down to the younger. Admittedly, the very frail can probably only enjoy the arts through being entertained. Stroke patients of all ages require mental and physical stimulus. Gentle workshops in the visual arts, puppetry, movement and creative writing can provide this.

THE FORGOTTEN GREY AREAS

The Creative Tree shows what can be done, and some of what is being done, but it would be misleading to make the picture look too rosy. In the United Kingdom and many other countries where people with disabilities are now enabled to participate actively in the arts, we still tend to forget or neglect those environments where institutionalised people are unable to speak for themselves, institutions where people with chronic illnesses or disabilities will remain for the rest of their lives, either because the family is unable to care for them, or because they have no one. Hardly any of us realise these homes exist. In them live the forgotten people of our society. They have little to do but watch television and wait. This is no reflection on these dedicated staff who look after them, and indeed their lives too can be isolated by the nature of their work.

In the United Kingdom there are contradictions. With all the sensitivity that is being directed to choosing the words by which people with disabilities prefer to be described, we still make no protest when some places are entitled 'homes for the incurable'. What an address if you have to live there for the rest of your life! Equally there is a contradiction that for all our progress what should be priority areas are still, creatively, so neglected. Both disabled and able-bodied people who have a voice in the arts must ensure that the forgotten people are remembered. Some of us who think of ourselves as artists can make a contribution to these environments by introducing ourselves, our work and its energy.

ART: INCLUDE US ALL

Art should include all the various pockets of a world community, from the abjectly poor to the wealthy, from the refugee in a transit camp to the housewife with security. What this chapter is suggesting is simply that those people whose circumstances are so very disadvantaged should have proportionately more encouragement and provision of opportunities than those of us who are more fortunate.

TAKE A RISK

The following chapters will advise you how to begin. That is the great thing – to begin. If you feel hesitant and think it is a bit of a risk, take it. Sometimes exciting ideas come to nothing because problems overshadow the moment of planning. To turn a concept into a reality there is always an element of risk. It is rarely possible to start with all the required assets; but if you really want to do something, it is surprising how often you can.

GINA LEVETE

1

Shape: How to Start a Link Service

In localities or countries where bringing the arts to disadvantaged people is a relatively new concept, one of the most effective ways of converting the idea into reality is through link or intermediary organisation. A clear definition of the role of such a service is described in a report issued by the Carnegie United Kingdom Trust of the Committee of Inquiry into the Arts and Disabled People.*

> Intermediary organisations have developed to provide a bridge between artists who are interested to work with people who have special needs and institutions and authorities which wish to utilise the arts but have neither the experience nor the expertise to know how best to proceed. The framework of support and administration which they have created has relieved artists from the problems of fund-raising, marketing their services and negotiating terms, while it has helped institutions of all kinds bring suitably skilled and experienced artists and works of art into their buildings, in many cases assisting in the raising of special funds for this purpose.

There are dynamic and effective link services in a number of countries. The ones we have heard about are listed in the Directory.

A PERSONAL STORY: SHAPE

I should like to describe briefly how Shape began. Interlink has visited a number of countries to establish intermediary services based on the Shape model. These countries have adapted the structure to fit in with their particular culture, environment and situation. By describing in some detail this personal experience I hope it may give readers guidelines should they be inspired to initiate similar projects, and perhaps demonstrate, too, the enormous potential of an intermediary organisation.

During the late sixties little was being done to provide disadvantaged people with arts activities. There was a communication gap between

Guidance for Funding Organisations and Applicants on Arts Projects Involving Disabled People, April 1986.

the disparate worlds of arts and social welfare. Later, when working for Interlink, I saw that exactly the same gap existed in other parts of the world. Our research work, too, showed that hospitals, special schools and institutions had a real wish to introduce new creative opportunities for their students, adults as well as children, but they had no idea where to seek advice and assistance. The same situation applied when we talked to cultural organisations or individual artists. Once they had considered the suggestion of reaching out and widening their area of work, they were most enthusiastic; but the question always arose 'How do I make contact?' As an artist myself I had asked the same question; so in 1976 I decided to create a link service that would try to solve this problem.

THE BEGINNING

The first thing I did was to draw up a plan in the form of a proposal and work out an estimated budget of costs. This information was submitted to funding agencies. At the same time it was necessary to find an organisation that was a registered charity to act as an umbrella for receiving and administering any money I raised just until the project could be registered in its own right. Through the help of Dr Claus Newman a London hospital agreed to become the umbrella.

I had managed to secure the finances for the administration costs and a small salary for myself; the next step was to choose a name for the project. Shape was a word I liked and it represented form. Ideas only work if there is a form in which they can be continued.

Shape installed itself in a tiny London office. At first the office was somewhat underfurnished: a telephone (essential to the project), a kettle and cups (essential to my survival) and a plant (essential because it was growing). Then I was lent a typewriter and given an old desk and three chairs. Letters were sent out introducing the service to institutions, rehabilitation centres and hospitals in and around the London area. The introductory letter was accompanied by a questionnaire which read: 'If funds were made available for one or more of the following activities, would you be interested in having them on a regular weekly basis?' The list of activities included dance, drama, music, puppetry, visual art, toymaking, photography, video crafts, flower-arranging. The second part of the questionnaire enquired if any creative activities were already taking place, and whether a setting could support new workshops from their own budgets. Eighty per cent of the questionnaires were returned, which alone seemed to justify

Shape's existence. Often questionnaires are not filled in or returned. Indeed a fifty per cent return is considered to be a success rate. There were eager requests from many different places including psychiatric hospitals, rehabilitation centres and prisons. The returned forms indicated a bleak and fragmented picture. A very few hospitals had infrequent music or art therapy sessions and the occasional drama workshop. Armed with this information (which was crucial to successful fund-raising), Shape appealed for financial sponsorship to meet these needs. Happily our appeals did not fall on deaf ears.

The next stage was to locate artists or artistic therapists who would like to work in these environments. By now I had found a colleague who took over the secretarial work. It made all the difference and life became less lonely because we could bounce ideas to each other. To find the artists we contacted arts centres and schools for the performing arts. We advertised in local papers. The copy was on the lines of 'Are you interested in working with new people in different areas of your community?' 'Have you thought how art can enrich the lives of those people who are disadvantaged?' At this time such a suggestion was practically unheard of.

Soon artists of different disciplines began to contact us. We interviewed everyone who came to the office, and compiled a register of artists, carding them in boxes under the headings of different art forms. The artists filled in cards with their details, including where they received their training and work experience. We asked them to state the group they would prefer to work with. For example, some people wished to work with only physically disabled people, others with the elderly. My colleagues and I made our own intuitive assessments which we wrote on the person's card. Occasionally we would decide not to link an artist who showed no real interest. After the interview it was a policy to see the artist at work, and we never linked without doing this first. A meeting was then arranged between the artist and staff of the institution or centre. The final choice lay with the staff. If they felt one candidate was inappropriate we sent another, usually making the link on the basis of the artist agreeing to work once a week for a two-hour session. This meant he or she could give two workshops and work with two groups of students. Shape agreed to remunerate the artist at an hourly rate which was comparable to the Education Department's rates of pay for visiting teachers. Travel costs were met and monthly claim forms were provided. We also arranged for theatre, dance, music, puppetry and poetry performances to go into centres for the homeless, prisons, hospitals, institutions and centres for elderly people. I still remember the pleasure of those audiences.

MONITORING

Our service was there to give back-up support and ensure that if there were any problems we could try to sort them out. My colleague and I made regular visits to watch the sessions, in fact to take part in the activities because it gave us a chance to be creative as well. Half-yearly reports were requested from both artists and staff and, whenever possible, students. At the end of the year an Annual General Report was written which was sent to our sponsors as well as to potential new funders.

FUND-RAISING

Shape was growing rapidly, more and more establishments were asking for help. It was essential to continue fund-raising in order to meet both existing and new commitments. To eke out our tiny budget we introduced artists on a 'free trial' basis. It was understandable that an institution could not commit the time and energy to finding the means to pay for a hitherto untried activity, but if after the trial period was over they wished the work to continue then it was their responsibility to find the small amount of money. Ninety per cent of the activities Shape had linked continued through this arrangement. We were then able to use the 'trial' money elsewhere.

Shape was by now bridging the communication gap and I felt it was time to make our work known to the relevant government agencies and local authorities' departments. We desperately needed grants from these statutory bodies so that Shape could have some security. My colleague and I had been living from month to month, never knowing how much longer we could keep the project going. After endless letters and a few meetings there was light at the end of the tunnel. It was agreed that we should receive small grants from the Arts Council, the Department of Health and Social Welfare and the Education Authority. This was a real breakthrough. One of our problems had been that Shape did not fit neatly into one box. Its functions straddled all three areas, and at first each department had said we were the responsibility of the other. Now they had agreed to joint funding.

REGIONAL SERVICES FOR RURAL AREAS

Shape's service only covered the London area, whereas there were hospitals, centres and institutions all over the country, with those situated in rural areas even less able to provide creative programmes than those in urban areas. Using the model of Shape and liaising with the regional arts and health departments, new Shape services began to emerge. Each scheme started with one full- or part-time coordinator and a very small amount of money. Providing a service for rural areas was a far more challenging task for the organisers. Hospitals were spread out, which meant the organiser had to travel extensively, and artists were difficult to locate. However, all these difficulties were overcome. Each service was independent, the organiser took the Shape model and adapted it to the needs of the location. (Later Interlink assisted countries to do the same.) Eight organisations came into being and since my departure from Shape another nine have been born. These seventeen organisations are now part of a national network.

CURRENT DEVELOPMENT

The range of the Shape activities is quite phenomenal and they are reaching many thousands of people right across the United Kingdom. Integration within the organisations has meant that people with disabilities are now practically involved in the artistic creation and future administrative planning. Indeed their main emphasis is focused on integrated programmes. London Shape and HAI New York (Hospital Audiences Inc., see Directory, another very exciting US link service) run subsidised ticket schemes which allow people who hitherto could not afford it to go to concerts, theatres and events (see chapter 13). Interlink has assisted India, Zimbabwe, Sri Lanka, Mexico and Colombia to start similar services that are also working to great effect.

FURTHER SUGGESTIONS

A service can be based from home or in the premises of another organisation.

Initially one person can run a scheme, but will need to be mobile or have transport if disabled.

Make sure the base is accessible for people with physical disabilities.

Invite people whom the project aims to benefit to be represented on the committee.

If there is a limited budget the service can start by focusing on one or two areas and gradually extend outwards.

Do not wait for people to contact you. They may not have heard about the scheme, or they may think it is inappropriate for the people they work with.

Do not concentrate solely on children. Adults can benefit from activities and in general are provided with far less stimulus.

It is essential to keep fund-raising all the time.

Sponsorship under 'adopt a project' (see chapter 11) can be used to link workshops rather than having to wait until all the required money has been found.

Keep the whole project simple with as little paperwork as possible.

Include staff and artist training courses (see chapter 14).

Inform the relevant local authorities about the scheme and invite one representative to be on your committee.

When the project is established some secretarial help can be very useful. It means one person can be based in the office while the other is out visiting. Otherwise – if available and if you can afford it – have an answering machine to take messages.

Arrange occasional general meetings with the artists working through your scheme. Artists can feel isolated in this work so it is valuable for them to meet and discuss their work with others.

Your scheme is a clearing house. The organiser needs to be able to relate to different situations and people.

The following brief account written by Seona Reid, then Director of Shape, describes the development of the project. Readers are recommended to contact other Shape network organisations in the United Kingdom, or HAI, USA, for information about current activities.

GINA LEVETE

SHAPE IN 1986

Shape is now ten years old and has grown and diversified considerably since the early days. It now has seven full-time and two part-time project-based workers in its main office, with four development workers based in specific boroughs in London. It works throughout Greater London. Each aspect of its work represents one part of the jigsaw which when complete will enable people with disabilities and special needs to participate as equal partners in every aspect of the arts. Equality of access and opportunity is the long-term goal.

LEFT *Shape: music workshop with people with mental disabilities at the Lewisham Academy of Music's community music centre in South-East London.*
BELOW *Weaving project with elderly people with physical disabilities in a Wandsworth, South-West London, day centre.*

Shape: ABOVE *A mask-making workshop with people with physical disabilities at Jackson's Lane Community Centre, London.* BELOW *People with mental disabilities prepare for a multi-media public event at the Albany Empire Community Arts Centre in Deptford, East London.*

As well as responding to requests from hospitals, day centres and so on, Shape is funded by London boroughs to undertake borough development programmes. These programmes are designed to increase the quality and range of the arts available to people with disabilities and special needs in that borough. Again they take many different forms. For example, the worker (often a disabled person too) has an office in a community arts centre. He or she sets up projects which bring people with disabilities into local arts and community centres or in which local artists and arts organisations run projects in homes and day centres where members are unable or reluctant to go out. The aim is to encourage people to make use of the arts resources which already exist. The worker ensures that the needs of disadvantaged people are not overlooked in the policies and practice of the borough's own arts department. Even in those boroughs where there are no workers, the projects established by other Shape workers pursue the same aims of encouraging people with special needs to make greater use of their arts resources.

The Arts Centres Project began in 1983 and has now worked with seven arts centres, each centre being involved over an eighteen-month period. The aim is to ensure that arts centres increase their provision for people with disabilities and that people are encouraged to become involved in the life of the centres. But for those people who prefer simply to go out to theatres, concert halls and exhibitions, there is the ticket scheme.

Shape also tours exhibitions, usually accompanied by a series of practical workshops or gallery visits. For example, the organisation worked with the Whitechapel Art Gallery, a major London gallery, to tour work from their annual Open Show to local hospitals and centres and to invite people into the gallery to see the exhibitions and participate in practical workshops.

Training has become a major focus. Training courses in basic workshop techniques are run regularly for staff from health, social services and voluntary settings. A variety of training opportunities are also made available to artists to acquire workshop skills and experience. Apprenticeship placements enable an artist with no workshop experience to work alongside an experienced workshop leader over a period of ten or twelve weeks. Short one- or two-day courses are organised for artists already running workshops to develop old skills or acquire new ones.

Meanwhile an increasing part of our work takes the form of providing advice and consultancy to disability organisations on developing the arts. There are many parts of the jigsaw still missing and equality of access and opportunity is not yet with us; but progress is being made.

SEONA REID

2
Visual Arts

BECOMING INVOLVED

For many thousands of years visual art has offered an inexhaustible enrichment of life. From cave painting to contemporary murals, prints and sculptures, works of art continue to be created, forming an expression and reflection of our times. We all have something to contribute. Anyone who expresses an interest in visual art should have the opportunity to explore further, whether alone or as part of a group – where there is the chance to share ideas and spark off new ones, to develop imagination, creative thinking and judgement by constantly trying out both new and familiar arts activities in a stimulating environment.

Once involved in creative activity your world starts to expand. Perception of your environment sharpens as you become more visually aware and interested in the nature of things and people around you. There is nearly always an element of surprise as you discover aptitudes in yourself of which you were completely unaware. I was recently involved in a large mural project with young people. One girl had never used a paintbrush before. I won't forget the look of utter amazement and delight in herself as she completed painting a palm tree twice her height.

A skill takes time to develop, so it is worth practising as often as possible, whether daily or weekly. The eventual sense of achievement is worth all the effort and other people will benefit from the results of your own artistic development.

ARTS AND THE ARTIST

If you wish to explore the visual arts as a group activity here are some ways in which you can begin. This section sets out the values of the activity and how to find an artist should you not feel ready to undertake the activity yourself.

Involving an artist in the activities An artist who has a lot of enthusiasm and specialised skill and is keen to work with your group can generate fresh energy and a new level of enthusiasm and creativity. He or she can introduce methods and techniques not normally possible within the work situation. The artist and students will find that they gain inspiration and new ideas from each other: the work produced as a result of this two-way exchange is likely to be of high quality. Working with the artist, staff will be able to develop new ideas, themes and techniques to use with students in the future.

Finding an artist If you feel an artist would make a worthwhile contribution in your workplace, begin by looking around your locality. It may be a local artist or someone who has a special interest and enthusiasm for a relevant arts activity. If you have an arts association, college, university or main library nearby, enquire there – they may have lists of artists in your area.

Look for an artist who shows genuine interest in sharing his or her skills with people, who has a flexible way of working, and whose personality feels right for your students. It is a good idea in a school, for example, to arrange first for the artist to meet the head, the staff and the pupils, to discuss everyone's ideas and interests, to find out which materials are already in stock or easily obtainable, how much work space is available, and what are likely to be the most appropriate arts activities to begin with. The artist can then start sensible planning of the practical arts activities. There are many ways of working and it is up to all concerned to discuss carefully the basis on which the artist is to work.

Ways in which the artist can work with a group Projects which have worked successfully include:

Workshops The artist comes in for one, two or more workshops a week over as long a time as possible – months, years – exploring and developing many different art ideas and themes with the students, and helping people with their individual ideas as well as working on group projects.

Short-term Projects The artist works with a group every day on a specific project for a limited amount of time (four to six weeks), to explore techniques and work in depth together. The finished artwork might be a large wall painting or a sculpture for the main entranceway of your workplace.

Residencies The artist is given space to work within your building on his or her own work for two or three days each week. The rest of the time the artist spends with individuals or groups wanting to learn about and participate in his or her particular skill. The length of time of the residency will depend on your requirements, space and funding possibilities. Residencies have been known to run between two months and two years.

Areas in which the visual arts have been used successfully Many people previously isolated from the arts have become involved with new creative initiatives – painting, printing, sculpture, drawing, mixed media, environmental art and so on. Visual arts projects, too, have been set up in different community settings – homes, day centres, youth clubs, prisons, community centres, rehabilitation centres, hospitals and schools, giving people of all ages, with and without disabilities, the opportunity to develop and extend themselves creatively.

I have not particularised ways of working with people of different age groups and with physical disability and so on, as I believe that the basic approaches to group arts activities, laid out in this chapter, have a general application if the artist and participants are sensitive to individual needs. For example, if a person with a physical disability finds he or she cannot grip small objects easily, a paintbrush can be adapted by wrapping foam or cloth around it to form a thick handle – a simple way of enabling the student to participate without compromise.

PLANNING YOUR ARTS ACTIVITY

Think of the particular requirements that are needed for the smooth running of your scheme. Give careful consideration to preparation: if that is neglected, the value of the arts activity can easily be undermined. Be sure that you have materials, space, equipment and time.

Aims The clear definition of aims is vital in the setting up of an arts activity. Together with the artist, develop a clear picture of immediate, short-term and long-term objectives and review them regularly as the activity grows in new directions. A useful way of thinking them out is to 'brainstorm' – write down as many words or sentences as quickly as possible, as soon as they enter your head, which describe how you would like the activities to develop. For example: discovering new ways of working with the techniques, developing a visual language which others can respond to, fun, everyone who wants to can participate, colour, liveliness. In this way you think big and imaginatively; you can compromise later if necessary, but this is far better than restricting yourself in the beginning.

Then, with all your 'brainstorm' ideas in mind, think of the initial activity. Let us suppose it is mosaics, with everyone having fun exploring and gaining confidence in a new set of materials. Set down your objectives: short-term – to complete a large mosaic to be displayed publicly, all the students having participated in the designing and practical work; long-term – for the students to gain confidence in their creative thinking and practical skills.

Funding Any proposed arts activity requires a realistic budget, taking into account the artist's fees (including research, design and consultancy), the acquisition of the necessary materials, travel and subsistence costs, and so on. Detailed records should be kept of all financial transactions. It may be a good idea to set an hourly rate of pay and arrange for a separate fund which the artist can use for the purchase of materials. Look into the question of insurance cover for those involved in the project (although this may well not be applicable in many countries).

Materials may be quite expensive, so consider all possible sources of funding – financial or in kind. Many firms are willing to donate materials in exchange for a public acknowledgement of their help and it is often useful to approach local timber yards, paint firms, glue manufacturers or paper suppliers.

You may like to begin with a short-term project. The success of this would inspire confidence, not only in your group, but also in those who could help you in securing your long-term funding.

Materials A basic list of materials which are useful for painting, drawing and collage include:

- brushes of various sizes (sponges on sticks also work well for painting on a large scale)
- pencils, crayons, pens, felt-tipped pens
- paper – various sizes and colours, brown paper
- scissors
- a selection of paints and inks in the primary colours – red, blue, yellow and also black, white and any other colours available
- plywood, hardboard and canvas if available
- collage materials – fabric pieces, colourful paper, old magazines etc

A basic list of materials which are useful for printing:

- printing inks or thick paint
- lots of paper
- printing screen – gauze stretched over a wooden frame
- squeegee and roller
- newspaper
- sponge which can be cut into shapes to print with
- any interesting objects and textures to print with

A basic list of materials which are useful for sculpture:

cardboard, wood, wire
plaster, clay
different textures – sand, sawdust and so on
any junk materials – wire, tins, tubing, small objects etc
tools – hammer, nails, chisel, saw, pliers, drill etc

Look into the materials available and leave a little of your budget over for additional items. Then, with the artist and students, think of suitable techniques and ideas. There are many possibilities which can be developed with growing confidence and imagination. Here are some ideas: ink paintings on paper or a large mural on the wall; sculpture using junk materials – a magnificent tree, for example, built with wire, tins, cardboard, fabric and so on, with many interesting small objects hanging from the branches; printing with sponges of different shapes forming a repeated design, or silk-screen printing; a mosaic using coloured pebbles forming an abstract pattern; a relief picture on board made out of clay or plasticine, depicting a local story or one of your own; metalwork figures or wood carving; simple instrument-making, such as music shakers made by half-filling two empty cola tins with lentils, rice or small pebbles, taping them together firmly, covering with thin card and painting with bright designs; a large painting on plywood or hardboard which can be fastened to the wall to be exhibited and then moved to another place as requested.

Some people may like to explore one art form deeply while others may want to try out many different techniques.

Space and equipment Find an area where a bit of mess won't matter. Ideally you need a fairly large room with natural light, a sink area and one or two large tables, preferably with easily cleaned surfaces. A large cupboard with shelves is useful for storing materials and good wall space is helpful in displaying art work.

Time When setting up a regular arts activity it is important that everyone involved can work at their own speed and not feel under pressure. Make sure there is enough time to prepare, settle into and explore the activity, time to concentrate and then to clear away the materials. Between one and one and a half hours seems to work well with many groups. This can be extended or shortened depending on the response of your group. When work is going well, time seems to pass very quickly as people get really involved – sometimes a whole afternoon is not long enough. Experiment, too, with leaving some arts materials out and available for people to use freely on their own between workshops – they may be used to continue their work or to explore a new idea.

GETTING STARTED

How many in a group? The number of people involved will of necessity vary and thought should be given to individual needs. A fairly small group usually works best: say eight to twelve students with three to four helpers. Colleagues or volunteers can assist the students taking part by helping to sort out materials with them, coping with any difficulties which might arise, and discussing ideas individually.

The arts activity should not be mandatory. If students really don't wish to be involved, try to help them find another outlet for their creative energies.

Beginning a group project Begin by finding a suitable level – start simply with an idea or theme with which everyone feels comfortable. If you start with something too complicated, it can discourage people. Once you get the feel of the group and people's requirements, then you can begin to explore more complex ideas.

In the early stages it is often a good idea to reinforce new techniques by repeating the same kind of activity several times – for instance, simple methods of printing. The results will differ each time and it is exciting for the students to see each person's progress over the weeks. In this way a balance can be maintained between learning new techniques and experimenting further with existing ideas.

Exploring and improvising Encourage a relaxed, fun atmosphere where the students can enjoy becoming familiar with materials – mixing paint, handling plasticine or clay, making shapes with cardboard or wood, discovering how different objects can be used in printing. Sometimes quick spontaneous pictures or sculptures can be more successful than artwork made over many weeks.

Encourage the students to put a lot of energy into their work and help them to develop their ideas from as many sources as possible. When developing new ideas try to explore freely with the materials available; concentrate on the process, not the end result. In this way you don't restrict yourself. You can often achieve great results quite unexpectedly; and this is part of the fascination of visual art.

Developing ideas and themes For an example of developing ideas and themes I will take 'Beginning a Mural Project'. The mural will be painted with emulsion paints, which the group has already had time experimenting with and using on a small scale. At this stage a theme has to be explored, using paper, pens and poster paints.

First of all we look at the site of the proposed mural and any features near it – water, large plants etc – which might influence our ideas. Then we go back to our room to think about a theme. The 'brainstorming' technique I described earlier comes in useful here as each person can contribute to the idea.

Say for this particular wall we choose the theme of a 'journey'. Some words may be: travelling, movement, roads through an environment, symbols, bridges, different climates, etc. At this stage everyone chooses one word from the 'brainstorm'. Then we divide into groups of four, and each group works on one large piece of paper making a picture describing each of their words.

Later everyone gets together again and displays their group's work. We pick out ideas and images from each picture which we feel would form a good basis for the mural. Then we all go on to develop the chosen ideas, thinking carefully of the composition, shapes and colours which would most suit the shape and situation of the wall; working to scale, we carry on until we are satisfied with the design. Then we get on our overalls and head for the wall.

When you are thinking about ideas and themes these are some suggestions which you may find useful: think about exploring self-portraits or abstract emotions – joy, anger, amazement and so on; fantasy themes such as life on another planet, the world turned upside-down; explore social issues, news, local stories, dreams and memories; draw life-size pictures of people, animals, objects; 'brainstorm' on the theme of the four elements – earth, fire, water, air; in fact any theme or issue on which you feel strongly. These are just some suggestions – you will have many more of your own.

Write down ideas when you think of them. Draw them. Try as a group to visit any arts exhibitions in your locality or to bring interesting and unusual objects into your workplace. Sometimes a library or museum will let you borrow exhibits. Work at the ideas and themes until you feel satisfied that you have produced your best. The finished work will reflect the amount of time and thought invested at this earlier stage.

THINKING AHEAD

Thinking environmentally It can bring good results to involve everyone right from the beginning in the decision-making concerning their environment. You could look around your workplace, picking out areas which could be used to display artwork, remembering that in most circumstances you will need to obtain permission to paint or make a sculpture for a specific area. When considering the subject, try to make your theme relevant to the proposed setting. A large blank wall, an archway, a spacious public area or entranceway – these places can all be transformed.

Displaying artwork It can be fun and helpful to concentration to work towards an exhibition. Many public places can display visual artwork – libraries, galleries, community centres, colleges and universities, art centres, hospitals, even outdoors. So, exhibit your prints, drawings, paintings and sculptures as widely as possible, not only in your work environment. Try to find an area within your own building which can be a 'changing exhibitions' area – a corridor or hallway where people gather, wait or pass through regularly. Every few weeks or months the display can be changed. It is a good feeling to see your work on display and others – you hope – reacting positively towards it. The environment, too, is enhanced at the same time.

Problems Inevitably problems will sometimes arise, caused perhaps by insufficient space or materials or by difficulties in the arts sessions themselves. It does help to have a colleague with whom you can discuss both problems and successes.

A problem which arose in a hostel for homeless young people was caused by the artist not having sufficient understanding of the area he was asked to work in. To him the aesthetic value of his work outweighed the needs of that particular environment. He was asked to produce a mural in the main entrance involving some of the residents. The images he produced were inappropriate and the staff and residents disliked them. He had not approached the residents beforehand to exchange ideas or invite them to assist with the mural. Eventually another person had to be asked to take over and, with the participation of the young people, a more appropriate mural was created.

Recording your progress Try to keep a record as the activity progresses. Ask the students involved to submit a short written report; and remember that photographs are really useful to support the written material. The record can enable you to assess how the project is developing and whether your group's aims are being fulfilled. It can also be invaluable when applying for funds for a subsequent project. Any conclusions

ABOVE *A one-day workshop on the theme 'Our Village and Surroundings', involving pupils from Dr Reijntje's school for deaf children, Sri Lanka*
BELOW *A circus mural in the physiotherapy gymnasium*

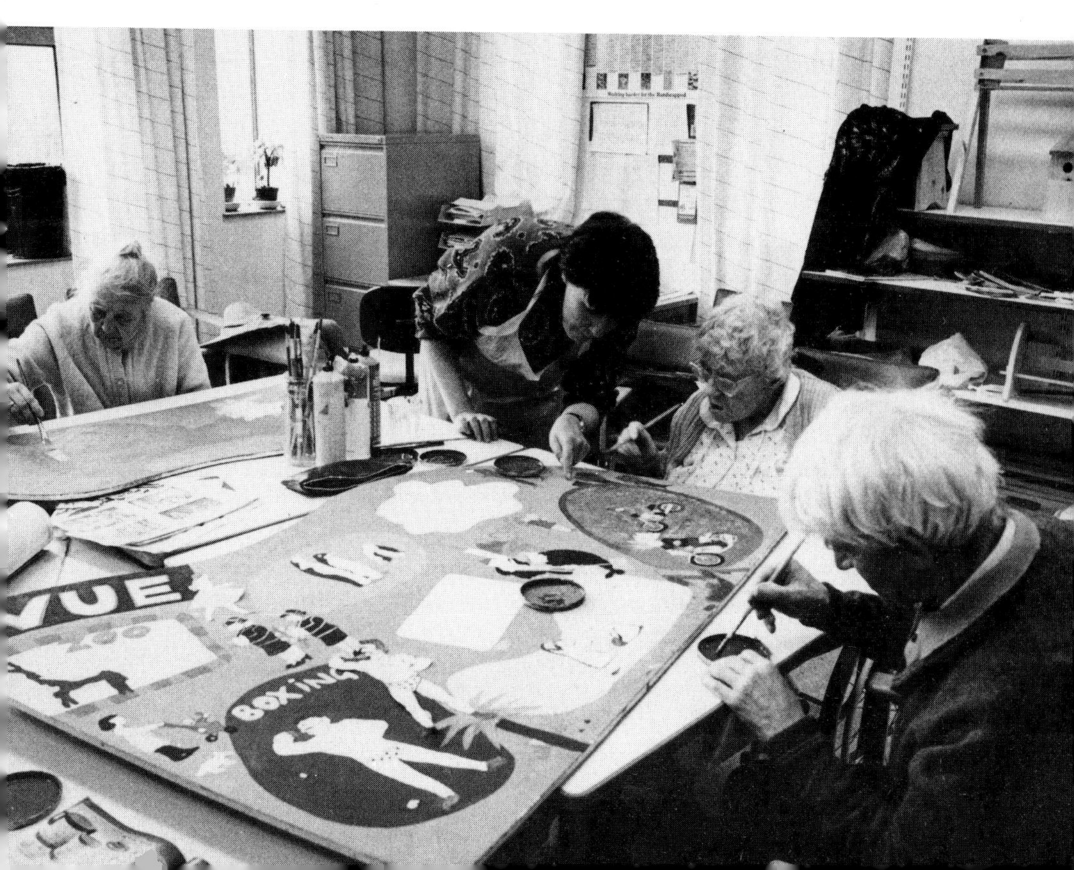

LEFT *A mural in progress involving staff and local artists at Chitra Lane School, Colombo, Sri Lanka*
BELOW *An art workshop with people who are elderly*

reached or ideas for the future are also worth recording and can be of considerable help should others want to initiate similar activities.

Training If you work in a school or other institution the artist can be very valuable in training staff in particular art skills and approaches. A training session could be held perhaps twice a month, or even, in a concentrated programme, every day for one week. Alternatively, if a member of the staff shows a special interest, investigate the possibility of that person being allowed to study art one day a week at a local college, so as to take over from the artist at a later stage.

Involving other art forms The visual arts can be used imaginatively with many other art forms. Music, drama, puppetry, dance, photography and visual arts can all be integrated successfully.

Try drawing and painting to different moods of music in an arts session. Think of the colours evoked by each piece of music. Paint a large cloth illustrating the theme of a play and act out the different scenes in front of it. Have a visual arts session making large colour drawings on card of characters from a well-known local story, then cut around the edges and mount on bamboo to make stick puppets, and perform the story to others.

Ask some of the students to dance, energetically or slowly and gracefully, while others draw their reactions to the movements; then they in turn can dance and move in response to their own paintings. Look at photographs or take them yourselves, and carry the ideas further visually by exaggerating, beautifying, making twice as dramatic, twice as big and so on – in this way you discover how you can modify or change an image to get the effect you particularly want.

Invite performers, musicians, dancers, painters, sculptors, crafts-people and photographers to demonstrate their work to your group and talk about it. If you are working on a certain theme – for example, the countryside around you – try to invite artists whose work is related to that theme.

Moving forward I have suggested practical possibilities of how students can participate in visual arts activities, which you can build on to meet your own requirements. Setting up a project involves careful preparation in the early stages. Begin on a small scale – the project will develop naturally as everyone's confidence grows. Think positively: if you feel the proposed arts project will be a useful and exciting activity, go ahead.

LIZ FAUNCE

3
Dance to Discover

Dance for many people can revitalise and restore, yet the word itself sometimes puts up a barrier. Often it is thought of as an activity for 'others'. 'If it is that thing "music and movement", forget it.' 'Keep fit possibly, but not *dance*.' 'Disco yes, but that's different.' In Asiatic countries other reservations are expressed. Dance is a ritual stemming from deep religious cultures. It is viewed as an art form, the techniques of which takes master dancers many years to perfect. Such dancers themselves at first find it difficult to appreciate the healing application. In Africa dance is as familiar as walking, but even here often that familiarity stops if you happen to be disabled. Indeed when there are opportunities to participate in a dance programme it is regarded as something out of the ordinary. But why? For dance is an absolute 'natural' in these very situations.

THE ROLE OF DANCE

If you want to dance there is absolutely no reason to feel that because of a physical or mental limitation it is not possible to do so. Every human being is born with a sense of rhythm and movement within. This can be outwardly expressed through the eyes, the face, the head, the fingers, the feet – through any part of the body that is able to move. It is not possible to describe on paper the enjoyment that a movement session can bring to people who have wanted to dance but hitherto had not realised that they could do so.

WHAT IS DANCE?

What is considered to be dance by one may not be by another. Someone may claim to have a 'sense of dance' but defining it is almost impossible. What is and what is not dance is relative to the situation in which it is being used. In this chapter I should like to focus on forms of dance which will not necessarily equate with the professional dancer's definition. The professional's body is trained to achieve a high standard of technique so that he or she can attain a quality of expression and movement which reaches far beyond the lay person's movement boundaries. Dance for such students becomes a way of life; they base their criteria of what is or is not dance on skill, technique and performance. Indeed without these measures there would be no standard of development or inspiration against which to set those less sophisticated aspects of movement which can also be described as dance.

WHO WANTS TO DANCE?

Not everyone. Nonetheless there are people everywhere who would like to try to experience dance movement in some form, and might enjoy participating in dance for the experience of feeling, rather than learning a technique. There are also those who feel too shy to do so because they think they are not the 'type'. What is the 'type'? Someone slender, agile, ethereal? The problem is that society is always boxing people in, and making judgements on who or what is suitable. What we should realise is that such categorisation is a form of discrimination. Because you are deaf, or terminally ill, because you are fat or elderly, because you are over fifty and wear a suit and go to business, because you are limbless, because other people don't think you would enjoy moving just for the sheer pleasure of moving, because, because . . . In the end you start believing it yourself. Let us ensure that, whatever the circumstances, opportunity and encouragement are provided to enable people to discover for themselves how far they wish to explore movement. As it is, our situations and responsibilities in adult life restrict us to all too infrequent opportunities that might help us discover the creative potential within ourselves. So it is essential that children and adults are given every chance to discover that indefinable 'spark'. For some, dance or creative movement is a way of finding this.

BODY LANGUAGE

Dance can communicate itself as a language. It can help students realise their own energy, rhythms and movement potential; they begin to understand that the body too has a language of its own. They can learn how this language can be used in everyday situations to ensure a feeling of well-being and confidence (and never more so than for the dancer with disabilities). Often there is greater truth in gesture and expression than in words. It is the dance tutor's encouragement and inspiration which will allow children or adults to discover the body's ability to say almost anything.

DANCE AS AN OUTLET

Dance can be used as a therapy or as a celebration. In many instances it is both at the same time. It can also help to alleviate social problems. Energy which is pent up and needs to be released can be channelled through it; energy which has sunk too low through despair or illness can be revived. Breakdancing, which began in the United States, is an example of how street gangs formed breakdance gangs and began to compete with each other, unconsciously exploring a means of getting rid of their frustrations through their ingenious and energetic movements. For the housewife who feels isolated, aerobics, keep-fit, jazz or other movement classes may make all the difference to her day or week. She may be involving herself in dance movement to help herself look and feel better, or perhaps dance is a way of chasing a fantasy; the reason is unimportant. If the outcome is greater self-confidence, then movement has played its part. For many ill or distressed people, dance – like other art forms – can play a healing role. I have worked with mentally ill people who began a session in a state of great tension, their faces anxious and their bodies strained. At the end of the workshop the same students seemed to have been smoothed out, their breathing was quieter, their energy and equilibrium more balanced, and, most important of all, they had smiling faces. For the mentally or physically disabled child who has a sense of dance this art form opens up a whole new horizon.

Dance as part of the life force within a community is completely natural to some nations, but much less so in the West – although it is slowly attracting attention as a community activity. Dancers in residence within schools, community centres, hospitals and institutions should become accepted placements rather than unusual ones.

SHARING DANCE CULTURES AND MUSIC

Exploring other nations' dance forms and music can be a way of encouraging understanding and integration, particularly for the child. Sometimes we are intimidated because we feel the rhythms, energy and dance style of another nation may not be compatible with our own energies and environment.

This is not true. Often music and movement from other cultures can enrich a student's own indigenous movement vocabulary; for example, I have found when working with students that music from a Zen monastery imposes no emotional attachment, yet has the effect of inspiring the student's imagination. African rhythms create an energy which can bring out the impetus and effort needed for a physically handicapped student to make a particular movement. Indian and

Chinese rhythms and gestures can lead a student beyond his or her normal dance boundaries. Equally, Western music may blend into other dance cultures. Perhaps purists will say this is 'playing around' with traditional and technically beautiful art forms which are already perfect, but we should be aware that by improvising and taking rhythms, ideas, styles and movements from all over the world we are allowing a student the experience of creating in a new and individual way. It crosses the cultural boundaries, and at the same time educates the student and integrates his perspectives.

WHAT IS IMPROVISATION?

Before embarking on a movement improvisation class it is necessary to examine the word 'improvisation'. It is something most of us have to do every day of our lives. We try to make the most suitable composition out of situations that face us, almost from the time we are born. When a baby discovers it can move, he or she experiments with ways of getting across the room. For the student who is training to become a professional dancer, mastering a technique of dance is of primary importance. In this instance improvisation is not enough in itself, but is still an essential part of the student's syllabus. Improvisation is a wonderful outlet for expression and a creative game for the imagination.

It is important to bear in mind that when using this approach you are not 'teaching', but simply 'working with' your group. Think of the words 'creative movement' rather than 'dance' for giving session. A well-structured session will allow students the maximum opportunity to 'stretch' themselves. The exciting part about improvisation is that there is no right or wrong way. This however does not mean a tutor should not focus on quality and development of movement. On the contrary it is the tutor's role to draw out the most original ideas and performance a student can achieve. Nor is dance improvisation an outlet for uncontrolled emotional release. Whatever emotional fantasy is being expressed students must be able to 'cut' and return to themselves immediately because they are in complete control of their expression. There should be no distinction of content made in a workshop for students with or without disabilities, since the themes are based on how each individual can stretch an idea. It is as if one says 'Here is an idea, now reach out and make it grow for you.'

IMPROVISATION/CREATIVE MOVEMENT

The rest of the chapter focuses on suggestions that can be applied when presenting a movement improvisation workshop. Improvisation is a simple and exciting way of introducing dance. I have given these kinds of workshops to many different students in countries all over the world, each with its own distinctive way of moving. The attraction of improvisation is that it works anywhere, but then I am biased because it has been the key to my own creativity.

SUGGESTIONS FOR PRESENTING A WORKSHOP

Can anyone give a movement session where no technique is required? My feeling is that whenever possible the tutor should be a person who has specialised in dance; failing that, someone with a love and feel for dance who has attended classes and experienced it personally.

SUGGESTIONS FOR THE TUTOR

The framework or structure of a session is to allow the individual's maximum potential to be drawn out, through movements, words and abstract ideas.

It is important to plan a programme in advance and whenever possible to learn it by heart, but also to have notes at hand.

Choice of music and sounds are very important. Choose and tape all music beforehand so that there is no fiddling about during the class trying to find the right track or part of the tape. Particularly with patients, this can sap up their concentration and confidence. A drum and percussion instruments are necessary. Each programme should have time devoted to students working without accompanying sounds so that they can discover their own rhythm centres. It is not possible to suggest music as this has to be the tutor's individual choice. It is essential that you like the music and feel it interprets your ideas.

Clear demonstration must always be given and clear examples when suggesting abstract ideas.

Flexibility to change a planned programme, if for some reasons students do not respond well, is essential.

Flexibility with regard to timing is also necessary. If students are tired, finish before the planned time. You will probably achieve a better result than if you rigidly adhere to your planned programme.

Only ever plan a session that you enjoy yourself.

Remember that first and foremost you are there to encourage people to have fun and extend themselves through this experience.

Suggested timing of a workshop: one hour for children, elderly people half an hour, adults one and a half to two hours.

Space: the larger the space the more exhilarating it will be for the students. Do not expect people to move in cramped conditions.

The workshop could begin with warm-up exercises and a formal direction which becomes less obvious as students begin to build their own ideas. For adults a session can focus the whole way through on one theme (let us say 'breath'). For children more emphasis needs to be placed on developing the quality of movements. For example, a session could focus on stretching and contracting movements; this theme could still weave in stories and games. Exercises to develop proper breathing need to be included at the beginning. Allow for a quiet period in the middle and time for relaxation at the end. The following workshop which is suitable for older children or adults demonstrates the structure suggested.

THEME: AWARENESS OF SPACE: TIME 2 HOURS

1 In a circle each student calls out a name and writes it in the space with any part of the body. Tutor directs: 'Shut your eyes. Feel the space where you are placed, stroke it, move in it.'

2 Travel around the room, making different floor patterns. On the drum beat join with a partner and create a space, at the same time looking into each other's eyes and call out 'Hullo'.

3 Slow warm-up exercises, being aware of how the body is moving to space. (Music.)

4 Sitting. Breathing exercises. Breathing and making isolated parts of body float in different directions on the in and out breath. (Music.)

5 Standing. Lean different parts of the body on space as if it were a solid substance. On the drum cue the space disappears and that part of the body collapses – rest your chin on space, your foot, your elbow . . .

6 Travel around the room with scarves, fans, or sticks. Let the object you are holding lead you (in other words, you follow the stick) into different levels of space and different directions.

7 Use the floor structure made from masking tape.

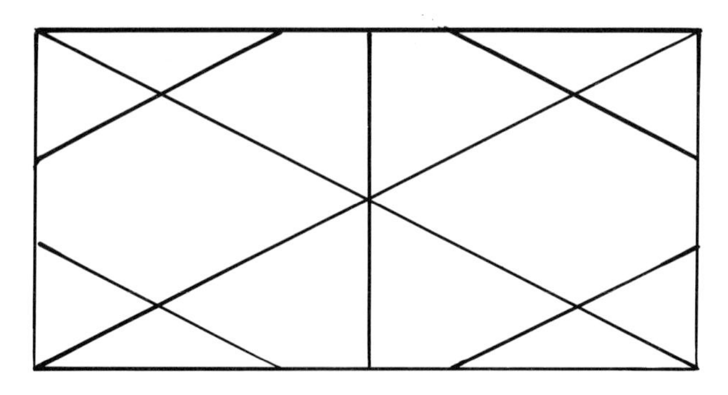

Create a dance sequence where you become part of the lines stretching out, and in the spaces you withdraw. (Music.) Floor structures can be useful frameworks for movement. For example: travel on the lines and balance in the spaces. Travel every time you come to a join in the tape change direction. Different spaces can represent different emotions or movement qualities.

8 Mould space as if it were a substance like clay. You can pick it up, stretch it, crumple it up, give it to someone else. Pick up some more. Create a dance with it. (Music.)

9 Sitting in a circle present a formal exercise to strengthen the back. Exercise the face by making ugly and gentle faces. Sit and without outward movement feel the different suggestions being made to you: feel as if your hair, back, nose, chin are floating in space. Each part of the body is taken in isolation. Feel as if your arms cover the whole room, feel as if you are as small as a pin. Feel as if you are an empty space . . .

10 Take a partner and with him or her create a dance composition where you create spaces with your body for your partner to move in and through. (Music.)

11 Listen to these sounds and draw the sounds in space with any part of your body. (For this I used Japanese Zen music from a monastery, but it could be any unusual sounds.) Now use the body to flow with the movement you are drawing.

12 Take the movement of circling, stretching, running and being still, and by yourself compose a dance sequence. (Music.)

13 Move freely, always travelling; as you pass others, brush gently against them. Feel together like a river where bubbles meet each other and disappear to become part of the flow.

14 Lie on the floor and rest. (Relaxation, talk through.)

STUDENTS WITH PHYSICAL DISABILITIES

Some students may be mobile, others not. Almost certainly the group will have very varying degrees of handicap. Do not worry. Each person will work within his or her own limitations. Encourage those with artificial limbs to discard them (with staff approval, of course). Have rubber or foam mats for the severely disabled to lie on. Make sure those who prefer to remain in wheelchairs are spaced out between the more able-bodied. Do not feel inhibited at referring to different physical limitations, and encourage students to improvise with as many different ways of moving as is possible so that they discover their movement potential. Do not be afraid because the class is physically handicapped. You are not teaching them how to move, you are asking them to discover their own ways of moving, and instinctively people know their own limitations.

MENTAL DISABILITY

Demonstrate very clearly. Develop a good control and quality of movement from the outset. The time to work on this is at an early age when students are first introduced to dance. By the time they reach the next stage they will possess a good standard of movement. From the outset make sure they are given the opportunity to improvise and experiment and think for themselves. Too often dance sessions for these students are just repetition of the tutor's movements.

PSYCHIATRIC PATIENTS

When planning movement improvisation for this group of people, know why you feel dance and creative movement can be beneficial. Sensitive timing is essential. Recognise instantly when the group is tired or the concentration is lost. Also, know how to stop any individual who may wish to talk or perform too long, and thereby tend to lose the interest of the rest of the group. This must be done in such a manner that the student does not in any way feel squashed.

Never overstimulate or tire. The class should act as a stimulus but students should not feel 'wound up'.

Participation must be voluntary, and the members of the class should be able to drop in, drop out, or just watch.

Particularly for psychiatric patients, structure a class so that if some wish to do their 'own thing', for example, sing, read a poem, dance by themselves, it is possible at some point.

VISUAL HANDICAP

Much attention should be focused on students' awareness of space.

Often it is a good idea to start the class in a circle holding hands so that everyone feels the circle shape. Move around together in a circle one way and then the other. One student can then weave in and out of the circle touching his colleagues as he travels.

Balance of the body needs to be worked on with simple exercises. For example: run; stop; stretch up on toes and remain still.

Put emphasis on working together physically in order that students become sensitive to the rhythm and timing of each other.

Touching objects and re-creating the shape and feel of them. Touching each other and re-creating the shape and feel. Repetition of floor patterns so that they can 'feel' space for choreographing movements.

STUDENTS WITH A HEARING DISABILITY

Dance movement for these students is a very important part of their learning. Obviously it is not possible to ask students to perform lying down movements unless they are absolutely clear about instructions beforehand. Music can be used, wooden floors transmit vibrations and rhythms can be picked up from observation rather than hearing. A drum is very good, as the action can indicate when to start and when to stop. I feel dance movement for these students is a very important part of their learning.

ELDERLY PEOPLE

The main reason why elderly people wish to participate in movement sessions is because they are anxious to keep their joints supple and tone up the parts of the body that are mobile. Stroke patients are motivated by the same reasons, but with this group of students it is important to encourage them constantly, as the very nature of their illness tends to make them feel depressed and enormous willpower is required in order that they don't give up.

Always explain the reason why you are giving the session. If you simply present the class as 'music and movement' without an explanation of how it can be beneficial, the group can too easily feel that they are being treated like children. Explain each part of the programme as you go along. Remember that half an hour of concentrated movement can be as valuable as a longer session, during which students may tire and lose their concentration.

MIXED MEDIA WORKSHOPS

It is a good idea to allow students frequent opportunities to take part in mixed media workshops so that they can be aware of how all art forms can blend together and enhance each other. They will also realise the way in which artists of different disciplines can work together, that integration through the arts includes integrating the creative work that takes place in the classroom – dance and visual art, photography and

ABOVE *Warm-up: Gina Levete working with students with mental handicap.*
BELOW *Workshop, Hong Kong 1986: improvisation with water.*

ABOVE, LEFT *Gina Levete workshop, Mexico 1985. Theme: 'stretching'.*
ABOVE, RIGHT *Dance workshop, Interlink, Sri Lanka.*
BELOW *Workshop: theme 'touch'.*

dance, dance and drama, dance and poetry. When students become accustomed to mixed media workshops with two art forms, a third can be included. I have worked with a photographer and painter giving all-day workshops based on one theme. It was a challenging experience to blend our work together and fascinating to see how the students stretched themselves – and, most important of all, had fun.

INTEGRATED WORKSHOPS

Whenever possible arrange sessions which invite disabled and able to work together. Always have helpers participate in the sessions. These times are for self-expression and enjoyment. If your students leave with a big smile on their faces you will know they have begun to discover dance.

GINA LEVETE

Passages in this chapter first appeared in Gina Levete's No Handicap to Dance (1982) *and are reproduced by kind permission of the publishers, Souvenir Press.*

4
Creative Writing

WHERE IS THAT PEN OF MINE?

Everybody has a story to tell. Some have many. Everybody has precious moments of memory. Everybody has opinions, fears, loves; ideas, fancies, imaginings. Everybody has pain to negotiate. Some have much. Everybody has perceptions of beauty and intimations of the unknowable.

We have jokes to tell, prayers to utter, desires to express. We have been in love. We have been out of love. We have hated our parents. We have loved our parents. We have seen our dreams shattered. We have seen our dreams come true. We have failed in our responsibilities; we have succeeded in impossible ordeals. We have been ill and recovered. We have suffered bereavements – and welcomed babies into the world.

We have such richness of common emotional experience but our individual experience is unique. You may never have sat on a small ledge high on a mountain after a climb, eating a meat paste sandwich with a tiny slice of lemon peel in it. I have. The zest of that moment I hope never to forget. You may not have had your backside and legs repeatedly caned and whipped when you were five years old. I did. The memory still brings me fear. On the other hand I have not stood in the dole queues of modern Britain, or attempted an overdose, or driven a school outing in a coach to the seaside, or played cricket at Lord's, or the guitar by a camp fire. We have much to tell each other.

That is why creative writing is so important. Writers have always known this but it is only comparatively recently, I think, that wider implications of this in terms of therapy, community social work and the like have been recognised. I have done quite a lot of work in this field with psychiatric patients, with delinquents, with prisoners, with elderly people, children, adolescents, school teachers and aspiring writers. It is with the practicalities of running a workshop that I wish to concern myself in this chapter, rather than further rationale. Sufficient to say that there are many people in the world who are deprived (once their physical needs are dealt with – food, water, shelter, and so forth) of the means of communicating their ideas and feelings. And (and this is just as important) who have come to believe that their ideas and feelings are without significance. The creation of literature by such people, whether in prose or poetry, is one way in which this deprivation can be alleviated. And where the people in question are not literate, or where, because of disablement, they are unable to write, then we can act as scribe for them.

THE WORKSHOP

Anybody setting up a writers' workshop should consider first, numbers and location. With able-bodied and articulate people I have run workshops with as many as two-dozen people (fifty, once, if I correctly remember), but smaller numbers are desirable. Somewhere between eight and twelve seems to me just about ideal, but if the people are severely handicapped or mentally ill, smaller numbers (say five or six) are probably better. A very successful workshop of mine at St Clement's Hospital, London, consisted of six patients (although the individuals changed a little from week to week) and never less than three helpers. Sometimes we had as many helpers as patients. And these sessions worked very well.

It is essential that each individual who participates in a workshop is enabled to feel that his or her contribution is of value. The less able to fend for themselves the participants are, the more time the leader or helper will need to spend with each and, to make this possible, the group will have to be small. Conversely, the more self-sufficient the members, the larger the group can be.

As to location, we are usually limited by what is available. However, some vision of what we want is certainly needful, even if in the end we are obliged to compromise. It should be as little like school, and as much like a comfortable democratic activity as possible. I always try to get a carpeted room with armchairs set in a circle (that most levelling of all shapes). If there are desks, I try and break up the stultifying arrangement of them in straight rows. The St Clement's group met round a circular oaken table in the midst of an enormous ward; somehow we managed to create our own island. Although comfort and security are important, occasional maverick sessions in other locations (outdoors, for instance, on a fine summer's day or a bright snowy morning) can yield wonderful results. Runners of workshops will help themselves and their workshops, I believe, if they constantly remind themselves that although their position in the group is that of expert and initiator, they should not in other respects be leader. We are not doctors, teachers, scoutmasters, dictators or other wielders of power, we are facilitators. And although we should accept our responsibility for the overall running of the workshop, we should avoid as much as possible the leadership roles adhering to our position.

At an early stage in the planning of any workshop we should also consider our overall aims and objectives. Why are we doing it? What do we hope to achieve? However grandiose some of our answers may be (and I believe in grand and ambitious schemes), we should also be able to ask and answer some simple, practical questions. I would like to explicate my meaning here by giving some small account of the St Clement's workshop.

My grand ambition was 'to provide a voice for the valid experience' of these elderly psychiatric patients. I had just six two-hour sessions, spread out at fortnightly intervals over a period lasting from October through to December. To achieve my overall objective I devised, in discussion with Debbie Rowles, the occupational therapist, a simple strategy. We would base the bulk of the work on recollection, reminiscence and personal experience. One session we would run differently and discuss and write about colours and the feelings they evoked in us. We decided to make this the fourth. For each of the other five we selected topics: childhood, courting, work, the war, Christmas.

At each session we would talk about, and then try to write poetry on, these subjects. We chose poetry partly because of my own experience in this medium, and partly because it sometimes achieves considerable success in a very short space. Several of the patients were not able to write, so it was necessary for me and the helpers to act as secretaries. Once the patients understood the project, they worked very enthusiastically, and at the end we produced a small booklet of poetry 'Memories, Memories . . . ', of which the authors were extremely proud and which provided much discussion not only among patients who had taken part, but among others who hadn't, and also among some of the hospital staff. Some of the poems were later published in an edition of *Positif*, the Interlink newsletter.

On the first occasion the two therapists and I met, and half an hour was spent in discussing our plan, after which we prepared the table and chairs. We made it as welcoming as possible, put a potted plant in the middle of the table and put lots of different kinds of paper and pens and pencils out. We then assembled our group. I talked to them for a while about memory, about poetry, about childhood. I read them a couple of poems. I asked them about their own childhoods. They all responded with reminiscence, little tales, wonderful nuggets of social history. This part also took about thirty minutes. The next half hour was spent 'writing', making close contact with each member of the group and writing down what they said. We made it very clear that we were writing poetry, and read back what we had written for the authors to correct or alter. We read around, then, to share the work, and then, when lunchtime intervened, the therapists and I discussed what had gone on so far, clarified our next session's objectives and typed up the work. Here are two poems from that session, the first by Mary McGowan, the second by Fred Roberts.

The Bed

We slept in a big bed
It was four of her children
And my brother and I
We slept alongside them.

It was tremendous!
It was an old-fashioned bed
I remember it
In fact
There was nothing else
But the bed
In the room!

Ploughing

I was ploughing when I was fourteen.
When first you start to plough a field
You choose a spot to start.
You don't start too near the hedge,
If you did
You'd plough the dirt into the hedge,
You find a place to 'cut in'.
You've got two horses when you plough:
One walks in the furrow
The other walks on the outside.
When you get to the top of the field
You turn the plough over,
You do it with one hand.

Ploughing,
Oh that was beautiful!

And we used to make our own cider
And when you ploughed
The birds followed you,
After the worms, you see,
After the worms.

You made the cider in a cider cheese
It was built in straw.
Oaten straw was the only kind you could use,
Wheaten straw would break.
I've seen pigs drunk on cider pulp.

Ploughing now,
That was beautiful!

Fred Roberts had never made poetry before. He was eighty. He was very proud of this and other poems that we published in the booklet. Fred, who had left school before the First World War and could barely read, had been at first reluctant to join the group. He grew to love it – and underwent such a change in his attitudes and behaviour as the weeks went on that he was discharged shortly afterwards.

The other five sessions followed the same pattern and at the end of the sequence we had enough material for a small in-house publication. I will give a few words on producing a book or pamphlet later.

My workshops at the North Middlesex Hospital are rather different. Here we have patients of varying age who have chosen poetry from among a number of options (woodwork, doll-making, drawing, etc.).

I read poetry to the patients for a while from a considerable stock of books, and they also read. Kathryn Hudson, the occupational therapist, is always a strong supporting presence at these groups and sometimes a nurse is there too. We read and discuss. After about an hour I set a writing exercise, which we *all* do, any staff in the room as well as the patients. This is, in my view, very important. We do not expect the patients to try anything we are not ourselves prepared to try. We do not institute or perpetuate a class system. When everybody is ready (usually after thirty to forty minutes) we read back. Discussion follows. We have a large file of writing and occasionally we produce a *book*.

These workshops are very popular with some patients, and indeed for some serve as a lifeline.

There are individuals to whom this form of expression is especially important. I would like to illustrate what I mean with a brief anecdote.

One of the group, whom I will call Gloria, is unable to sit still. Her tongue lolls out and she has not much control of her physical movements. She speaks very indistinctly, she does not much enjoy the company of other patients, especially those whose behaviour is odd. And she expresses this by turning away from them. Gloria often mutters to herself, but it is difficult to understand what she says.

She writes very beautiful poetry, skilfully wrought, with an advanced vocabulary, threaded through with vivid imagery. In her own country, Ceylon, she has published poetry. Although she normally speaks indistinctly, when she reads poetry she makes a lot of effort and speaks with a laboured clarity that is lovely to hear.

When some nurses who knew her only as a patient attended a session, they refused to believe that she had written the poem she read. 'She never wrote that herself. She's incapable,' one of them said to me over lunch. I assured them that she had and later showed them some of her other work. Their attitude altered. But for over a year they had taken Gloria for an idiot.

I have written largely about work with mentally ill people because this work particularly exemplifies some of the problems and aspects of the creative writing workshop. But I would like to emphasise that such workshops are also valuable to other members of the community.

I have also concentrated on the piece of individual writing. However, with people of limited ability (and sometimes with highly sophisticated people) group poetry can be very exciting to create, and very satisfying to perform. I will describe just one method of doing this. Workshop leaders will, no doubt, be able to think of many more. Choose a subject of universal interest and get each participant to write a single sentence. Subjects might be: 'The Day My Childhood Ended', 'My First Memory', 'What I Fear', 'My Idea of Heaven' . . .

Devise with the group a rhythmic phrase to introduce and close the verses and then arrange the sentences you have obtained, singly and in twos and threes.

It might read like this:

What would be Heaven for me?
What would be Heaven for me?
To lie in bed all Monday morning.
That would be Heaven for me.

What would be Heaven for me?
A kiss from Robert Redford.

A cure for my grandson's illness.
A letter from my old mum.
Bananas and cream in the bath.
That would be Heaven
That would be Heaven
That would be Heaven for me . . . and so on.

EXERCISES

It is of tremendous help in the workshop to have a number of exercises to help initiate work. Here are some which I have used in the past. Many of them are written in rather a simplified form and are capable of almost infinite extension.

1 Play a record or tape of music and ask the students to write a response to what they hear.

2 Write a poem in the first person written from the point of view of an animal.

3 Write a poem which asks questions of an animal, perhaps after reading and discussing Blake's 'Tyger', or another poem in this form.

4 Take in objects which are in some respect interesting, handle them, look at them and write poetry based on the object. Or alternatively ask the participants to provide objects. The following poem was written in such a workshop:

The Needle and Cotton

A needle and cotton can mend so many things.
You can sew on buttons and zips and things.
Stitch a seam and sew a hem
And mend a tear in that pretty dress.

I'd like to take a needle and thread
And sew up the troubles of the world.
Stitch a seam between EAST and WEST,
Mend the tear between Catholic and Protestant
Embroider food for those without.

PENNY HAYDEN

5 'In A Few Words': a formula for simple poetry which might give confidence and a sense of achievement to a young or inexperienced writer. Write a noun; then two adjectives, then three verbs; then two adverbs; then another noun or the first noun repeated.

Bee
Furry, stripy
Flying, buzzing, stinging,
Suddenly, sharply.
Bee!

SUZY KING (aged eight)

6 Rather complicated, this: the students write five true statements about themselves (e.g., I live in Hackney. I have three children); then they write five untrue statements about themselves (e.g., I often dine at Buckingham Palace); and then five statements that could not possibly be true (e.g., my mother hasn't been born yet; I have never wept; I am a toy dog; I ate my breakfast on the moon today; I breathe solid rock). Having done all this the students will no doubt have much to discuss. You have not finished yet.

The next stage is to get the students (I call them this for want of a better word) to develop the logic of 'impossible' sentences for two, three, or four more lines. The result is often a venture into surrealism:

I am the knight in a chess game.
I step obliquely.
I will kill you from an unusual angle.

G.B

7 The students close their eyes. A small interesting object which they haven't seen is passed from hand to hand. The object is put out of sight and then the students write.

This often gives rise to interesting metaphorical writing. Handling a buzzard's skull, for instance, sentences were written about bubbles, lace, a boat, a scimitar. These formed the basis of poems.

8 'A Blitz': hold up an object. The students write, as rapidly as possible, for a set period of time (ninety seconds, say). They look at the object and write – just a list of words. If they block, they write again the word they wrote before. At the end of the time they stop and then read out out what they have written. Do this three times with three quite different objects: a violin, a cabbage, a coat, for instance. Some of the lists already have poetic quality. Set the students the problem of re-ordering the words they wrote to make a poem. This exercise is surprisingly effective.

9 Get two students to cooperate on a piece without conferring. The first writes a question. The second writes an answer, the first writes another

question, the second another answer and so on, until they feel the poem is finished. A subject could be given or it could be quite open.

10 Provide the students with a stock of magazines and ask them to make a collage poem by cutting out the words or phrases they want and pasting them onto a background. This often gives rise to high creativity. The student feels absolved from responsibility for the words and 'goes to town'.

11 Cut a known poem of rich vocabulary (for instance 'Now Sleeps the Crimson Petal') into its individual words and give them to the students as raw material for a poem.

12 Write a simple acrostic, rhymed or unrhymed.

Horse

*H*e follows the wind
*O*ver the hills
*R*unning so fast
*S*howing his beauty
*E*ver onwards.

TRUDIE CANNON (aged nine)

In facilitating the composition of prose, exercises are also helpful. These tend to be less prescriptive and elaborate. Here is a baker's dozen of examples:

1 Write a passage or extract of a story in which the *place* is given prominence (e.g., a room or street or even a land).

2 Write a story or extract containing strong physical action between two people.

3 Write a dialogue between three people in which two of them are in conflict over a possession.

4 Write a family meal-time scene.

5 Write a story in which are hidden elements from a well-known myth or legend. (Or you might prescribe the legend, e.g., 'Write a modern love story based on the Eden myth'.)

6 Write a story about a journey.

7 Write an episode round a specific object, which you describe.

8 Write a love scene.

9 Describe a fight.

10 Write a first-person narrative as a character of the opposite sex.

11 Write an episode about a child and an animal.

12 Ask the students to include ten specific words in a piece of writing.

13 Write a piece using only one-syllable words.

Exercises such as these are fairly easy to devise. You could use your or your students' current reading to isolate techniques or areas of subject matter. For instance, after reading Hemingway you might set an exercise in extended dialogue with no individual utterance containing more than five words.

THE BOOK

As I mentioned before, it is a good idea to produce an anthology of work from a workshop. It can also, in some circumstances, be very helpful to display writing on a bulletin board or on the wall. (I sometimes do this with my own work in progress.)

Techniques of book production are very varied. I will make some suggestions about one possible low-budget method which may be of help.

First make your editorial selection. I like to do this in collaboration with the student group but this isn't always viable. Where humanly possible, be sure to include material by *all* members.

Choose a title for the anthology. Very often a phrase or line from one of the poems will serve. Check through the poems making sure they are in mint form and obtain permission from the authors to include their work. Give titles to poems. They formalise and, as it were, authenticate the work, but preferably the author will already have done this. Type the poems and cut them out, so that you know their physical size. Using A4 paper turned landscape-wise and folded down the middle, design a layout and when it is finalised paste or staple the poems onto the page. You will have your own editorial principles – but it is perhaps worth saying that poems on similar subjects often go well close together, but not always, especially if they are very alike.

The cover, which will be thin card, should be designed and, of course, carry the title. The next stage is to retype on a long-barrelled typewriter, so that the paper can be put in sideways. Remember that one typed page represents two reading pages and space your magazine accordingly.

The next stage is to photocopy, being very careful which pages back onto which. When you have all your sheets and your cover you fold each sheet separately and insert them within the covers. Staple or sew.

CONCLUSION

I hope that in this short space I have been able to offer some strong, practical help in operating a creative writing workshop. Flexibility is perhaps the most important factor, and of course discussion is paramount. Our common experience is so worth exploring, and language is a tool we all have. I wish you joy.

I would like to leave the last words to Caroline Akumu, a member of one of my workshops.

The Pen

The pen to write with,
Communication to friends, relatives,
Good news, bad news, the pen is always needed.
Children use it to scribble on walls,
On places that they shouldn't.
Junior children want and wish for
The day when they can progress
To using a pen, like grown ups
Instead of a pencil.

Teenagers hunt for a pen to write their first secret
Thoughts into their diary.
Adults use the pen for little notes.
Employers use the pen to assess the potential employee.
Teachers mark with the pen, reports to parents.

Everyone needs the pen; little shopping memos
To do weekly trips to the shop for a mother.
The pen is a form of communication from the
Blind to signing the Official Secrets Act.
The pen lays down the law.
It can be used by the illiterate if they only knew how.
Messages left by pen.

The pen, the most powerful instrument used world wide.
Where is that pen of mine?

GERARD BENSON

5
Puppetry

Everyone is attracted to a puppet, perhaps for its beauty, its pathos or just for that magical quality which has universal appeal and where age and handicap is of no significance. It is a quality which attracts the child in all of us, the child who is buried under the pressures of 'real life'. Puppetry has been a constant source of joy to me, a lifting of the spirit, an ever-present interest which develops in so many ways that I never fail to marvel at its diversity: a colourful history of a 3,000-year-old art form, opening the gates to many cultures and traditions; a therapy which has already been proved to be of great value in the treatment of mental and physical ills; a theatre form which admits no barriers of language or culture? Whatever paths you wish to tread, puppetry can be the gateway to all of them.

Its practical advantages are numerous. First, it is inexpensive, so a lack of funding for your project need not cripple the enterprise. Puppets can be created from many ordinary household objects, from bottles and tops, cutlery and discarded packaging, clothes which are no longer of use, and from many of the small bits and pieces which are often thrown away. All you need is imagination and patience. It is useful to remember that few puppets need a theatre, and that those which do will perform quite adequately from behind any screen which hides the puppeteer. I shall come back to the ways in which you can improvise a stage.

Puppetry is truly small-scale theatre. You will need only a corner of a room, with a table if possible, for planning and making your puppet characters. You do not need much space to start with. I have worked with puppets of all sizes, from finger-size to about two metres high. The whole cast for one of my demonstrations can be packed comfortably into one medium-sized suitcase. Very large puppets are possible of course, and some puppeteers specialise in this kind of work – I have seen figures over six metres high in an outdoor theatre production. However, remember that they need large amounts of material and the employment of at least two manipulators – and this means expense. If money (or the lack of it) is an important factor, keep the puppets small.

Puppets are able to express concepts and information without the need of a common language. It is an effective and creative method of communication and ideal for that part of the educating process which is concerned with building closer relationships between teacher and pupils. A teacher who introduces puppets becomes a special person, one who has brought magic into the lessons – and many barriers are broken in this way. I would urge teachers, especially those who work with disabled children to try puppetry; it will open so many doors, for them. Students working together on a puppetry programme will gain in self-confidence and learn to work as a team.

Other art forms can be integrated into your programme. Music is one, whether singing, playing, composing or listening. Painting, drawing, sculpting, needlework, design and dance can all be incorporated and so too can writing and making plays, songs and poems. These are subjects which help to develop the creativity of your students. Added to all this, you are offering students the chance to carry on an art form which is over 3,000 years old, yet as up-to-date as today, and an occupation for their leisure time which is intellectually satisfying and great fun.

How do you set about a puppetry project? First, try to contact one or a number of puppeteers. Look in theatre advertisements, in newspapers and magazines, ask your local education department or the library. Have you a college of dance, drama or visual art near by? They will surely be able to help. There is an international puppetry association called UNIMA which is the Union Internationale de la Marionnette. This is an association for all who have an interest in puppetry of any kind, whether performance, teaching, writing or simply general interest. UNIMA has centres in more than sixty countries, and any one of these centres will know what you need. There are also many puppet guilds and associations in Europe, and in America there are branches of Puppeteers of America in most states. In Britain the BPMTG (British Puppet and Model Theatre Guild) has plenty of members, all of whom will be happy to help. In Britain, too, we have two flourishing puppet centres, one in Birmingham, part of the Midlands Art Centre and one in London in Battersea. The North West Puppetry Forum has recently been formed in Manchester to help puppeteers with meetings and courses. From your enquiries you should get the opportunity to see some puppet performances, and find a tutor. A list of useful books and addresses is included at the end of this chapter.

There are three main ways of tackling a programme of puppetry. Whichever way you choose, you must first make some puppets, either from a book or, ideally, with a tutor. The first way, *you* do all the work, *you* make the puppets, learn how to use them, and act with them. Then through the puppets *you* teach your students rhymes, songs and stories. The second method begins as does the first, *you* must make some puppets. These should be geared to the skills and ability of your pupils. After you have shown what action is possible with your models, you will then help the pupils make the puppets and use them in a play, with music, and/or in a theatre group. The third method is used when your project is to be the formation of a theatre group. You must begin with a number of puppets and write and produce an entertainment which will involve the students. If funding is not a problem, you can buy ready-made puppets, but they are usually expensive if they are to work well. I would advise you to try making a puppet first. The choice is yours.

The next step can only be taken when you have decided whether your project is to be limited to one session – 'short term' – or 'long term, which involves a greater amount of time spread out over some weeks. If your project is for one session or one day, it is best, I feel, to begin with a demonstration. Follow this with a practical workshop, allowing at least two hours; this will provide a session of interest and stimulation. It is simpler, if you are only there for a day, to keep to one type of puppet – for example, glove or rod puppets, marionettes or shadows. This kind of short-term activity can be particularly useful for a holiday scheme or festival. Try to arrange for your students to visit a theatre and see a professional puppet performance, which will most certainly enhance their interest and possibly stimulate their appetite for further activities.

Long-term projects are very different. Here you have the time to investigate more thoroughly the different kinds of puppets, and to decide which appeal to you most, which you will try first, and what kind of theatre, if any, you will need. A long-term project allows time to build up a stock of puppets and materials for shows, exhibitions and workshops.

If you intend to work on an extended course like this, it is useful to know something about the different kinds of puppets. There are five main types: finger puppets, which are usually used for very small children, hand puppets, rod, string, and shadow puppets.

Finger puppets are small, fit onto the fingers and can be used as characters in stories and rhymes. Children find them quite intriguing when they are used in nursery counting games and songs. You can have a box or a pocket full of these small puppets for a morning's activity. Some years ago, in a hospital, an experiment with finger puppets proved highly successful. It had been noticed that children who had undergone surgery to straighten deformed fingers and toes could not be persuaded to move them. Finger puppets were tried, and exercises carried out without the children worrying about the possibility of pain. They were too busy making their puppets perform.

Hand puppets should be at least as long as the length of your arm from fingertip to elbow. There are two kinds of simple hand puppets: glove puppets, where the head is attached to a robe which covers the puppeteer's hand and arm, and sock puppets, which are easily made from large socks. Glove puppets are very direct, for the movements made by the fingers and hand are translated precisely into puppet head and body movements. You can simulate clapping, waving, bowing, walking, jumping and running, and picking up and managing stage props. With sock puppets, the toe of the sock is tucked in, making a moving mouth which is held from inside by the fingers. A good vigorous movement for singing or speaking can be produced by opening and closing the fingers. Care must be taken to synchronise movement with the required words.

Perhaps the first of the rod puppets in Europe was the jester's stick or *marot* used in the European courts of the Middle Ages. This was a very simple puppet consisting of a head fastened to a stick with a suggestion of a dress in the decorations hanging from it. Nowadays a flowing robe hides the whole of the rod, and hands and arms, attached to the main rod, can also be manipulated by separate rigid wires (umbrella spokes are ideal). The rod puppet has great dramatic possibilities with its sweeping, graceful movements: practise in front of a mirror – you will be charmed. It is ideal for representing gods or royalty and other powerful characters. Its possible variations make it suitable to be made by children or adults.

String puppets, or marionettes, seem to intrigue people the most. The puppet figure can be made from a variety of materials, from wood and metal to synthetics and natural fabrics. You must, however, make sure that the limbs are loosely jointed so that they move easily. Humanoid figures can perform a variety of ordinary movements with nine strings: two to the head, two attached to the shoulders, two to the arms, two to the knees and one to the small of the back. There are also types of marionettes which are manipulated by metal rods attached to the head and the hands. In India some have long flowing skirts and no legs, and are controlled by one string which runs from the centre of the crown and is attached at the other end to the back of the figure.

Though this is quite acceptable for the limited movements which are required for these performances, it is much simpler to attach two strings to the head, one above each ear. This gives more directional control to the puppeteer – in other words, the puppet will walk where you want it to go.

These days it is unusual to perform in an elaborate marionette theatre with a bridge for the puppeteers. Instead, wearing dark clothes, the operator works behind the puppets (but in full view of the audience) and necessary pieces of scenery can be free-standing. It is quite amazing that even if there is no complicated lighting, the puppeteer seems to disappear into the background as all attention is concentrated on the puppets and their movements. These marionettes may vary in size from diminutive figures of six inches to characters which are half life-size, though the usual height is about eighteen inches. A safe rule to follow in all branches of puppetry, but especially with marionettes, is 'Keep it simple'. Complicated stringing can soon become irretrievably tangled and each string is an added difficulty when manipulating your puppet.

Shadows are the only type of puppet which cannot function without a stage. This takes the form of a screen covered with a taut piece of translucent material and having a source of light at the back, which could be the daylight through a window, bright light or a complicated console of electric lights and dimmers. The puppets themselves are silhouettes made from card, thin plywood, metal or wire, and animated by rods attached to the back of the shape. They are sometimes used as plain, solid figures and sometimes pierced with designs so that the light can shine through. When any kind of translucent coloured fabric is fastened behind the pierced motifs, the dark shapes of the basic figures are transformed. Eastern shadow puppets are usually made from fine leather and pierced with intricate designs through which the light can shine. They are also painted elaborately with bright colours as the audience can sit at the back or the front of a performance. Shadow puppets are my favourite, they are very easy to make, magical to view and inexpensive to operate. As they must be stored flat, it is important that the rods which move them can either be removed or folded down when not in use.

There have been hundreds of books written about puppetry. Many public libraries have a selection, and the puppetry associations have extensive collections and can give you information about suitable reading. When you feel that you have accumulated some basic knowledge about this subject, try to find a puppeteer who will work with you, either alone or with a small group of would-be teachers. This will be your first major financial outlay, but it will give you greater confidence if you can make your first puppet under the guidance of a competent tutor. Once you have made a puppet, you have a basis from which to launch your first workshop, though you will, of course, be restricted to the kind of puppet you have learnt to make.

How will you run a workshop? Let us presume that you begin with glove puppets. First make at least two very different characters and begin to collect all the materials you will need for the session. Ask everybody who is to be involved to help to collect wool and fabric, and aim to have enough material to make two puppets for each student. The most expensive items will be scissors, needles and pins, thread for sewing and glue. Perhaps the local school might help you here, in exchange for puppet shows for the children.

At the workshop there must be an adequate working space for each person. Try to get an experienced puppeteer to run the first workshop for you and your team of helpers. After the teams have made their first puppets, encourage them to read and experiment with the puppets together. You should practise in front of a mirror.

Now you are ready to manage on your own. First lay out your materials. When you are ready to show your puppets, point out what they can do. Make them walk, look round, clap hands, bow, pick up small objects, smell a flower. Use any or all of these actions. It is preferable if you can play background music as an accompaniment to the demonstration. Rely on the puppet to captivate your audience. Point out the materials, and get each student to collect all that he or she needs for a puppet. Then set them to work. Be there with help and advice, and try to allow different ideas to develop even if you do not think them attractive. As each puppet is finished, encourage your students to practise simple movements. If possible have mirrors so that they can see how they are getting on; and have some kind of screen for a theatre. Finally, play some bright music for the puppets to dance to. You can think later about their performing more serious movements.

Here are a few ideas for improving stages:

1 Tie a rope to the backs of two heavy chairs and drape a cloth over it.

2 Get behind a cupboard, a piano or bookshelves.

3 Turn a table on its side and perform behind it.

4 Drape material over one arm and, holding your arm out, let your puppet perform behind it.

5 Fasten a cloth to the two sides of a doorway, having the top of it at a convenient height for most of the group.

There are many ideas for more permanent theatres in the books I have recommended at the end of this chapter.

I have structured many puppet programmes, both short and long-term. My short-term work has included demonstrations with all kinds of puppets. When I gave a demonstration in the geriatric ward of a local hospital, some of the women were so interested that they asked for an immediate workshop. There was a good supply of tools and materials, so I stayed to help. Later, good 'follow-up' work by the staff resulted in a puppet show given by the patients to people in other wards of the hospital.

A workshop for mentally retarded adults, mostly men, showed them how to make 'no sewing' marionettes. It was a delight to see the rapt attention they gave to choosing of material, of buttons for eyes, and of wool or fur for hair. These adults showed a far more highly developed aptitude and creative ability than had been appreciated, and they were overjoyed when their puppets moved successfully to the music.

A day-long course for a group of teenagers, combining physically disabled and able-bodied young people, resulted in many fine puppets. Strangely enough, although they all worked well together, not much interest was shown in manipulation until the students were assured that the puppets they had created were theirs to keep. Only then did a relationship between puppet and maker seem to develop. Perhaps it is appropriate here to stress that a puppet belongs to its creator and should not be taken away by the tutor for future use. This applies particularly to short-term, 'one-off', workshops. On the other hand, in long-term projects the puppets may have to be kept until a show is over.

Another interesting short course was with a group of teachers and lasted for three hours. There were twenty-five in the group, and we worked in a large space. Each student had brought tools, glue, and a selection of materials. My demonstration of all kinds of puppets lasted for almost an hour. The teachers then had a 'hands on' experience, when they tried out different puppets. We spent a short time discussing suggestions for craft lessons, poems and stories. The teachers were then told where to find materials and encouraged to make a puppet which they could use with the children when they returned to school. Some were interested in the craft side, making simple puppets which young people could easily manage; others made finger puppets for teaching rhymes and songs. One music teacher made a series of cardboard rod puppets, each representing a different musical instrument. He intended to have musical 'conversations' so that the children could learn to distinguish the sounds made by each instrument.

My longer projects have included six year-long courses with junior children. Believing that puppetry could be used to teach all the skills usually acquired in a year's lessons of art and craft, I decided to try out my ideas with a class of children of seven and eight years. All types of puppets were included in my plan and the children were allowed to work at their own pace. Although I began with lessons for the whole class, I found that the children soon divided into groups working at a similar pace. A special area was designated for painting so that possible accidents could be confined. We experimented with all kinds of materials and made our puppets. Sometimes these were used for other lessons, for drama, music and movement, and for creative writing. They learned, in a year, to make all five types of puppet and use them successfully.

Another project of ten weekly workshops was run for leaders of community centres and workers in nursery establishments. These sessions opened many new avenues for after-school activities and holiday-time projects. All the group enjoyed these periods of creative activity. There can be few occupations which are as much fun, as magical or as satisfying as an evening of puppetry. Other long-term projects lasting from five to eight sessions have included work with disturbed teenagers, a term with a class of retarded infant children, sessions with unemployed young people, assisting in training programmes for library staff, and holiday schemes for children. I have worked on many university programmes, taking classes to show the advantages of puppetry in teaching English as a second language. At the other end of the educational scale I have found that the experience of working with children in nursery schools has been wonderful – the puppet removes all the strain of understanding and speaks to the heart. Small children do not hide their feelings.

I have also helped in prison rehabilitation programmes. Perhaps the secret of success in this type of work is that initially puppetry does not offer any great difficulties, or seem to be teaching anything, yet through the puppet many emotions can be expressed.

Although puppetry is essentially a visual art, and I have had no personal experience with those who are totally blind, I imagine that listening to the music, enjoying a more detailed description of the events, and having a 'hands on' practice afterwards, would prove a

ABOVE LEFT *Rod puppet dancers;* RIGHT *All sorts of container tops make marionettes.*

LEFT *Junk puppets ready to go.*

ABOVE *Shadow puppets need a screen.* BELOW *'I just love him.'*

rewarding experience. I did once work with a group of partially-sighted children and enjoyed seeing their delight in the puppets as they explored them with their fingertips (I had tried to use many different textures and kinds of materials). They seemed to find the large figures particularly satisfying. Deaf students can derive much joy from puppetry programmes and become competent manipulators.

It is hard to calculate the financial costs of any puppetry project. The only assurance I can offer is that it can be done cheaply by using discarded materials and oddments of scrap and waste. Most puppeteers, too, are happy to answer questions and give advice, being only too pleased to stimulate interest in their art. So try it – it is a joy.

UNIMA President: Dr Henryk Jurkowski, Ulica Krucza 5/11 M 49, 00548 Warsaw, Poland.

UNIMA Vice-Presidents: 1 Meher R. Contractor, Nowroki Vakil Compound, Shahi-Bag, Ahmedabad 4 380-004, India; 2 Margareta Niculescu, Teatrul Tandarica, Rue Eremia Grigorescu, Bucarest Sector 1 153288, Romania; 3 Taiji Kawajiry, Puppet Theatre PUK, 2-12-3 Yoyogi, Shibuya-Ku, Tokyo 151, Japan; 4 Michael Meschke, Marionetten, Kungstradgarden, S111 47 Stockholm, Sweden.

UNIMA General Secretary: Jacques Felix, BP 249, 08103 Charleville-Mezières Cedex, France.

British UNIMA: Secretary: Percy Press, 16 Templeton Road, London N15; **Membership Secretary:** Stan Parker, 10 Hurley Road, Little Corby, Carlisle CA4 8QY, Cumbria.

British Puppet and Model Theatre Guild: Honorary Secretary: Gorden Shapley, 18 Maple Road, Yeading, Nr Hayes, Middlesex UB4 9LP.

Chairman of British UNIMA and Director of The Puppet Theatre: John Blundell, Midlands Arts Centre, Cannon Hill Park, Birmingham 12.

The Puppet Centre Trust, Battersea Arts Centre, Lavender Hill, London SW11 5TJ.

North West Puppetry Forum: Secretary: David Mason, 20 Norburn Road, Longsight, Manchester M13 0QQ.

Puppets of America: President: Kathy Piper, 12013 S.R. 521, Sunbury OH 43074, USA.

There is no book which deals with all aspects of puppetry but I have found the following useful:

FOR FINGER PUPPETS

Hutchings, Margaret, *Making and Using Finger Puppets,* Mills & Boon, London.

FOR GLOVE AND ROD PUPPETS

Paludan, Lis, *Playing with Puppets,* Mills & Boon, London.

FOR STRING PUPPETS

Bramall Eric, *Making a Start with Marionettes,* G. Bell & Sons, London.

FOR SHADOWS

Cochrane, Louise, *Shadows in Colour,* Chatto & Windus, London.

GENERAL INFORMATION

Philpot, A. R., *Let's Look at Puppets,* Frederick Muller, London.

MANIPULATION

Engler, Larry and Fijan, Carol, *Making Puppets Come Alive,* David & Charles, Newton Abbott, Devon, UK.

EDUCATION

Hunt, Tamara and Renfro, Nancy, *Puppetry in Early Childhood Education,* Nancy Renfro Studios, Austin, Texas, USA.

ALL TYPES OF PUPPETRY (NOT FOR BEGINNERS)

Currell, David, *The Complete Book of Puppetry,* Pitman.

PAT BRENNAN

6
Drama for Beginners

Drama allows us to reflect on our past history, it mirrors the present and allows us to speculate about the future in a way which brings each chosen subject to vivid living form. It allows us to develop our emotions and to experience situations which we might never encounter in our everyday life. It gives each one of us who practise it permission to play and to understand ourselves more deeply.

Drama can be used to express anything that we wish, whatever our physical or mental condition. During the past twenty-six years I have worked with many people in a wide variety of special situations – people who are mentally or physically disabled, offenders in prison, children in schools, the young unemployed, as well as many elderly people. Invariably, once a group had experienced a drama session they wished to explore it further.

There is something deeply satisfying in the idea of playing a role, of being someone other than yourself, of being able to express ideas which may be totally new to you or which you would agree with but would normally never have the confidence to express in real life. Drama gives us a vehicle for overcoming prejudice and ignorance. It is common to all cultures and is easily communicated between peoples and nations.

GETTING A DRAMA GROUP OFF THE GROUND

If you are going to run a drama activity then you have to try and interest as many people as possible in participating and giving support to ensure the group's survival.

Members of staff must be considered as well as the patients in a hospital. How will the activity fit in with the hospital day? The same approach applies equally to other situations. Contact local professional actors or directors of any theatre, television or radio stations in your area and ask the artists to involve themselves in your project, perhaps by coming to perform to your students or by leading workshops. There may also be good amateur theatre companies in your area who could be invited to work with you.

Make use of local radio and newspapers to advertise your plans to establish a drama scheme, and invite people to come forward to join as students or volunteer helpers. If you do not feel confident enough to run the workshop yourself, there is usually someone in your community who will have the skill. In any event I would advise you to try to enlist the help of actors to take the sessions in the first instance.

SIZE OF GROUP

I find the ideal number for a new drama group is between eight and twelve people. This number is large enough to allow some support for everyone from their colleagues and small enough for there to be a comfortable atmosphere. If I work with people who are severely disabled I need extra helpers who can work on an individual basis with the students.

SPACE REQUIRED

The space needed for a session is a room large enough for the group to move around without feeling that it is either too small or too large. Usually a school classroom is large enough. The room can be quite bare – there is no need for furniture unless chairs are needed for those unable to sit on the floor. Often a bare space will stimulate the imagination more successfully than a cluttered arena. If you're lucky enough to be able to work out of doors, find a location which is not too large so that people won't feel lost in it. If presented with one of those vast auditoriums with a stage at one end, then I use the stage, *not* the auditorium! If the space is equipped with lighting and sound equipment that is a fortunate bonus; but it is not crucial in the early stages of a workshop activity.

EQUIPMENT

Although drama can begin with just an idea, I like to add sounds, lighting, make-up, costume and properties as the work develops. I also find that in addition to my own equipment, nearby educational establishments, theatres, hospitals or community centres will lend me things. However, for ordinary workshop activity not much is necessary, so no one should allow the lack of materials to deter them from creating a drama group. The following is a list for an ideal situation, *not* for the beginner:

Tape recorder
Record player or compact disc player
Spotlights and stands
Lighting dimmer board

Electrical leads for lighting and sound
Microphone
Amplifier
Musical instruments
Make-up and costume
Mirrors
Materials for scenery and props

Remember that collecting equipment often means having extra storage space and possibly a vehicle for transportation, so acquisition does bring its own problems.

GIVING A WORKSHOP

Some readers may wish to know how to structure a drama workshop, so let me describe the way that I set them up and a sample session that I have given. Everyone has to work out his or her own method of approach but the following description may help you get started.

I would suggest that a workshop of one hour is enough to begin with. As the students and leader become acquainted with each other and develop their working relationship the period of time can be gradually lengthened.

Before commencing the workshop I try to assess the overall atmosphere in the room. If I consider the students would benefit from a warm up, then that is how we will start; but if relaxation and concentration need to be obtained, then I begin with a quiet concentrated exercise.

Thereafter the workshop is split into four sections. I begin by asking the students to sit in a circle and I present an introductory exercise which is designed to encourage people to be settled and ready for work. This introduction can last ten to twenty minutes, depending on the group. Some people take longer to relax and to develop their concentration than others. Secondly, a short stimulus is presented, sometimes with words, sometimes music – again to develop concentration for the main theme of the session. This stage will last between ten and twenty minutes.

Thirdly, I encourage the students to split into small units of three or four and begin to create an improvised piece based on the subject introduced in the second section. During this period I constantly advise and help the group as they improvise. This third section of the workshop takes the longest time and is the period when the participants must rely on their own creativity. We can work on this section from between thirty minutes to one hour, sometimes longer.

Fourthly, I encourage each small group to present their work to the other groups. Some people consider this not to be a good idea as it may inhibit those people who prefer to present their work in performance. All I can say is that in my experience this section is often the most productive part of a workshop, provided the students view their drama activity as a fellowship and not a competition. In any event it is my responsibility to develop the right atmosphere from the outset.

WARM UP

The students are asked to find a space somewhere in the room for them to move without touching anyone else. Then: 'Stand with feet slightly apart. Shake your right foot in the air. Loosen the ankle. Then the other foot.' I continue in this way until every set of muscles has been loosened. I use music. With some groups, particularly the elderly, the exercise period requires adaptation.

RELAXATION

The students are asked to lie on their backs on the floor. If this is not practicable, then they can relax in chairs. Then: 'Place your hands palm downwards on the floor [or arm of chair], and during the next few minutes I would like you to listen to my voice only as you relax. Relax your eyelids. They feel very heavy and they close. Relax your tongue in your mouth. Let your mouth open and your jaw relax. Let your shoulders feel heavy. Let your arms feel heavy. Concentrate on your breathing. With each gentle rising and falling of your abdomen let your trunk relax, your chest, your stomach, your pelvis, then your legs and finally your feet and ankles. Let the relaxation travel right to your fingertips. Feel as if you are floating. Remain in that position relaxing even more deeply. Concentrate on seeing a black space in your mind's eye.'

FIRST SECTION

Following the warm up or relaxation, the students are asked to sit in a circle ready for the introduction. After they've introduced themselves to each other they are asked to describe their neighbour's appearance, to touch their neighbour's face, to feel the texture of the skin. In this first section I try to enhance people's sensory awareness for the rest of the session, by including exercises which allow for observation, hearing, touch, taste or smell.

I ask them to identify sounds outside the room, to listen to sounds inside the room, to whisper a message to their neighbour. Make him or her strain to hear. 'Concentrate on smells – wood, polish, hay, damp. Taste your own lips. Lick the skin on the back of the hand. Is the taste different from the taste on your lips?' I ask them to choose a partner and work in pairs. They sit facing their partners, quite near, close their eyes and trace the outlines of the other's facial features with the tips of their fingers, memorising and feeling shapes and texture as they go. 'With your partner, imagine you are caring for a wounded person – *or* repairing broken machinery. With your partner, imagine that you are looking into a mirror and with one person leading, try to observe each other's movement so closely that you produce a perfect mirror image in movement.'

SECOND SECTION

Following this first section, I then introduce the main subject for the workshop, which in this instance is to be an improvisation based on a 'space' theme. I use the voice to describe a situation which each of the students is asked to follow individually. Later on there will be an opportunity for people to work on the development of this.

Notice that during the directed passage the words in bold print demonstrate that the accent is still on developing the individual's sensory and emotional awareness. The students are asked to find a space to sit or lie down. Then:

'You are lying on the floor in a star position [or with arms and feet spread out in a sitting position]. You **feel** with your hands and you realise that you are lying on a couch. Judging by the texture of the material on which you are lying, you figure that the couch is made of soft vinyl or some other similar material. You **touch** the luxuriously soft cushions, **feeling** their texture, the smoothness, the slight chill. You **look** upwards and **see** a large console with a great variety of knobs, levers, switches, sliding bars and other electronic controls. You begin to manipulate these controls and, as you do, you gradually become aware of the noises in this place. You **hear** the sound of engines, powerful engines, throbbing somewhere far beneath you. You **hear** the sound of very controlled voices describing the countdown for a rocket take-off. You realise that you are **listening** to the space control centre, and that you and the people next to you are all about to be hurtled into space! You can **hear** voices over the intercom instructing you to make the necessary manoeuvres with the controls. You can **smell** the newness inside the small cabin. You can **taste** the salty sweat on your lips as you lick them in anxious anticipation. You **hear** the controller's voice saying: '10-9-8-7-6-5-4-3-2-1-zero!' You **feel** the vibration as the enormous engines thrust you and your companions into the atmosphere. You can **see** smoke through the windows as the engines struggle. Gradually the speed increases and the vehicle surges into the upper atmosphere and thence into space heading for outer space. There is blackness outside the windows of the space vehicle now. You remove the space suit that you are wearing, the **sound** of engines has now disappeared. If **feels** as though the space ship is hurtling through space. Suddenly you **see** a storm of meteors hurtling towards the ship. You can **taste** fear. You can **smell** your own fear. You manage to guide the ship through the meteors. Suddenly you **sense** the lurch as the ship goes into overdrive and you **see** beautifully coloured stars and planets flash by. You and your companions prepare for your first night aboard the space ship.'

Following this introduction of the main theme in which students work individually, we arrive at the part when they work closely with one another, contributing their own ideas for the continuation of the story that has been introduced. I encourage them to investigate their own imaginations, to ask themselves questions about what is likely to happen next, to ensure that a lively but concentrated atmosphere continues. The students then develop the theme either in pairs or with three or four people. If you are taking a workshop try to ensure that people are concentrating, otherwise improvisation can become chaotic. Add your views about how they are working together and the way their improvisation is progressing. Your suggestions can help to link the ideas of the students.

This second section is important for the workshop. In addition to the subject of the talk-through described you could pick themes from taped or live music, songs, cuttings from newspapers, a box of stage properties, costumes, make-up, extracts from plays, novels, poems, current affairs, the environment and the current political situation.

THIRD AND FOURTH SECTIONS

The third section is when I encourage the creation of a new composition which the students themselves devise. The fourth section is the time when they present their work. Initially, I look at that work from the viewpoint of what the piece is trying to say; then I encourage the whole group to make constructive suggestions about it. The students are asked to consider how they could highlight the dramatic qualities of the improvisation by introducing background music, special effects or stage lighting. I always allow people time to organise their 'set', which may involve the available furniture and anything else to hand which has become part of the improvisation in the students' minds.

When they have presented their 'performances' we form a circle for the conclusion of the workshop to discuss how the improvisation could be developed in the next session. This means that some ideas can be worked on by students together between workshops. Finally, as students need to have a short relaxation period at the end of the session, I usually use live or taped music linked to the subject of the workshop to which they can listen and relax.

I have used this model workshop theme on a number of occasions – and it works. With a group of students with mental disabilities it led to the making of a video film. With a group of physically disabled people it led finally via an outer space theme to a consideration of the word 'space' in relation to the daily needs of the physically handicapped. The resulting performance had humour, tragedy, reality and fantasy in a fine mix. One group of elderly people created a wonderful improvisation about travelling from the Earth to a far distant planet on which they set up a new civilisation. They were having another go at life, trying to get it right all over again – reliving their past experience, evaluating it and planning for change.

TRAINING

I have received a very mixed training which has proved useful to me in my professional life. Teacher training, drama training and that invaluable experience which comes through *doing*. I did not train specifically to work with disadvantaged groups. It came through a natural development and combination of teaching, performance and theatre direction and an awareness that a significant part of our society obtained little access to the arts.

In the United Kingdom and elsewhere there are various universities, polytechnics, training colleges and community colleges which are providing training and qualifications in drama. There are artistic therapy training courses in some countries (see Directory), and a growing number of such therapists are working in hospitals and institutions. There are, however, very few places which provide specific training for artists wishing to practise and communicate their art forms in special situations. Indeed it may not be necessary – most of the artists that I have met who work in this way came to do it because of change of direction in their artistic lives. Obviously some drama training will be of great help if you wish to set up a drama activity, but if that is not practical do not allow your present lack of training to deter you.

I have been keenly aware that as an artist working in these areas I should be encouraging others to participate. Now I invite people from the local community to come and work with me so that I may be able to give them some training alongside the actual workshop. Doing the job is the best way of learning the best methods.

Make sure that everyone is kept fully informed about the drama project because then they will be able to help you more. Even those people who find drama difficult to understand can eventually be led to see the benefits both for themselves and their charges. Recently I held a six-week hospital staff training course. The initial object of the course was for the students to learn about the presentation of work for patients. Though that remained the principal aim, the accent moved to a more personal consideration of drama and the people taking part gradually realised that they were gaining a great deal from the experience for themselves. As a result of the course they wanted to have a regular workshop for their *own* use, never mind the patients!

When you make the decision to set up a drama project, whether you decide to take the long road towards personal training or the shorter route of inviting an artist to set it up for you, the rewards will far outweigh the hard work involved. The delight on people's faces as they welcome you for the week's workshop says it all, particularly if you know that if it were not for the session, that person's opportunities for self-expression would be very limited.

I always remember the character Tom in Tennessee Williams's play *The Glass Menagerie* who comments to the Gentleman Caller that people should not be content for a few professional actors to 'have all the adventures for us'. Not everyone will want to participate; but the option should be there, based on experience of working in the medium.

DICK ALLWOOD

THEATRE IMPROVISATION

The previous section suggests structures that first introduce students to drama. As they begin to feel confident, theatre improvisation can be incorporated. It must be remembered that in improvising the mood is not of competition and displaying talent, but of exploring one's abilities and creative energy.

Theatre improvisation is often based on abstract ideas which the student works on spontaneously with little or no guidance from the tutor. It is an approach which can open up a new world within the imagination. Using improvisation in this way requires students to work by themselves in the first instance. There needs to be that private space which allows them to explore before they have to have to consider fitting in with other people's imaginations. The ideas suggested here would require people to work individually (all at the same time), followed by partner work, to culminate in a group improvisation. All these suggestions have been used with able-bodied or disabled children from seven years upwards, and with adults, actors and amateurs. The framework for a session can be as follows:

THEME FOR THE WHOLE WORKSHOP: THE WORD 'WALK'

1 The improvisation begins with a movement warm up.

2 All the students are asked to walk around in a circle and discover as many different ways of walking as they can. Silly walks, serious walks, slow, fast, walk on the toes, side of feet, heels, walking bent double, walking high, over to one side. Students are asked to put on faces that they feel suit the walk. Some students demonstrate their walks.

3 Everyone walks normally, going round in a circle in the opposite direction. The tutor calls out: 'Someone is following you'; each student continues to walk, breaking away to respond to that suggestion. Perhaps they walk slowly, stop and look around. Is the response one of tension, fear? Does this affect the whole body or just parts of the body? The tutor encourages the student to become aware of the body's response; thus each person begins to build the beginning of improvisation around 'Someone is following you'. The next stage is to 'set the scene'. Each student sets out for a walk and discovers he or she is being followed – the idea/story is developed. (These exercises are quite short, perhaps a few minutes.)

4 Each person takes a partner for spontaneous improvisation. The only decision to be made is who is to be the 'follower', and who the 'followed'. The walk begins again anywhere in the room. On a drum cue from the tutor, the person being followed turns to his or her partner: 'Why are you following me?' This sentence has been given by the tutor; from there on the dialogue, movements and expressions are generated by the students themselves.

The partners 'being followed' (on the drum cue) all speak at the same time ('Bedlam'). When the tutor feels it is time, another cue is given to 'cut'. The reason that everyone speaks at the same time is to prevent any feeling of shyness. At this stage the dialogue is simply between the two people.

5 Individual partners are then asked to improvise for the rest of the group. Because this is 'spontaneous dialogue', they are asked not to repeat the first conversation. This time they do not need a cue for when to begin; it is up to them. Extraordinary conversations can evolve. 'Why are you following me?' 'Me, following you?' 'You cannot be serious . . .' 'Because I wanted to know where you bought that packet of cornflakes . . . ' 'Because I have nothing else to do . . .' The conversation flows on until the tutor says 'Cut.'

6 By now the students will have created their own characters. There can be a rest period where they discuss the appearance, mannerisms and clothes of their fantasy people.

7 Now the partners rehearse their piece with these ideas more clearly focused, so that it moves further towards a 'set presentation'.

8 Before going on to work in larger groups the focus is turned again towards the individual. The following exercises may seem difficult, but in my experience neither young nor old have found them to be so.

By discovering that a person's energy, emotions or sensations can be directed to an isolated part of the body, we are made more aware of how we live in a whole body, rather than just in the head (which is where most of us think we are). If we do realise this it can help alleviate mental stress. To 'act' or 'portray', people must feel their own energy, body rhythm and the potential of being able to communicate with any part of the body.

Students sit in a circle and exercise all the face muscles, wrists, hands, fingers, ankles, feet and toes in isolation from the rest of the body. Special attention should be placed on the back. Then, with eyes shut, they concentrate on their own breathing rhythm, observing inwardly the in and out breath. After a time the tutor asks them to change and focus their attention on the words he or she will say. For example: 'Without physically moving outwardly, "feel" as if the toes are laughing, your hands are sad, your back is listening, your chest is tired. Your arms are full of energy, you are walking on mud, or soft grass [this takes the student back to the theme], there is energy in your walk, gentleness, anger, joy . . . ' After this period students open their eyes and act out these suggestions with different parts of the body.

TAXI
CAB 2T

RIGHT AND BELOW *Drama workshop: theme 'hands'.*
OPPOSITE, ABOVE *A young mentally handicapped person in a make-up workshop.*
OPPOSITE, BELOW *Cheerful traffic.*

9 Still working individually, they are now asked to walk, and at the same time talk to themselves using the word 'walk' in many different sentences: 'I love walking, it helps me sort out problems.' 'I wish I could walk, it must be wonderful.' 'I walked all this way and you were not there.'

10 For the final part of the session the students work together, four to six people creating an improvisation based on the theme (the word 'walk') which can also include a few props or sounds. Each group has different props, which have to be part of the improvisation. These can help the improvisation come together. For example, a scarf, a pair of shoes and a plant; the sound of running water (on tape), a cardboard box and a pencil.

The students rehearse and work on the improvisation and then present it to the others. The tutor suggests ideas wherever necessary and makes constructive criticism about the end presentation so that all the students can be helped to develop the quality of their acting and imaginative abilities. (Obviously this framework can be modified to fit the particular situation – being in a wheelchair or immobile makes no difference in such a session.)

The following are theatre improvisation ideas which could be used as themes to fit within the suggested framework:

Sounds (taped) Running water, breaking glass, sea, a clock ticking, an aeroplane landing, taking off; *objects* Cardboard boxes (each person would need one), a candle, a stick; *words, phrases (abstract)* 'Be careful it is fragile', 'What have you done to your hair?', 'Stop', 'Hide', 'You can come out now', 'I have bought you a present.'

EXERCISES

Improvisations can be based on poems or paintings. For example, the tutor brings in a landscape painting and the students are asked to create characters or animals that they feel might live in such a place.

Conversations that take place with the hands, or feet.

Gibberish conversations (sounds that mean nothing) – in other words creating your own language. (Children love this.)

Becoming the object Students are asked to look at an object and then become it, giving it a personality. For example, a broom for sweeping: perhaps the broom is full of life, is bossy, ordering everyone about, or cannot stand rubbish or is missing some bristles and is feeling very sorry for itself.

Telling a story The tutor tells a story and the students become the characters (again it should be fairly abstract). For example: 'The sun was shining [one person represents the sun throughout the story], a small sea shell had just been washed ashore and was half-buried in the sand, which the shell did not like because it was rather vain and thought everyone should see it [one person is the shell]. A jelly fish [another person] was right next to the sea shell longing for the tide to take it back to the sea. The jelly fish never stopped complaining . . .' Gradually the dialogue or characters evolve and when the tutor feels it is appropriate the students spontaneously pick up the story and interact with each other.

Props for expression Using props to express emotions – for example, provide a large bowl of water: students sit in a circle; they are asked one by one to wash their hands and use the water in a manner that will convey how they are feeling. The rest of the group tries to recognise the emotion. Perhaps someone washes their hands pensively, aggressively . . . Emotions can be conveyed by different ways of putting on shoes, sitting in a chair, brushing your hair . . .

Intonation Different ways of saying the same word or phrase. 'Oh yes' can be said with different intonations that will convey different meanings. Conversations that change speed on a given cue, from very slow to very fast – silence – regular pace. This can be changed to movement and then back to dialogue.

The Stages of Man Students are asked to express through body movements, getting up in the morning, eating, going to bed at night . . . the manner the same act would be performed by a child, a teenager, a middle-aged person, someone very old.

Meeting places Dialogues that take place in the laundrette, the sports stadium, the café, the playground.

What is so attractive about theatre improvisation is that it belongs to people's own fantasy and imagination and it need have little to do with a person's immediate life or circumstances. It allows us to explore the nicely 'crazy' part of ourselves, and surely giving someone the opportunity to do this is an extremely sane thing to do.

GINA LEVETE

7
Video

Of all the art forms available to you, video has to be the most expensive, technical and problem-ridden. So why do so many groups and individuals want to use it?

At its simplest, it is great fun to point a camera at people and then watch the results – a lot of people like the idea of being film-makers or indeed film stars. The problem, however, is that the initial enthusiasm may soon start to wane: the fun of seeing yourself on the television screen begins to fade; not everyone wants to take part in your dream movie, and the problem of making programmes often puts off all but the most motivated group.

So why video? Principally because it's an exciting medium, capable of simultaneously recording good quality colour pictures, sound, instant play-back (no waiting for weeks) with cheap re-usable tapes. Look at it like that, forget television. Instead, think what could I do with a medium like that? And given a bit of imagination the possibilities are enormous. That is what this chapter is about – looking at some of the possibilities, sorting out the technical jargon, pointing out the pitfalls and suggesting video project ideas.

WORKING IN VIDEO

Having got away from the idea that you are making a television programme, you can plan projects on a human level. You should understand that the process is as important as the final production, and while the production may only reach a limited audience it is still more than worthwhile.

SUGGESTIONS FOR EQUIPMENT

The suggestions and references made about video equipment apply in the United Kingdom and a number of other countries. However, the systems and current situation will not necessarily be the same the world over and the reader will need to make enquiries locally. If you know very little about video and are planning to get some equipment, it seems that there is an enormous range to choose from. Video, like all the new technologies, surrounds itself in jargon, abbreviation and sales talk. It is difficult to get reliable advice from many dealers and magazines swamp you with terms and frequency responses. So here is some basic information to help you get started.

Video equipment can be divided into two categories: (a) domestic; (b) professional or industrial. Domestic equipment, i.e. equipment designed to be used in the home, is relatively cheap and simple to use. It is ideal for showing films and recording TV programmes; it is excellent for many of the activities listed in this chapter; it will record on to three-hour tapes, and work in low light levels; it is simple to use, and the quality of both sound and picture is good on the first generation, that is, your original tape. The quality falls very considerably when copied or edited. Therefore, domestic equipment is ideal for recording events, plays, meetings, and simple documentaries.

Different manufacturers of domestic equipment have designed different systems for the home market. All of these are approximately the same price but are completely different, so that tape recorded on to one machine cannot be played back on another. All the systems are colour and have sound and are of similar technical quality.

The major systems are:

Beta Max (Designed by Sony) Although good quality, it is now being phased out of production in the United Kingdom but may well be used in other parts of the world.

2,000 Here the same situation applies. Designed by Philips, the only European company in the video field, this was their third attempt to produce a successful domestic system. Like the other two, 1500 and 1700, it was of a high quality but has now been phased out in the United Kingdom.

VHS (Video Home System) Overwhelmingly the most popular system in Europe. This system, designed by JVC, is both very reliable, widely available, and has the greatest share of the pre-recorded market. JVC have also developed a system called 'C' format VHS. This is a miniature version of the same standard, designed to be used in portable systems. To play these in an ordinary VHS machine requires an adaptor shaped like a standard VHS tape.

Video 8 This is the latest system available on the market. Leading manufacturers have agreed to adopt this standard eventually but this will take a few years. The advantage of this system is the cassette size. With the cassette being only a little larger than an audio cassette, it means that equipment can be made smaller and more portable.

SO WHICH SYSTEM TO CHOOSE?

Usually the choice will be between VHS and Video 8. In the United Kingdom VHS is slightly cheaper and has the greatest range of pre-recorded tapes. It is more often found in institutions such as schools, colleges, day centres. If you plan to show tapes to other centres, then VHS makes more sense. Video 8 has good quality and is portable, and will get more popular as it becomes more available.

Having made the choice which system to buy, you are still faced with decisions. If you buy a VHS, you can either buy a Camcorder (a camera and recorder in one), or as separate units. Personally, I prefer separate units when working with students as they are more flexible (they can be used with cameras, as a play-back deck, or for recording television programmes). They tend to be of sturdier construction. Also, separate units mean that more people can be involved in checking that everything is working. Lastly, Camcorders tend to be very complicated to use and this can be a disadvantage, especially when working with people who have a physical disability.

Professional or industrial equipment, the second category, is designed for making productions of a high quality for mass duplication. Whilst the industrial equipment is technically superior (better quality pictures and sound), it is much more expensive and of very little use for showing and recording television. If you decide to work on the industrial or professional format then you should take professional advice – this equipment is very expensive. Low Band U Matic is the most popular format for good quality at a reasonable price in the United Kingdom. Other formats, including High Band U Matic and Bea Cam, are all of broadcast quality and very expensive. Each country may have a different situation and the reader will need to make enquiries.

Finally, if you are buying or hiring equipment, remember to budget for a reasonable tripod, a television light or two, extra batteries and a microphone. All these will substantially improve the quality of your productions.

HOW TO USE VIDEO

The most important thing is to become confident and capable in using your equipment. That is to know how to connect it all up, what all the pieces do, simple fault-finding and how to connect the accessories, the microphones, the headphones, tripod etc.; and how to connect up to a television for play-back. These things can be learnt from the manuals, some of which are very good and others which seem designed to confuse. It is not possible in this chapter to explain all the procedures for setting up equipment. The list below gives you suggestions of the things you will need to know how to do.

Connecting up all the equipment.
Running the batteries.
Connecting the equipment to the mains power.
Connection to the TV.
How to focus the camera.
How to use the zoom lens.
White balance (a method of producing accurate colour under different light conditions).
Use of tripod.
How to use the microphone.
Audio dub (to put new sound track on existing pictures).
Simple fault-finding.

If it is at all possible you should have some training in using the equipment. This may be available formally or informally at local colleges, universities, community video groups or adult education institutes. A little training can vastly improve the quality of your tapes and have an impact on the representation of those you portray.

Once you have learnt to use the equipment thoroughly, it is important that you pass the knowledge on so that it becomes a genuine learning experience for your group. They should be involved in camera work, sound recording and recorder operation. Quite often a small group can come together and, after everyone has tried the equipment, become technically very competent, experimenting with new ideas and using all the facilities. This means that the tutor is not always tied to filming and gives the students much greater control over the final production; but remember that for this to work the initial training must be thorough.

Here are some general suggestions for good working practice and simple ways of improving production quality. Set the camera to the eye level of the subjects. Too many people set the camera at a height that is comfortable for the camera operator – which means the camera is pointing down on the subject. This can make the subject look intimidated and will detract from the content of the tape. It is especially true when working with children or with people confined in some way, either to bed or in wheelchairs.

Most amateur video tapes are ruined by poor sound. The microphone on the camera will often pick up comments from the camera operator and noise from the camera motors rather than the sound you had hoped for. If you want good sound then you should use a separate microphone as near as possible to the subject. As a rule do not film against windows unless you are using lights. These points are important. Often the people you work with may have low self-esteem and if they see themselves on tape out of focus with inaudible sound, it does nothing to increase their confidence. Well-made videos, used sympathetically, can enhance the self-perception of the subject.

The range of possibilities for using video is enormous and the results can be very exciting if well planned and carefully executed. Unfortunately, because of the way video equipment is marketed, and through poor training, too many people who use video are disappointed by the results and never use it again. Your work must be well organised.

ROLE-PLAYS

Role-playing is often used to help people prepare for a possible real-life situation; they are asked to act out themselves in the situation with which they may be confronted. The scene is then played back so that they can watch themselves on video. Video role-plays are frequently used for training purposes in industry, where the subjects tend to be confident and go-ahead and more resilient to the searching demands of the method. It would be inappropriate for our purposes to allow role-play to be a demoralising experience – it has to be approached in a sympathetic and sensitive manner to help increase people's confidence. The most common use is to record imaginary interviews – perhaps for a job or a place in college or university. In this imaginary situation the interviewer should know how to conduct the interview and have the correct information about the work, as well as information about the candidate. The role-play should not be recorded in the presence of an audience. It should be set up with the camera looking straight at the interviewee from the waist up; the interviewees can then see themselves as the interviewer saw them. Then, when the tape is being played back, set up a comfortable space, with just the interviewee and one other person who has experience in pointing out the strengths and the weaknesses of the result. The interviewee can then take notes and work on them in a constructive way.

MONITORING PROGRESS

Video is an excellent medium for monitoring progress. For example, a centre for children with disabilities that I worked in wanted a way of assessing the success of different types of therapy. So we set up a system where every two months a child was filmed performing a similar exercise, piling bricks on top of each other or playing a simple game. Each child was allocated his or her own tape, which meant that therapists could look at the film in detail to analyse the child's difficulty and, by looking at previous sessions, assess progress. Similarly, a physiotherapist used the video to record a programme of exercises with a child. There tapes could also be shown to parents and to encourage the children themselves.

MEETINGS ON VIDEO

Many groups within different environments of the community hold regular meetings. To record the meeting on video provides, at its simplest, an accurate record of what happened. I wouldn't recommend doing this too often for its own sake – you will end up with a huge library of very boring videos. However, it also enables you to see how decisions were made and how the group worked. By closely reviewing the tape you can see who was the dominant force in the group, how much time other people spent contributing to the debate.

Video can also be used to stimulate discussion. You can first show filmed tapes of topics that should provoke discussion, and then video the discussion itself. You can set certain rules: for instance, only one person can speak at a time and only on the subject in hand. The structure imposed by video means that discussion can be kept brief. It can also be directed to encourage those who want to speak, but often cannot. Then in future meetings the group can view the video and consider some of the points raised.

VIDEO AS AN ARTS MEDIUM

Video has a range of possibilities when linked with other art forms. With dance, for example, it can be used to record a performance or it can be used in rehearsals so that those taking part can see how they look and note their mistakes.

Another possibility to be considered is designing a video project that combines several art forms. A play or film can involve more than just actors and video operators and very often, particularly in hospitals and day centres, there will be some who find it difficult to participate in the filming or acting activities. They could be involved in painting the title sequences, working on computer graphics, making models, making sets, playing sound-track music, producing special effects, helping others to learn words, sewing costumes, making puppets. If the video project is designed to use all the talents available, then everyone feels part of it.

MAKING A FILM

When working with young people you might in the early stages look at science fiction films from the video shop for ideas. Good science fiction should be more than *Star Wars* style. Develop a story line with the participants. It may take time to find one that works, is subtle and raises some issues about the future. For example, in the early stages the most vociferous member of the team will assume he will be the captain and go around giving orders and killing aliens, but involve him in discussion on how young people see the future and he may well change his ideas. Perhaps design a story line around the environment in which you are filming. There should be no more than ten scenes and you draw them out on a storyboard (that is a series of squares showing what happens in each scene). If it makes sense and there is general agreement within the group, the next stage is to write the script, sort out locations, design titles and build sets. Exciting science fiction sets can be built using cardboard, sand and toilet rolls and other improvised materials. Puppets can be used as aliens, computers for titles or for flight decks. When all the scenes have been planned, rehearse them. If actors have difficulty remembering their lines, you can add them afterwards using the audio dub feature on the recorder. Finally, when all the scenes have been rehearsed, film them carefully in sequence and include any new sounds. Making a film like this should be fun, as well as creative and educational.

Often the groups of people you may be working with will want to make a video about something they have in common – for instance, being in hospital, having a disability, being unemployed. It may sound unadventurous, but it can work out well as a first project. One group I worked with wished to make a tape about how they experienced society's reaction to them. Although there was some interesting material, they all agreed it was visually boring. We made it come to life when individuals acted out common situations. These scenes were quite successful, so we went on to create a simple drama, where the roles were reversed. The unemployed person became the manager, the disabled person took the role of the able-bodied character. The end result worked well and provoked discussion both amongst the students and the audiences to whom it was shown. My students were then confident enough to attempt a more ambitious project.

VIDEO MAGAZINE

Many of the people this book considers are isolated, even though they may be living in the heart of a community. A video magazine project may be a way of their being in touch with each other. It can show items of common interest, ideas for shared events, feedback on other programmes. The video magazine can then be shared by other similar groups who in turn can make their own editions. Magazines need only be very simple, lasting ten to fifteen minutes. They can be easily made with basic camera work and no editing. Copies can be made between two machines and then posted out to other centres.

ORAL HISTORY

Oral history projects give people time and space to reminisce and have their history taken seriously. If the process of telling their stories is well organised, with the help of newspaper cuttings, old magazines, personal photographs and other sorts of memorabilia, people can begin to appreciate the importance of their own histories and enjoy sharing the process with others.

If you want to make these histories into a permanent record, you can make scrapbooks, put them on to audio tapes or record straight on to video. The latter can be done in two ways. Either you can film the people talking and include their photographs etc. (this will sometimes mean the tapes are very long), or you record the interviews on to audio tape, edit them, then record some shots of people going about their daily lives – plus their photos, press cuttings, home etc.; then audio dub the audio tape on to the video. This process requires a fair degree of confidence with the equipment but can, in the end, produce a good-looking programme.

Remember that oral history projects need not be limited to the elderly; everyone has a tale to tell.

VIDEO FOR THE DEAF

People who are deaf find video exciting because they are able to make simple programmes for themselves and others. The attractive thing about this is that the tapes can all be in sign language. If the tape reaches a wider audience it can be subtitled.

ROCK VIDEOS

When you talk to people and say you make video tapes they may assume you mean rock videos. Making rock videos of the type seen constantly on television is a very expensive process. However, people who enjoy music will often get a lot from compiling images on video tape that for them express the mood of the music and how they feel about it. When the images are recorded, the sound track can be put on with the help of the audio dub feature found on most portable recorders. One of the good features about this exercise is that it allows people to make very personal tapes that mean a lot to them.

An interesting variation on this is to record short scenes, then see the effect of adding different types of music.

You can have a lot of fun with video. It is a fast-expanding medium, with endless possibilities for imaginative and creative work.

GEOFF STOW

OPPOSITE *Ashley/Sandpit Centres video project.*

8
Music as a Language

Music is a way of talking to other people. Sometimes we use words and music together, sometimes we communicate using music without words. How do we learn this language?

From the moment a baby is born he or she needs to relate to other people in order to survive. The baby cries to express needs; gurgles and coos to express satisfaction. He or she uses the vocal chords to communicate; and all over the world people use baby talk to respond. Within the different national variations of this there are many similarities. People use high-pitched sounds for excitement, low-pitched sounds for grumbling, middle-pitched sounds for expressions of comfort and affection.

The developing baby imitates this flow of sound, experimenting and inventing a language which is shared with the people in the family circle or community. He or she also listens to the sounds in the environment – people talking, the sounds of cooking, eating, household activities, older children playing.

It is from these sounds, each of which, like the sounds of a violin, flute or drum, can be scientifically analysed in terms of pitch, duration loudness, tone colour, that a repertoire of sounds is built from which the growing child can develop understanding and use of language and communication, both verbal and musical.

It is from this beginning that the art of music has developed.

Watch the child waving his arms, discovering the sounds of banging a spoon on the table, exploring the sounds of floor, walls, chairs, a tin can, anything that is available, learning all the time, adding to that store of sound-knowledge. If there is a drum or tambor on which to make the discoveries, so much the better. If there is someone else with another drum, you can both play, and listen, and play, imitating and making up new ideas. You can add vocal sounds – oo's and ah's.

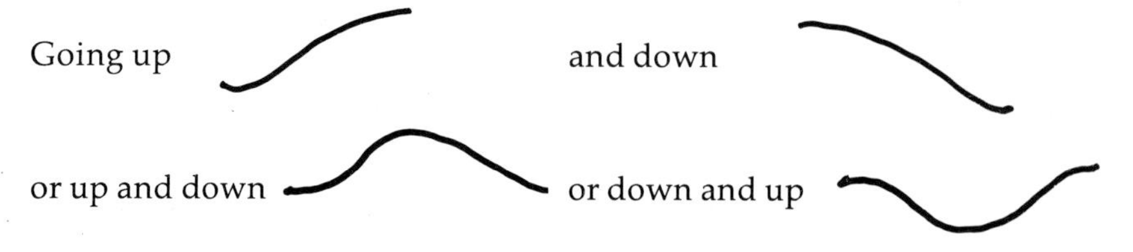

You can make two separate sounds.

Throughout the world the first pitched notes that a child uses are the same. If you want to know what they are, listen to a mother and child playing together when the child is beginning to walk. Mother will use these sounds instinctively, and the child will respond.

What happens to all this spontaneous use of sound? Why doesn't it grow logically into music-making? Why do people grow up estranged from music?

MUSIC AS AN ART FORM

In every culture there are rules about the development of musical skills. The natural ability is formalised, and the pupil learns structure and discipline. Scales have to be learnt, rhythmic patterns and forms have to be mastered, musical literacy has to be acquired. Musical instruments and tuition are expensive, and parents want results from money invested, so music exams have to be taken.

The methods used to get quick short-term results can destroy the natural development of musical ability. For those children who go on to achieve the requisite skills there is success – but at a price. All too often the fear of getting it wrong destroys the ability to communicate without producing the musical skills of a performer. A few will gain sufficient technical expertise, but they too will often have lost the spontaneity of early expression, and need to rediscover the lost art of speaking for themselves in music.

LEARNING MUSIC WITHOUT FEAR

The greatest inhibitor to learning is fear. Fear that you will get it wrong; fear that you will not understand; fear of punishment. It is essential, therefore, that learning should be enjoyable, and that the learner should take pleasure in his or her achievement. When a baby is learning to talk we reward any attempt to communicate by talking and smiling and warmth. The child responds to this encouragement, and learns both vocabulary and grammar from our use of language.

The language of music has structures similar to verbal language. It has single sounds, or two sounds together, short phrases, sentences, question and answer, development, logic. We know how important words are to reinforce practical skills, and help the learner to grasp concepts. Music is also a support to other learning. It is a guide to movement and body control. It is a support and a stimulus in using words, in joining words into phrases, in using phrases to communicate with others, and turning sound into meaning. It also develops the skills of listening which are so important to learning.*

A person can learn a language at any time – it is never too late. But someone who learns as a child will use it more confidently, and use that language to support other forms of learning.

'Hullo, Mary how do you do'

This is a favourite rhythm for a song with a group with whom I work. The children aged eight months to five years have learning disabilities – mostly Down's Syndrome. Parents and children sing the 'hullo' song to one another. Another song they sing is:

Joe is learning to brush his hair,
Joe is learning to brush his hair,
Joe is learning to brush his hair,
What a clever boy.

We hear what each child is learning to do, and sing about it, using the rhythm of the words and a simple tune which was made up by Joe's mother – who was quite sure when she joined the group that she was 'no good at music'! In another song –

Bobby Bubble beat the drum,
Bm, bm, bm, bm,
Bobby Bubble beat the drum,
Bm, bm, bm,
Let's play Bobby's tune,
Bm, bm, bm, bm,
Let's play Bobby's tune,
Bm, bm, bm.

– the children enjoy learning to sing and play alternate lines, or listen to

*Music is a stimulus to all learning. In Hungary a research experiment looking at how children learn found that where music was the basis of the syllabus in kindergarten and primary school, the academic record of the children was 'much higher'. Benefits are listed – such as memory training, reasoning capacity, enrichment of emotional life, stimulation of activity, development of expressional and creative abilities, speech fluency, manual dexterity, adaptability, improved chest expansion. See Sandor, Frigyes (ed.), *Music Education in Hungary*, Boosey and Hawkes.

others sing, and then play. If music is to be enjoyed without a sense of failure it is important that people are given space to join in vocally when they are ready to do so, and not forced to sing. This is important for children and adults. When they are not singing they are hearing and memorising the sounds for future use. For the same reason people should not be forcibly made to move. They can be encouraged, helped if help is wanted, supported where that is needed, but never forced.

For instance, the activity of clapping hands to music is a response to the stimulus of sound which passes from the brain, through the spinal column, and down the arms. If someone takes your hand and tries to make you clap they interfere with the neural pathway of the stimulus. This causes muscular discomfort. Where the capacity for movement is weak, and help is wanted, the helper should work from behind like a mobile armchair. In this way any movement stimulus can be sensed, and both pairs of arms can work together.

The helper should be very sensitive to any movement initiated by the learner, and be there in a supportive, rather than a directive role. This allows the weaker person to use the strength of the helper, rather than being manipulated. Where the neural stimulus is weak this may mean that the clap does not synchronise with the beat. Remember that the person is *learning* to use his or her muscles to clap. If the musical stimulus, and the desire to move, are there, the person will make the adjustments necessary to get a musical result.

The results of learning without fear are confidence, with which comes improved posture and concentration, and an increasing skill which can be shared with others, either informally, or if people have reached a stage of musical competence where they can give pleasure to others, in concerts.

I work with a group called Special Jam. The skills are varied. In addition to playing together, some are solo singers, others are solo players. They are all performers – people who can give pleasure to others through their musical talents and ability, and want to communicate through music. We give concerts, and we have appeared on television.

The type of music we perform is varied. We do classical, jazz and popular music, and I and other band members compose, or make up our own numbers. We also extemporise togther. Someone plays a musical idea, and someone else replies, developing the idea round the group, talking with music, like a conversation. Sometimes we use a song structure, making up our own verses, as in:

Singing for ourselves, singing for ourselves,
We like to sing, we like to sing,
Singing for ourselves, singing for ourselves,
Thinking, and singing for ourselves.

Each person then has space to sing a reply which they have made up. Typical replies are:

I like the Post Office Tower,
It stands in London.

or

Me and Louis, coming on the bus,
We caught the 38 this morning.

The adults in this group are particularly interesting. They all have learning disabilities. Some have spent years of their lives in subnormality hospitals. One was diagnosed as ineducable. Yet each one is musically very talented. They all have instrumental skills, and sing in tune. How has this been achieved?

The most important thing is that they all enjoy music, and want to spend time making music and listening to it, and developing their skills. It has not been possible to teach by traditional verbal methods. Music has been taught through the medium of music. All members of the group are aware that music is written, because when they make up a tune they want to recall I write it down, and when I make up music I bring the written copy to the session. If we are using published music I usually have a copy. But there is no pressure to read or write msuic, although they recognise its usefulness. Only one member is interested in reading music, and in owning written music.

The rules of music have not been learned first as rules, and then applied. They have been absorbed through the experience of music – through listening and doing. The students have had space and opportunity to develop their own sounds into music without needing to conform to style (classical, pop, etc.). They are free to use musical notes, either in a once-only exploration, or to develop a musical idea, working together to produce something that can be repeated. Even when we have developed a piece of music, new ideas can be added or we can explore new ways of playing the piece, so that the students continually think in musical terms, rather than repeating learned tricks.

BEGINNING TO USE PITCHED INSTUMENTS*

When working with pitched instruments the use of a selected scale is valuable. Pitched instruments usually have a scale of five to twelve notes. The common Western scales have seven notes (eight including the octave). To select your own scale, you give each player three or four notes on which he or she can make a full musical contribution in harmony with others who are using the same notes (say, C,D,F,G, in Western notation). It is important that everyone should be able to make a full musical contribution using their own musical skills. If notes are chosen so that no two pitches clash, and a rhythmic beat is sustained, people begin to make music without fear of failure.

Gamelan music works on this principle. Each Gamelan orchestra is tuned to its own four or five pitched sounds. In the Kandyan drumming of Sri Lanka the same priniciple is used without pitched notes, but with higher and lower sounds on the drum. In jazz the principle is found again, although here all the twelve notes of Western music are used. In each of these forms of music there are traditional patterns, a repertoire of ideas to be learned, and a range of expertise to be gained, from basic skills to virtuoso. But in each case you make music with other people from the beginning, using your instrument (or group of instruments) and using your own musicality.

In the early stages of development known tunes are not very helpful. They bring with them the fear of getting it wrong, and produce tension in the arms and back, and a tendency to falter, or go back and start again – or give up. If a flowing rhythm is used the players can respond, using their own body rhythm to produce sounds which blend with the playing of others into a satisfying whole. As confidence is gained tunes of three to five notes can be introduced. This is an opportunity to make up your own tunes. 'We are good at music' or 'What do you like on a Saturday night?' I suggest words, because everyone understands the rhythm of words, and it gives the piece a structure.

Here the emphasis is not on getting it right as quickly as possible, but on the search, the growing understanding of the rise and fall of sound, and the continued use of movement without tension. As the group become more skilled, more notes can be added – usually one at a time, and a part for rhythm instruments – drums (not too loud, or they will drown the tune) or any percussion instrument.

*Instruments with a scale of tuned notes.

The importance of gaining an easy, flexible, free-arm movement cannot be overstated. When you watch expert instrumentalists you see the confident use of the whole body in partnership with the instrument. The beginnings of music-making should inculcate this physical oneness with an instrument, and promote a sense of well-being and confidence.

I use the rhythm of words a lot in this context. For instance, 'What goes down the road?' Car, minibus, lorry, van. One group can play car while another group plays minibus. Make sure that they listen to one another, and play together. Or you could ask 'What food do you like?' and build up rhythm patterns on that. You are using what people know to introduce them to something new – making music together.

When people are given encouragement, and a musical environment, and accepted for themselves as people of worth, music will happen, and it will be shared and enjoyed. The development of skills will happen over time, as people continue to enjoy making music.

WHAT PEOPLE ARE WE TALKING ABOUT?

Music is important for everyone. It is particularly important where the opportunities for communication are limited, by reason of disability or limitation of verbal language. Where words have become barriers against feeling, or feelings are too deep for words, it offers a vehicle for sharing and validating experience and exploring potential.

There are those for whom past experience, or perhaps failure or ridicule, have built a wall of fear that is difficult to scale. Where such people are still wanting to make music, great care should be taken to ensure that there is a sense of achievement, and that the courage shown in trying again is recognised. A person in this situation feels exposed and vulnerable, and needs support and reassurance.

Singing is the most personal expression of feeling, and anyone wanting to help someone develop this skill must be very sensitive to the dignity and humanity of the singer. The singer is speaking from his or her soul; listen and share. Eye contact is important here. Give the singer your whole attention. If you can play an instrument a soft accompaniment may be helpful, as long as it does not overwhelm the singer or divert your attention. Singing *softly* with the person can also give confidence. 'Thank you' when the singer has finished shows your appreciation. Whether or not you thought it was in tune out of tune is not very important.

Singing in tune is learned by experience, and by developing listening skills. The ear hears the notes, the brain records the sounds, and the vocal chords (which are muscles in the throat) reproduce what is heard, which is reported back to the brain via the ear. It is a continuous circle. Some people achieve this easily, but for others it is more difficult. If people are finding it difficult to sing in tune, encourage them to sing softly. This makes it easier for them to hear the sound they want *and* the sound they are making, and bring the two together.

Playing an instrument is a satisfying experience. For those who are as yet unskilled it is important to make it successful. There are many instruments where gross motor movement (i.e. the movement of the whole arm) can be used to achieve a pleasing musical result, and stimulate the player's desire to do more.

All instrumental playing should start with relaxed, balanced, easy gross motor movement, before fine movements are attempted. (Yes, this does include the piano!)

There are now electronic (and expensive) instruments which produce music at the touch of a finger. While this may seem an advantage to an audience it is in effect not playing, but listening. To play an instrument is to use your muscles to make music – by the response of the instrument to your direction. A musical instrument is anything on which you can make a musical sound.

I spent a satisfying hour playing duets with a two-year-old recently. I played a chair, and he played a table. After a while he made the discovery that the table made a better sound without the tablecloth. We made important, slow and loud remarks. We talked softly; we made jokes, and laughed; we got slower – and then suddenly faster. We concentrated on the quality of sound and the flow of ideas. We spoke different verbal languages, but shared a common musical language, where we could listen and respond to one another, make music together, and enjoy one another's company.

Everyone should have the chance to make music at their own level. It is important not to assume what that level is by assessment of skills in other areas, or by assumptions based on present attainment. Where motivation is strong people can exceed the expectations of pathology, and do things previously thought to be impossible.

For those who want to develop their musical potential the opportunity can be given, *if* those in authority recognise its importance. Unfortunately this often has to be rationalised when one is seeking to provide musical experience and tuition for people who are disadvantaged or disabled, because those in power do not accept its relevance.

However, the case can be made, whether we are talking of children or adults, young or old, people with physical, sensory or learning disabilities, people who are socially disadvantaged or displaced, or physically or mentally ill. If people want to learn and use the skills of music making, we can make a case for it that others should find acceptable.

DEVELOPMENTAL AND SOCIAL BENEFITS

There are many subsidiary advantages in music-making.

Music develops listening skills, and the capacity to communicate. Where people are refusing to communicate with words it offers an alternative which can be less threatening.

Diction is improved by singing, and people with minimal speech can learn to understand and use short verbal phrases with the support of a tune. This is particularly useful with children whose language development is delayed.

Where children have had hearing loss in the first years of life the use of resonant instruments can help to replace lost aural experience.

Good breathing habits can be developed by singing and by playing wind instruments.

Gross motor movement is used in all instrumental works, and is a pleasurable way of exercising limbs that need stimulation, with the help of the regular beat of the music. Each movement produces the reward of sound which is an incentive to repeat the movement.

Achievement in music greatly enhances self-concept, which aids posture and behaviour.

Music is a group activity where people work together, sharing, and supporting one another. Each person is important and individual at the same time as being a group member.

Music acts as a stimulus to memory, both short-term and long-term.

Music-making is an outlet from the frustrations of disability; it can reduce tension and hyperactivity, *and* act as a stimulant to the lethargic.

In fact, music opens up a new world of possibility for those who have the opportunity to enter that world.

WHO CAN LEAD MUSIC SESSIONS?

The people who are best able to make all this possible are musicians – the people who themselves use music to communicate. Through their own experience of developing musical skills, and their use of those skills, they understand from the inside the meaning of music.

Musicians do need to be reassured that they are not expected to produce educational, exam-oriented results. They need to be encouraged to produce the essence of music in a satisfying and personal experience for all concerned. Any judgement of the results should only be made in terms of musical values.

Musicians who have not worked with people with special needs before may be anxious about the nature of those special needs, and need support and help when they start.

If you are planning to start music sessions do not buy instruments until you have talked to the musician who will be taking the sessions. There are two reasons for this:

1 The musician will know where to get the instruments he or she wants at a fair price. All too often money is wasted buying instruments which look good, but make a bad sound, or are overpriced, or not wanted by the person running the session.

2 The musician will know what instruments he or she is best able to work with. Every musician will have different ideas about this, and in every locality instruments will differ. There are no 'handicapped' instruments. In cases of physical disability there are instruments which are more suitable to the individual. i.e. instruments that can be played sitting down for a wheelchair user.

I use a basis of keyboard-type instruments because I am a keyboard musician. I also have two Chinese stringed instruments, some kazoos – an English folk wind instrument, and percussion, some of which is Latin American, some a modern version of Kenyan drums. I also use harmonicas. That is my choice, made on the basis of my skills ands the skills, interests and needs of the people with whom I work, and the money available.

WHAT SORT OF MUSICIAN DO YOU NEED?

Someone who is skilled at playing or singing, or both, and gets on well with other people.

Someone who is compassionate, but not so sympathetic that the music gets buried in pity.

Someone who is not obsessed with the need to produce results – i.e. concerts, performances etc. – at the expense of musical experience.

Someone who understands and uses the language of music, whether in a classical, traditional, or popular mode.

Someone who is flexible, able to respond to the needs and aspirations of others, and use their skills to develop skills in others.

ABOVE *The resonance of the metallophone enables Laura to enjoy her own playing despite severe hearing loss.* BELOW *Kenny, John and Bernard playing the chime bars.*

ABOVE *Special Jam perform.* BELOW *Music-making in Galle, Sri Lanka.*

He or she does not need to be a teacher. Indeed, that can be a disadvantage, as teachers sometimes find it difficult to forget traditional educational expectations.

WILL IT BE WORTH THE EFFORT?

I find it difficult to answer this question because I feel so positive about it. I have had so much joy sharing music with other people – with children, young people, middle-aged and elderly people, people with learning or physical disabilities – or both, people who are under stress or confused.

For some of the people with whom I have worked, music has been the key which has unlocked the door to life, and changed existence into living. I have seen people develop musical skils against overwhelming odds, and recognise their own competence and worth. For others it has been less dramatic, but nevertheless an enjoyable and useful experience. It has been stimulating, exciting, hard work, exhausting, satisfying – and I love it!

If you believe that giving people a chance to experience a fuller, richer life is worthwhile, I recommend music-making.

SUGGESTION FOR WORKSHOP PLAN

Work to an overall plan which does not vary. This gives security. For instance:

1 Introduction. 'Hullo' song, or theme tune, 'Good morning' piece.

2 Developmental. The piece you are currently working on – e.g. traffic rhythm music. Give opportunity for two or three people to play together while the others listen, working round the group so that everyone has both played and listened to others playing. Let the whole group play together.

3 Repertoire. Pieces you know and enjoy playing or singing.

4 New idea, or opportunity for people in the group to make sugestions or make up a new tune or song.

5 Listening to music. A chance to relax physically, and concentrate on the skill of listening.

Remember, these are only suggestions. Work out a scheme which suits you and the group.

Don't try to use too much material. Playing or singing through a lot of pieces every session is boring. Allow time for work and learning.

Give the group opportunity for choice. Choice of instrument, or notes, or activity.

Note individual special abilities, and develop a group activity around these. A good solo voice, or instrumental skill, can be accompanied by the rest of the group.

Enjoy it – and make it enjoyable for the learners.

JANET WYATT

9
Hospital Arts

If the arts have any value for society, then they must have relevance in important places such as hospitals, where there is a basic human need for beauty, humour and spiritual uplift. Art within hospitals and health care buildings should aim to complement not only the architecture but also the healing service. Hospitals, hospices, health centre and clinics can provide marvellous opportunities for artists and craftsmen to use their skills in a very real and creative service.

WHAT IS IT?

The term 'hospital arts' has arisen from the work I initiated in the hospitals of Manchester (UK). A large multidisciplinary team of talented artists have worked for the health authorities since that time. Our work has pioneered many ways in which the skills and creativity of the artist can contribute to the visual and social environment of the hospitals and health clinics of Manchester. The emphasis of our work has been on involving the staff and patients in a wide range of visual and performing arts and crafts activities, resulting in paintings, photographs, murals and three-dimensional forms which help to decorate the buildings. None of the work is intended to be therapy or detract from the valuable work of professional art therapists. The work of these people is not always clearly understood, but to quote from the *Attenborough Report on the Arts and Disabled People* (1985), p.73: 'Arts therapy is a form of therapy in which the art activity and any resulting art form becomes a method for diagnosis and therapeutic intervention.'

The project is now known as Hospital Arts-Manchester and a number of other places where similar work has started have adopted the title 'Hospital Arts'. I hope people will feel free to associate with what I believe should be an international concern.

BREAKING DOWN BARRIERS

The hospital community is made up of staff, patients and public (relatives and friends) and all can be touched or involved in some way by hospital arts – by brightening up an old hospital building possibly by making bland and often rather anonymous new buildings more welcoming; by providing a more cheerful environment for patients and public. Staff usually applaud such improvements. They work in what is usually considered to be a stressful environment and performances of music, mime, puppets, poetry, theatre or other entertainment provide a welcome change both for patients and themselves. Some hospital arts programmes include artists and craftsmen giving workshops where staff and patients can be involved in making something to be displayed in the hospital. This can be applied equally well in a health centre or clinic. A more congenial cared-for environment can lead to an increase in staff morale, particularly when efforts are made to consult and involve them. There develops a correspondingly caring attitude towards the appearance of the place, with the result that the fabric of the buildings is kept cleaner, trolley damage to walls is minimised, litter and general untidiness often decreases dramatically.

The introduction of painting, sculpture and murals gives a particular identity to the buildings. Providing performances, events and demonstrations by artists and craftsmen, whether these be occasional or regular, helps to change the atmosphere in hospitals; it makes them less austere and shows that there is a place for positive and cheerful expressions of life. Such occasions can unify a hospital community.

In all ages and in all societies art has played a very significant part in the faith, beliefs and practices connected with health and healing. It is easily forgotten and often difficult to imagine how long and tedious can be the days for people in hospital – particularly those confined to bed. Staring out of the same windows or at the same walls hour by hour, you notice every detail over and over again. Art can be used in so many ways to fill blank walls and vacant spaces. 'When people are relaxed, happy and interested, they are in the best condition for healing to take place': I quote a senior medical consultant. There are many patients, some of them resident in hospitals, for whom healing is not possible, but for whom enjoyable occupation is essential to caring, well-being and comfort.

A hospital arts scheme should include a wide range of arts activities: dance, drama, drawing, painting, pottery, puppetry, poetry, music, mime, mobiles, movement, photography, film and video, sculpture, story-telling, creative writing, literature, weaving, embroidery, all the crafts and many aspects of design. Different art forms will be particularly effective in different departments – for example, puppetry for paediatrics, mobiles in the maternity wards, craft demonstrations for cancer patients, music and concerts for 'long-stay' patients.

WHAT DOES IT COST?

There is much which can be done on a voluntary basis. There are many resources which can be used, people can lend their art and their skills to get something started. However, this should not be abused or taken for granted, and any hospital authority which wants to ensure a lasting commitment should think in terms of some genuine contribution, either in the form of facility, or in actual payment to the artist. For instance, if an artist lends his paintings for display, the hospital should arrange for insurance and security and perhaps provide transport for the artist and friends to view the works; the hospital might offer free rehearsal space to a music or theatre group in exchange for a number of performances for patients and staff.

HOW TO START HOSPITAL ARTS

The development of an appropriate and carefully considered programme has to involve a person with considerable artistic enthusiasm and sensitivity. It requires someone to concentrate fully on integrating and involving both patients and staff and to become known and accepted by the health service community as responsible for the arts programme. Someone with involvement in the arts could well take the initiative as arts coordinator, arts administrator or hospital artist. It could be someone from the nursing or medical staff or an enlightened hospital administrator. However carefully considered the provision of the arts might be when introduced by people from outside the hospital, there cannot be daily dialogue with the community about the work unless the artist is on the spot. The most appropriate hospital arts scheme takes account of the needs of the people and the particular context in which it will exist. This is only really ascertained through involvement in that community over a considerable period of time. Not all artists have the necessary sympathy and understanding for working in health care environments. They should want to talk to people and be prepared for questions from people not necessarily used to the arts. Always look for the highest standards and if unsure get advice from an art college or arts and crafts organisation. People studying the arts can be involved, but will need guidance and careful supervision. Get to know a hospital: the organisation and structure, how it works, who is in charge of what, and who is responsible to whom. If you already work in a hospital, look around you and consider the needs and ways in which the arts can be useful. Then, if you are involved with the arts and feel you could set up a scheme, contact a senior health service person. Other members of staff may be more accessible but sooner or later you will need agreement and support from the people with the overall responsibility.

In the beginning it is unlikely that you will already have any money for the project. So expect to volunteer your services initially while investigating the scheme's practicalities. Start in a small and simple way; it is much better to make a success of something with modest beginnings than to attempt an ambitious programme which you eventually realise you cannot fulfil. Gain people's confidence and trust, be realistic about what you can achieve in the first instance and then build on that. What about a poster, six paintings, or several decorative signs? Or a staff art and crafts exhibition where the staff's art work is shown. The staff must be involved.

DRAW UP YOUR PLAN

Your plans should clearly and concisely state:

1 The *Needs* as you perceive them.

2 The *Aims* you would hope to achieve.

3 The *Ways and Means* of achieving these aims: organising, preparation, implementation, programme of work and time scale.

4 The *Support* you need: costs, manpower.

5 How you would monitor, evaluate and review the work.

EXAMPLE: PLAN A

Needs There is a building or department which you feel could be improved by having twenty paintings displayed in it.

Aims To stimulate the visual environment; to stimulate the interest of staff, patients and public.

Ways and means To get the agreement of those concerned to try it for six months and then review the situation; to borrow twenty paintings and get them hung somehow; to hire twenty paintings; to purchase twenty paintings; to paint twenty paintings.

Support Obtain transport to collect the works; obtain help or cooperation from staff to hang the paintings; photograph the before and after effect. Will the hospital help with (a) transport (b) hanging the work; (c) paying for hire of paintings; (d) supplying you with paint, boards and frames?

EXAMPLE: PLAN B

Needs Several wards and departments would like some musical event.

Ways and means Find a suitable venue for this event; decide with staff what music and musicians to use (amateur, professional, students, etc); contact and book musicians; make the necessary financial arrangements (cost of tickets or fund-raising); inform all interested parties and publicise the event; organise chairs, lights, flowers, photographer etc.

Support Cooperation of wards and department staff before, during and after the event; cooperation of porters, selling tickets, arranging seating; arranging refreshments; clearing away.

RAISING THE MONEY

Take your plan to the appropriate person in authority for approval. Any caring health service will surely want to support a programme of arts activities which aims to contribute to the comfort, happiness and well-being of the staff, patients and public who use the service. Be confident that what you are introducing is a 'good thing' and worthy of their financial support. Refer to the considerable documentation which exists of work in this field. It will help if you have already identified a number of people in the hospital who have an interest in your project. It is essential to show that you are not alone in recognising the need for an arts programme.

If some of your friends offer to raise funds, so much better. Persist with the theme of partnership between the arts and health, because people need to recognise the value of both. If the hospital makes a commitment to provide space for the arts coordinator plus secretarial help, telephone and postage, this is a valuable contribution and a beginning.

COMMITTEE

Form a committee as soon as possible. This could be organised by a senior officer of the hospital in consultation with the arts coordinator and should include members of staff. The committee will be able to monitor and review the work, help raise funds and be responsible for their distribution. Most funding sources will be reluctant to assist unless such a committee exists and assumes financial responsibility.

NEW HEALTH BUILDINGS

In many ways the ideal time to consider the arts in hospitals is when a new building is being planned. Everyone connected with the scheme will hope that their new building is going to be both beautiful and functional. Enhancing the building with art is not always in an architect's brief from his client, yet for the people who may live and work in the building it can be as significant as the furniture and fittings. You need consideration at the planning stage for art on the walls, sculpture in the grounds, concerts in the wards and so on. Planning a space for an arts centre in a new development is the best way of ensuring a long-term future for a programme.

THE CENTRE

Let us assume the project has begun and there is a base in the centre. It is essential for everyone to know that there is a place which serves as the centre for arts activities, somewhere staff can visit for advice and help and patients for a welcome break. It should be a place for artists and craftsmen to work and have a dressing room for visiting musicians and actors. If large enough, it can be used for workshops in which patients and staff can participate. It can be a store for paintings, prints, etc. – though racks need to be built to prevent damage to the works. Ensure the base can be locked up.

HOSPITAL ARTS IN PRACTICE

There are many ways of providing the arts in hospitals and some will be more appropriate than others. For instance, if a mural is required for a wall it can be painted 'on site' by the artist or artists. If this is not practical, then a panel for the site can be prepared and painted in the artist's studio. A good solution, however, is for it to be painted elsewhere in the hospital, perhaps in the arts centre, so that staff and patients can visit to see the work in progress. Another solution may be to have the mural designed in several sections. The design could involve patients and staff contributing ideas and helping to draw out the design, each section being worked on by different groups under the guidance of an artist who should ensure that each section complements the whole. When people contribute even a few details they identify with a project, and it is delightful to see how much interest this generates. Having an artist or craftsman in residence, for a period of not less

ABOVE *Staff workshop, Hospital Arts Centre, Manchester.* BELOW *Mosaic mural by staff and patients of the Psychiatric Day Hospital, Manchester Royal Infirmary.*

ABOVE LEFT *Murals by Hospital Arts – Manchester in the main corridor.* ABOVE RIGHT *Decorative sign, also by Hospital Arts – Manchester.* BELOW 'Hollywood Faces' *by Liz Faunce, painting in hospital corridor, Manchester.*

than three months, is an eye-opening experience. The scheme should allow for the artists or craftsmen to spend time doing their own work, with people able to visit them wherever they are based in the hospital. There should be opportunities for them to exhibit their work and talk to people about it. Similarly, visiting actors and musicians will have greater effect if in addition to their performance they can talk about their work and give 'workshop' sessions. Exhibitions of photography are useful, lower in cost and easier to handle. All schemes must take aspects of health into consideration, as well as safety and fire precautions.

ADDITIONAL HELP, VOLUNTEERS

Volunteers who make themselves known to you must give a regular commitment and agree to work on the terms and conditions which you should clearly define. Extra pairs of hands may theoretically make light work, but unless they know what to do – i.e., have the necessary skills together with good direction – it can be more trouble than it is worth.

The activities described in this chapter are in the United Kingdom generally referred to as hospital arts. There are many places abroad where similar work is being undertaken. It is therefore particularly helpful for people engaged in such work far and wide to know what others are doing in the same field. They should find this book useful as it contains many worldwide contacts. In April 1987 a National Health Care Arts Centre will be established in England. The centre will supply information and advice on all aspects of arts activities in hospitals, except in the area of therapy. Written, photographic and audiovisual documentation of existing arts activities in British hospitals and hospices will be available to anyone wishing to intitiate arts schemes and to artists who wish to work in this field. Contact with this centre should be made through Hospital Arts – Manchester (see Directory). Information on the work of arts therapists in the countries of the European Economic Community is being undertaken at Hertfordshire College of Art and Design (also see Directory).

The value of hospital arts needs to be seen to be believed. Hospital arts facilitate more interaction between artist, staff and patient. In small but significant ways this is helping to expand other people's horizons and the involvement in creativity is a positive move away from negative thoughts into healthy, normal activity. Here is a challenge for art and artists – to work with and for people whose main concern must be to the body, its order and disorder.

BOOKLIST

Coles, Peter, *Manchester Hospitals Art Project*, Calouste Gulbenkian Foundation, 1981.

Coles, Peter, *Art in the National Health Service*, DHSS, 1983.

Coles Peter, *The Arts in a Health District*, DHSS, 1985.

Moss, Linda, *Arts for Health's Sake*, Carnegie UK Trust, 1987.

Pearson, Anne, *Arts for Everyone*, Carnegie UK Trust and Centre on Environment for the Handicapped, 1985.

PETER SENIOR

10
An Expression for Pain

Oh death
I have such
Mixed feelings
For you
Sometimes
I dread you
Sometimes
I wait thee
I know not
When
Thou shall embrace me

Oh, death
I do have a favour to ask thee
When thou comest
Oh, please dear death
Do come but
Unannounced
For there are crushed hearts
Within these walls
Hearts that love, adore and care
Hearts that bleed
Inwardly
And show not a care
But they do care
For the one
Whom you await to claim
Let them be asleep
Or take me in my slumber
For partings are so painful
Especially for those
Who reared me . . .
From a seedling to a flower

* * *

I am named
GITANJALI
After the famous book of Tagore
I wish and pray
Oh! help me God
I so live that . . .
I live up to the name

Gitanjali was born in India and died at the age of sixteen after a prolonged illness of cancer. Gitanjali's poems were found by her mother after her death. They were hidden in her room behind books, sofa seats, inside cushions and under the mattress. The reason was that Gitanjali knew that she was terminally ill but wanted to conceal that knowledge from her mother, as it might hurt her more. A strange chain of events eventually led to the poems being published and Gitanjali's mother asked for all the royalties to go to charities in India. The book has been read by many thousands of people across the world. In some schools the poems are introduced to open up the subject of death. Gitanjali's expression of pain through poetry has and will continue to touch life. It is an example of how the medium of art can help to relieve or express pain. Life is a cycle of moments, and there is no contradiction in confronting the end of your life whilst at the same time delighting in new beginnings – a spring flower in bulb, children listening to a story.

Consultants, doctors and psychiatrists now begin to recognise and value the healing role that art has to play and allow it to have its place, although obviously not all patients will respond to a creative approach. The greatest comfort when undergoing the stress of pain is to have someone to hold your hand or give you a hug, someone to talk to or shout at. Nevertheless, using the mediums of visual art, writing/poetry and music is a means through which fear, pain, memories and joys can be described. The end result of work produced often has a quality of artistic expression that is intensely truthful and occasionally quite beautiful. Introducing an arts programme for those who are terminally ill needs to be carefully planned; it is essential that all the staff should be aware of its existence. The activities should be offered to all patients, whether they are in the hospital or hospice or receiving care in their homes with the help of a nursing support team. There is a danger of introducing a single once-weekly activity and regarding that as an arts programme. It is almost certain to be insufficient.

The artistic therapist is better equipped than the artist without a therapy training to undertake this demanding and sensitive work. That having been said, it is usually the artistic therapists who regard themselves primarily as artists who are more successful than those who think of themselves primarily as therapists. Artists not trained as therapists can and do make a contribution in a more general way, particularly when it is not possible to employ a therapist.

The following are ideas that may help a reader plan a programme.

1 Invite family and friends to work creatively as well as the patient. Esther Dreifuss, a Swiss art therapist who worked with terminally ill cancer patients, made a point of including the family. Her approach helped them to go through the ordeal together. After the patient had died she continued to visit the family at home, encouraging them through their art expression to come to terms with the loss.

2 Creative writing, poetry, keeping a diary. One writer working in a hospice feels that what her patients most enjoy is being able to read books or listen to talking books, and most of her time is spent finding books of their choice.

3 Arrange for someone to read aloud to individual patients.

4 Provide a music library of tapes (recognising that musical tastes are very different).

5 Invite a visual artist to come in and sketch, from a photograph or description, someone or something the patient would like to remember or give away as a memento.

6 Plan the garden of your dreams with the artist. Either the patient (if well enough) or the artist can transcribe the idea visually, and perhaps someone in the family can plant some of the suggested flowers in a real garden.

7 Even if the patients are too frail to be active, the artist can still invite them to create a picture. They choose the subject, the colours and detail and the artist, working in the ward, portrays this on a canvas. A project like this can be carried out on a once-weekly basis and although some will not live to see the painting completed they will know that their contribution is part of it. It also allows people to talk informally with someone who is not identified with their illness.

8 Intimate music, dance or puppetry performances – for patients well enough to appreciate them – bring great pleasure.

Happily the majority of people nowadays recover from serious illness. The UCLA Jonsson Comprehensive Cancer Center in Los Angeles issued an inspiring report, *Creative Approaches to Coping with Cancer.** It describes a year's demonstration project. The hospital introduced arts activities as therapeutic, non-threatening experiences. A large part of the programme took place in the waiting room, with friends, escorts and family encouraged to participate. The 'art cart' enabled people confined to bed to take part. The art therapist wheeled a trolley containing a variety of art materials from which the patient could choose what he wanted to work with. Often the art therapist worked on a one-to-one basis and thoughts and emotions were released that had been hidden away.

A German music therapist, Silke Jochims, makes an interesting use of music as a means of non-verbal expression. Modern medical care enables road accident victims to survive severe head injuries but despite the improvement in their physical condition many patients remain in a state of emotional shock for a long time. Silke Jochims can 'talk' and encourage these patients to 'talk' through musical instruments. Patients rediscover the pleasure of communication.

Art heals, too, in situations of shock, trauma or loss. A visual artist working through Interlink visited Colombia to give workshops for people homeless after the 1986 volcanic explosion. Laurie Booth, a dancer, worked on another assignment. He visited the Sudan to work in a refugee-affected area. Laurie gave workshops to young people who were not on the point of starvation but were just waiting and suffering from the feeling of loss at becoming a refugee. The following extracts written by him describe the experience.

> Every day started with physical training and every day the training developed. We developed group games and after a few days the workshop was providing its own energy. We began to perform to each other, small incidents described with movement and sound.
>
> Finally we decided to perform. The audience sat around the outside of the room, looking into it. The room was actually a huge porch; it made a very good theatre.
>
> The audience was in fact about one hundred and fifty people and they spent most of their time laughing. The party continued for another three hours.

A letter from a workshop participant described the party. It 'remained

*For further information about this publication write to Devra Breslow, Director for Special Programs, Jonsson Comprehensive Cancer Center, UCLA Factor 10-247, Los Angeles, California 90024, USA.

as a cornerstone for remembering us. The Night, that unique night really is unforgettable and inexpressable in words. In my own part, it was just like a re-birth and my body was filled with joy.'

This chapter can have no better summary than an extract from another of Gitanjali's poems.

My Mother

She is like a pillar of strength
To, all, each one and sundry

She radiates the warmth
Even when she passes by
She showers the
Blessings through her
Lullabye

The emotions overwhelm her
The tears flow silently
And yet the eyes smile
And blink a message
of love and understanding

I hold my breath (in pain no doubt)
And look up in amazement
And try my utmost best
And slowly and silently I
Close my eyes; with Thine
Expression to cool my own

I once wondered how it
Thus could be
A frail soul could bear
The brunt of life smilingly
But it seeped through me
Like water through the plant
That no matter what may come
You've got to fight the weedlings
For the survival of your young

With sadness weighing heavily
In the precious eyes
That I adore

She creeps silently and softly
Into the little den
Which is my very own

And in those eyes
I seek and find
The friendly glow of confidence
That pulls me up
When all else fails
Including the hand of God . . .

(Gitanjali's poems are reproduced by kind permission of Oriel Press Ltd., Branch End, Stockfield, Northumberland, England, publishers of *Poems of Gitanjali.)*

GINA LEVETE

Dr David Frampton, MB, BS, MRCGP, Consultant Physician at the St Joseph's Hospice in East London, expresses his views about art in hospices.

TIME TO LIVE

Acres of unoccupied time . . . ! Sometimes as busy professionals we long for such a luxury; time just to be, time perhaps to indulge ourselves.

Time to our patients is an enigma. Mostly they want more of it, they don't want to die just yet. But how much time is often wasted hoping and wishing for more of it, and how much of the time they have left are they able to use in any way constructively? How many can react as positively as the lady with spinal collapse and paraplegia from a breast cancer who wrote:

1985

No thought of the body.
A healthy machine.
Needing:
nourishment and sleep,
for a full, happy and busy life.

But clock watching, clock watching.

Suddenly, catastrophically,
cancer closes all previous doors.

Paralysed, half-aware,
emotionally and spiritually dead,
long days, long nights . . .

Still clock watching, clock watching.

Slowly, through great skill and loving care,
the body becomes a manageable machine.
Through the selflessness of others,
there is a new freedom . . .

Freedom to develop family ties.
Renewing old friendships,
and the making of new.
Freedom from the petty tasks
of day to day living.

Time now for reading and writing.
Time now for laughing and crying.
Time now for praying.

The clock on the wall
is rarely consulted.

The whole environment of hospice care has of course been directed towards easing the patients' feelings as well as the more obvious sufferings. Warm, loving places, 'listening' medical and paramedical staff, social workers with specialist counselling skills, chaplains etc., all working as a multi-disciplinary team to limit the damage inflicted on the patient and his family by the terminal disease.

Having the emphasis on the patient 'doing' rather than 'being done to', however worthily, must therefore break some of the moulds of the sick role and help him to live and die as a whole person, restoring to him his own inherent dignity. It must be said, however, that there are many patients who do not want to keep or to regain responsibility for their own lives. Here we must be careful not to infringe on their rights as individuals and attempt to push them into creativity they do not want. There are, too, those who seem able to continue their naturally active and creative life style almost to the end without any more help than symptom control and nursing support. These avid readers, letter writers, needle workers, artists and autobiographers are all most rewarding to work with. They make such good use of the comfort we can bring them and are, to us, an inspiration.

Excursions into the world of the arts have tended to be seen as 'entertainment' or 'diversion' for our patients, and much credit is due to those who have worked hard in a variety of ways to bring high-quality and professional performances to hospices. Restoring creatively through art with the help and encouragement of experts is already showing signs of influencing the course of the illness in some patients. Unfortunately health care professionals tend to be blinkered in that so many activities tend to be seen in 'therapy' terms, so that if one tries to avoid the word it becomes difficult to find an alternative. Even 'reading therapy' has recently appeared in a semi-organised form. Reading tends to be good for all of us for all sorts of reasons – but we don't normally refer to it as therapy any more than art classes for senior citizens are referred to as 'art therapy', though indeed there are spin-offs other than artistic ones.

In a number of hospices professional artists, musicians and poets are making valuable contributions, encouraging those patients who are able and willing to make the effort actively to create, or share in creating, something which is 'theirs'. So it is that creativity may be therapeutic, but that is not the aim. The aims are primarily artistic and personal. There is of course also a place in hospices for those trained in the artistic therapies, such as music and art therapy, as evidenced in Susan Munro's book *Music Therapy in Palliative/Hospice Care.** Reading this one discovers the wholesale adaptation of the professional skills which has been necessary to respond to the palliative medicine environment. However good an artist is, it is clearly important that he or she should be carefully interviewed before being considered for work in a hospice or home environment with a dying patient.

In this country finance is for many hospices a major obstacle. While medical and nursing care are perceived as mandatory, arts therapies are not and trained therapists are expensive to employ. On the other hand, amongst the bands of energetic volunteers with which so many hospices are blessed there are often unrecognised artists with skills which could well be used, with encouragement and careful training, for the benefit of patients. Not only have well-recognised art forms such as painting, crafts, poetry and music been used with success, but origami, flower-arranging, herb-posy-making, silversmithing, doll-making and

*Magnamusic – Baton Inc., Canada, 1984.

fabric-painting (to name but a few) are being used at the bedside in hospices on both sides of the Atlantic. What artistic personnel are available dictates to a large extent the shape of the creative programme which patients of any hospice can explore. Certainly imaginative and creative care, through the doctors, nurses, physiotherapists, domestic staff or volunteers, can do much to ameliorate some of the pains of loss and isolation and some of the emptiness of waiting.

(Sections of Dr Frampton's article first appeared in the *British Medical Journal* and are acknowledged with thanks.)

11
Fund-Raising

Whether you are going to set up an ambitious arts programme or introduce just one or two regular creative activities, the first hurdle, indeed it may be the only hurdle, is how to find the money. I should like to make a number of suggestions which can apply to any country. These suggestions are as a result of my own fund-raising experience. For the past eighteen years the initiatives I wanted to introduce could only become a reality if they were funded. Fund-raising can be a painful and time-consuming task, though there is an element of excitement about it – rather like a lottery, waiting to see who will meet your request. Once or twice, after writing endless appeal letters (which happily secured the funds), I vowed never to do it again; but then along came another scheme which could only start through the charity of a donor, and the letters began all over again. The purpose of this chapter is not to put you off, but to make the task easier.

HOW TO APPLY FOR FUNDS

Let us assume you are seeking funds for a one-year pilot project for a large scheme or programme.

You should first draw up a proposal of your project, stating why the money is required and who will benefit from the results. You should include an estimated budget of costs – administration, fees, travel, materials and so on. Other details a potential sponsor will want to know are: how many people will benefit from the project, i.e. number of students; how the project will be monitored, i.e. assessing the results of the programme; for how long do you need the funds; how do you visualise the long-term development of the programme; and (always a tricky one) long-term funding, i.e. where you see the money coming from after the trial period. If you are very bold you could ask for a two- or three-year grant, but I do not advise this until the project or activity has proved itself. Perhaps the initial pilot project of one year is best. If you are also able to give examples of other similar successful programmes, not necessarily in your own country, this will help. The *Creative Tree* data can be used as information should you have no first-hand experience.

Make the application clear, simple and brief. No one wants to read pages. Try always to address the sponsor by name rather than as 'Sir' or 'Madam' – it shows you have done your homework. If the letter can be signed by someone who is respected in a related area of work, it may well add weight to the request; but don't worry if you are unable to find such a signatory.

In your letter ask if a meeting can be arranged. Follow this up with a telephone call about ten days later. If you are able to present a visual description through photographs, slides or a video, this will enhance your application. Make sure the display is brief. There is nothing more tedious for a busy sponsor than having to work through albums of photographs or sit through a lengthy video. Fifteen minutes is an ideal video length; it definitely should not exceed twenty minutes.

TO WHOM DO YOU APPLY?

This will depend on a number of different factors. This chapter is making only general suggestions, as each country will have very different economic situations in relation to charities or monies provided for social welfare, rehabilitation etc. Also some countries may have a much easier structure when it comes to seeking private sponsorship. The United Kingdom is fortunate in having many charitable foundations, each of whom supports specific projects that come into its grant-making categories. In some countries one state-established charitable foundation will hold the funds for all the large charitable donors of that country. Therefore it is necessary to do some research and find out which organisations may be interested in the subject of your appeal. Equally this will apply to industrial, commercial or trading companies. If you live in a less economically developed country it is likely that your country is the recipient of overseas aid. In this instance you should establish which agency would be the most likely to give assistance. Here your appropriate ministry or government department will be able to give advice. It is always advisable to inform the official channels of your plans, whether you are applying through them or not. They may well help you later. Otherwise, established local charitable organisations such as the Spastics Society can direct you to likely sources. Remember that the size of your project will also determine where you start looking.

In some countries libraries have books providing information of local grant-making bodies. In others relevant ministries may have lists of international aid agencies. It is a question of using your initiative and imagination to enquire locally about sponsorship from industry, trade, commerce, wealthy benefactors, local authorities and your government agencies which cover education, welfare and culture.

BECOMING A REGISTERED CHARITY

In nearly every country where substantial grants are required an individual is not able to be the recipient. You have to become a registered charity or the equivalent. This may take as long as one to two years and often cannot happen until it has been demonstrated that the project is working effectively. Therefore you will need to find an already registered organisation which is willing to umbrella your project until the scheme becomes registered in its own right. This need not involve other organisations in too much work. They would merely have to open a separate bank account and ensure the funds were administered correctly. On the other hand they might prefer to become rather more involved by becoming a member of your committee. With the projects Interlink has introduced in various parts of the world umbrella organisations have always been found.

If you are an institution applying for funding, you are in all likelihood already registered. In some countries even if you are registered you will still need permission to receive overseas aid from your government.

FUNDING SMALL SCHEMES

Should you only wish to introduce let us say one or two arts activities on a regular weekly basis, the above may not need to apply. Sponsorship could well be sought from within your local community. You could suggest an 'adoption scheme' whereby you invite a local company or trader to adopt one artist and one institution and pay the costs of that weekly activity for one year. The sponsors could be invited to come and see the activity from time to time or reports of its progress could be sent to them. Alternatively, a number of local organisations could combine to contribute the required amount. From a small beginning this type of scheme can mushroom rapidly.

PAYING THE ARTIST

If you are engaging an artist to work on a regular once- or twice-weekly basis you will need to arrange a teaching fee. It is unfair to expect someone to make a regular commitment on a voluntary basis, though this does not mean you should disregard offers of voluntary help. Enquire locally either through an education or health department, university or arts faculty, or from other arts centres, for advice as to the appropriate rate of pay.

FUNDING TO ESTABLISH A THEATRE GROUP

In Zimbabwe Interlink assisted the formation of 'Tose Sonke', a group of amateur actors with physical disabilities. This was a case of what can happen as a result of regular workshops where those with a very real talent wish to go further. If you are a group like them, wanting to set up your own performing group, the method of applying for financial support will be similar to the suggestions already made for larger schemes, but it will almost certainly be necessary to invite potential sponsors to see you at work. It would be politic, too, to agree to acknowledge their support in any written publicity material, such as programmes, leaflets and articles.

FURTHER SUGGESTIONS

Try to find someone with time to spare to form a fund-raising committee. Jumble sales and so on are hard work and best left to such a committee. Until you have secured regular guaranteed grants, fund-raising is a task that is going to be with you, even after your project has got off the ground.

If out of a hundred letters you receive ten interested replies, two of which turn out to be positive, you are doing really well.

If you need materials for activities it is worth writing to manufacturers; they might donate them in return for acknowledgement in any publicity.

If you are able to persuade a well-known entertainer to give a benefit concert, this could be well worth the effort.

Men's business or philanthropic clubs are worth writing to.

You may find that raising money for the purposes we are writing about will cause a few eyebrows to be raised, particularly when the approach of the arts in a healing or therapeutic role is a relatively unfamiliar concept. Artists also tend to be thought of (often most unfairly) as being poor at organisation and administration. It is up to you to inspire and persuade the donor that you have a valid and seriously thought out scheme.

Many sponsoring bodies are prepared to give away money for specific projects – a decoration scheme, for instance, or a writing project – but will not accept liability for the administration costs. This is a short-sighted and unfair policy and has caused many worthwhile schemes to fail. To run a successful project you need an effective administration, be it only one full-time and/or part-time person. Resist this attitude in your sponsors and try to convince them of its dangers.

Fund-raising is hard work, but if your reward is the enrichment of people's lives, it must be well worth the effort.

GINA LEVETE

12
Integration

The Oxford Dictionary's definition of the word 'integration' summarises the intention behind this chapter: 'to bring into equal membership of a community'.

All of us are conditioned to separation from the moment we are born. Labels are affixed to us which box us with others bearing similar labels, the process continuing through education into social life. It is as if we are to fit society rather than society accommodating us. We form opinions, 'better, larger, smaller, good, bad, beautiful, ugly, strong, weak, mine, yours'. How can the world not be in confusion with such a subjective and isolated approach, rather than 'being and let be'? If we could realise that we are all part of a universal circle and members of a world family, then perhaps we could be free enough to be part of each other's smile.

People who are isolated by their circumstances need more encouragement and support to become 'everyday' members of the community. Why is it that so often they are not? It is partly their situation, the boxes and labels; it is partly the world of charity itself in which – for honourable reasons – help is sometimes given in such a way that it builds up a good feeling in the doer and yet more separation for the receiver. We need to recognise the enormous feeling of isolation that exists through lack of public understanding for people suffering, for instance, from epilepsy and mental illnesses; the loneliness that can be experienced through poverty, homelessness or unemployment. To become elderly can mean to become lonely. Indeed, loneliness is the greatest social disease in the Western Hemisphere.

There has been some general progress in making it possible for disabled people to become more active members of the mainstream community, but we should not delude ourselves. In everyday life how many disabled people are shopping in supermarkets, sitting in cafés, restaurants, bars, moving along the streets, working with others? Very few.

INTEGRATION THROUGH THE ARTS

Arts organisations still do not realise how much their involvement can help the integration process. The first stage is to place arts programmes into the environments where disabled people are situated. The second step is that those students who are well and mobile enough should participate in the arts with the rest of the community, by working in community arts centres, houses of culture, schools for the performing arts or adult education centres.

The director of a dance centre (which was open to amateurs and professionals) was asked whether a studio could be made available for students with a mental handicap to have a creative movement course once a week. The director agreed and the class was booked in. As this was to be an integrated course, dancers and staff were invited to participate as well. A dancer with experience of working with students with disabilities was the course tutor.

The first week the students and their teacher arrived looking somewhat anxious. They used the changing rooms with other dancers who also seemed a little uncomfortable. After three weeks everyone had relaxed. The students had become familiar with the surroundings and were completely at ease. They made use of the cafeteria after the class and enjoyed watching through the studio windows the professional dancers at work. The dancers no longer stared or took any undue notice. What did surprise the dancers and staff taking part in the course was the students' movement ability, imagination and concentration. Another outcome which helped to build the students' sense of confidence and independence was travelling to and from the centre on public transport with their teacher. For many it was the first opportunity to do so. Buying their own ticket and having to be on time all helped to given them a sense of belonging. Regular visits to museums, exhibitions and galleries can also provide stimulus and a feeling of being included.

Before embarking on a similar scheme it might be necessary to make some extra arrangements that your group may require. Ensure that you have suitable access and toilet facilities for physically disabled students; and organise alternative transport if public transport is not available or appropriate. You will need extra helpers for people with visual handicaps, a sign-language interpreter for deaf students. Although there will be extra work in making the arrangements it is more than compensated for by the individuals' response.

INTEGRATED CHILDREN'S PROGRAMMES

Arranging integrated children's projects can break down barriers of misunderstanding before they arise. A system of special schools 'twinning' with regular schools introduces children to each other in a natural way. In these schemes it is often the arts activities which are done together. Summer camps and holiday arts programmes where the children enjoy activities on equal terms haved proved themselves to be a success.

Other ideas are: picture exchanges – a scheme similar to a pen friends exchange; children of secondary school age occasionally working as volunteers in homes for severely disabled or ill adults; educational theatre where actors with disabilities perform and give workshops for able and disabled children. Such interactions can do much towards a spontaneous understanding. Life-sized puppets, made with different disabilities, originated in the United States. The purpose was not only to entertain but to show the 'normality' of the characters and the problems they face. It is an idea now adopted by a number of countries, the latest being India where the group is called 'People of This World'. In community circuses children are invited to learn basic circus skills from the simplest to the more adept forms. It is a project which enables everyone to be good at something. Sound playgrounds where children have structures which can be climbed on or that can make music, thus catering for both mobile and less mobile children.

VOLUNTARY WORKERS' INTEGRATION

Voluntary workers play an important role in bringing people together. They can help with the administration that all projects require, provide transport as well as being a friend or companion. 'Foster Grans' was introduced by Arts Reach, a community arts project in Australia. Elderly people took part in drama workshops at a special school for severely disabled children. They worked under a tutor on a one-to-one basis. They adopted a child during that time and sometimes were the only family the children had ever had.

INTEGRATION THROUGH SUBSIDISED ENTERTAINMENT AND TICKET SCHEMES

Volunteers play an essential part in the ticket schemes run by two intermediary services, Shape UK and Hospital Audiences Inc., USA. These organisations provide a service which enables people who could not normally do so to go to the theatre or other entertainments and sporting events. Tickets are either donated by venues or negotiated at reduced prices where necessary. Shape and HAI then offer the tickets to hospitals, institutions, centres, housebound individuals, and other deprived groups. The Shape scheme provides a newsletter with details, and a free booking service. A pool of volunteers give the necessary back-up support, either by providing transport, being a companion for the evening, or meeting and welcoming a group. Through these imaginative schemes new audiences are being introduced to the arts. Entertainment administrators, however, have now to think more carefully about meeting their physical needs – induction loops for the hearing-impaired, access for physically disabled people and, not least, a smile of welcome.

CRAFT TRAINING SCHEMES

Teaching people a craft that may eventually bring in a small income is a positive practical way towards independence. The directory describes some imaginative training programmes happening in different parts of the world, including schemes where severely disadvantaged people are able to make high-quality crafts that are marketed. A problem with many craft-training programmes is that the design of goods is dull and has not moved with the times. High-quality traditional work will sell, but the 'grey area' products that are frequently made become charity objects which a few people feel obliged to buy. A skilled craftsperson and designers who are aware of the current market trends need to be brought in to manage these training schemes. The directory lists a few organisations who will give advice on marketing and distribution.

PUBLIC AWARENESS THROUGH THE MEDIA

Television and radio can make a real contribution by developing public awareness. Programmes where people represent themselves rather than being talked about not only bring understanding but can bring a new dimension to the listener's or viewer's own life. Radio networks in hospitals provide a sense of community life within that environment, as well as putting patients in touch with each other. Video, too, is a medium with great possibilities for integrated work.

Many newsletters are being produced by various groups. They are an excellent source of communication, and an effective written forum for self-help and information. The Sydney (Australia) Manic Depressive Self-Help Group issue a newsletter which contains a mixture of poems, remedies and personal experiences. It is an 'encouraging' publication.

So I'm off. Mania has me in its grip
Its hold is a demon in its fist
Work, work all day long
But things are collapsing what can be wrong?

Pills and therapy do me no good
I cannot confide as I know I should
How can I explain a knotted brain
How can I tell it will always be the same? . . .

Positif Issue no. 13, 15

We will be an impoverished society until we have been able to bring about 'equal membership of a community'. Integration through the arts is not the whole answer but it is a beginning.

GINA LEVETE

13
Projects Worldwide

This chapter describes a few of the imaginative projects happening around the world, though they are not necessarily more exceptional than any others listed in the Directory. Interlink heard about them through its quarterly newsletter *Positif*.

At the time of writing some of the schemes may have come to an end, whilst others are flourishing. It does not matter because they are included – like the Directory as a whole – for the ideas behind them. Some of the self-help groups that express their concerns through an artistic medium are mentioned as well, and you will see that all the projects work towards giving a person a sense of independence and dignity.

CRAFTS

Network, an excellent Australian community arts newsletter, describes the project 'Forest Tapestries'. This scheme was the brainchild of master weaver Lili Krams. Krams believed that her craft could offer some solutions to the current problems of unemployment. She decided to make a large tapestry that would depict the flora of the local park as well as motifs from the community's past and present. Four unemployed people were recruited who learnt all aspects of the theory and practice of weaving. Training for a skill which was relatively rare could offer potential for self-employment. Indeed it did. The team has been expanded and is now working on its first commission. The new tapestry will be hung in an international Hong Kong hotel.

The Gatehouse Centre (Zimbabwe) has shown unemployed women how to make hand-made carpets. The women are encouraged to become responsible for running the project. 'The outward visible sign of change that is happening inside our people is the ability to create something beautiful' is how Lyn Hall, founder of Gatehouse, describes the women's response to carpet-making.

Ernabella Arts (Australia) helps aboriginal women use traditional craft skills in an innovative and marketable way.

Camphill Village (USA), a non-profit making volunteer community of about two hundred people, half of whom have a mental disability, weave high-quality products which are exhibited across America. The

Museum Director, Lilo Markrich, believes weaving to be an especially valuable craft for discovering the potential of students with disabilities.

Ramses Wissa Wassef's School of Weaving (Egypt) was set up in 1951 by Ramses Wassef, an architect, as an artistic, social and educational experience. He wished to demonstrate that people are naturally creative. Originally the children came from poor families and were not selected for having a particular talent. He chose weaving because it was an ideal combination of art and craft. He said: 'It is not possible to separate beauty from utility, the form from the material, the work from its function, man from creative art.' There are two generations of weavers – the first, now in their forties, are still working. Their tapestries are larger, about six by nine feet, and the themes are taken from nature, with images of birds, animals and legends. The later generation work with a more direct sense of colour, a more stylised relationship between image and background, stronger detail, a greater variety of tones and finer weaving. The tapestries have been exhibited in many countries. The school of weaving has transformed many of the weavers' lives.

PROJECTS FOR OLDER PEOPLE

Collage, the *National Council of Aging (USA)*, focuses on arts projects for older people. One scheme they wrote about was the Jewish festivals. *Quilt (Canada)* workers aged between sixty and eight-seven were taught basic quilting. Each worker embroidered a square which represented a different Jewish festival. The weavers wove a biblical quotation around the border of the quilt, 'Even in old age they shall bring forth fruit, they shall be full of vigour and strength.'

Savoir Culinaire (Culinary Arts) (France) was a cultural project around the theme of food. It aimed to discover alternative ways of eating communally. Older people living in a residential home had their own plots of land for vegetables, so that they were able to participate in the growing of food for their own consumption. An exhibition was mounted in Deux-Sèvres entitled 'Kitchens, Food and Table Manners'.

Among the problems of old age are isolation and lack of mobility and motivation. *Dancers of the Third Age (USA)* have found an antidote. Liz Lerman is founder of the group, which works with both young and old dancers. They give performances to many different audiences within their community. Lerman comments: '. . . although older people are not fine technicians, other strengths compensate. When they move in harmony with an idea or emotion, with a movement vocabulary that is natural to their body, the result can be very beautiful.'

Bonnie Vorenberg, founder of *One Niters Senior Theatre Ensemble (USA)*, made a nationwide search for new plays featuring older actors. She wrote:

> A central focus in the new play search was to find plays which negate the many myths of ageing. Such fallacious ideas include 'old is sick', 'old is senile', 'old is a lonely time when you just wait to die'. In *Up Rose a Buring Man*, Ev Miller depicts an elderly man who is able to make decisions affecting his family and personal relationships while he views life with added clarity and insight.
>
> The scripts received covered a wide variety of settings. That few were set in nursing homes reflects the fact that fewer than 5% of America's seniors reside there. However, a great number of plays took place on park benches, which were settings for most tales of woe and life stories; bridge and chess games were also popular choices. Although these places have some validity, such stationary locales inhibit movement, making for a more static play. Other settings do not bear this ageist stereotype.
>
> Playwrights writing for seniors should bear in mind the skill level of the participants. Though a few senior theatre groups are comprised of actors with extensive professional or semi-professional experience, this is not a common situation. Usually, senior actors bring to the theatre much life experience, but little or no theatrical training. Moreover, senior adult actors face, often for the first time in many years, the frightening, yet satisfying task of memorisation. Playwrights can assist them by ensuring their script flows logically from idea to idea.

The Skills Exchange programme run by *Age Concern UK* enables young people to learn from the elderly. Older people are encouraged to teach the young the skills they acquired when working. The organiser, Hazel Rider, advertised locally for older volunteers and the programme varies from arts to crafts, foreign languages to soldering and cable forming. Local schoolchildren visit the centre. Many of the younger students enjoyed the relaxed atmosphere. One of the older tutors commented: 'What they've learnt they'll never forget.'

COMMUNITY/EDUCATIONAL PROJECTS

On a completely different tack, *The Product Life Institute (Switzerland)* is a non-profit-making organisation which provides an unusual service. A consultancy, it aims to create new products from wasted resources in different environments and countries. (Wasted resources can mean people, buildings, land, discarded goods.) The Institute proposes initiatives for local organisations to continue.

Down to Brass Tacks (UK) is another recycling scheme, under which unemployed people are trained in craft and restoring skills, to 'breathe new life into unwanted goods'.

Recycling of a different nature is promoted by the *Dandelion Puppets (UK)*. These young puppeteers specialise in using their medium for education in ecology. Invited by an environmental charity to visit the Nile Province of the Sudan, they are working there on a four-year programme to help teach village people about the urgency of preserving and growing trees to prevent the encroachment of sand dunes. This is done through performances and follow-up work.

Evelyn Roth is a Canadian multi-disciplinary artist who has developed a variety of unique art activities in recycling, sculpture and dance. Her interest in aboriginal cultures and ways in which our Western society can integrate art and life has made her a world traveller for the past five years.

Conservation and ecology issues in the sixties led her to develop a variety of recycling techniques and events, such as knitting fur and leather wool into wearables and home environments, crocheting reject video-tapes into 'car-cosy' and shade canopies. She also formed the Evelyn Roth Moving Sculpture Company and held performances with the group in art galleries in Canada and Europe. The film *Woven in Times* shows these sculptures in natural Canadian environments. Roth webs are crocheted play environments which hold hundreds of children.

Nylon Zoo is a children's participation dance theatre in which the people are the show. A series of nylon costumes and sculptures, each representing a particular native culture, are set up in a large park area with either the inflatable salmon or the Spirit House as the main setting. Evelyn was introduced to the Indian culture on the Pacific north-west by the famous Haida artisan Robert Davidson. She was inspired to build a large inflatable salmon. The thirty-metre structure was stitched from 2,000 pieces of colourful nylon fabric and became the focus of a Salmon Festival held in Massett. Following the success of the very portable 'Salmon Dance', Evelyn constructed a large, inflatable Spirit House. This dancing house is twenty-five metres long. The Spirit Dancer and twelve actors represent four world cultures: Candian Indian, Europe, the Far East and Africa.

Another project she worked on is a tactile family centre. She is a remarkable and creative lady: if there were more Roths in the world, there would, without question, be more fun.

David Werner, Director of the Hesperian Foundation, sent Interlink a description of *Project Projimo* – a village-run rehabilitation programme for disabled children in Mexico. The concern for every aspect of a child's rehabilitation – 'exercises, medicine and love and understanding' – is what makes the project special. Based in a small village, Ajoya, it has a unique community involvement in its work. It is an attempt to respond to the enormous need for basic low-cost rehabilitation in rural areas of developing countries. Families of disabled children stay at the centre or with volunteers in the village while being treated.

One of Projimo's greatest concerns is education, both about disability in general and the project itself. Popular theatre is an effective way of getting the message across. The progress of an orphan crippled by polio is acted out: he learns to walk, acquire rehabilitation skills, and finally becomes a capable member of the Projimo team. Theatre skits are also used to educate the villagers about the dangers of over-medication or the advantages of polio vaccination. Role-play is another method. If children pretend to have a handicap they understand the difficulties of being disabled. They then discuss what could be done to improve the situation.

The project's creativity, however, lies not so much in its theatre and crafts activities as in the very evolution of the programme itself and the constant exploration of effective, friendly, low-cost ways to meet the needs of disabled children and their families.

Mobile Creches (India) was started in New Dehli in 1969 as a response to the needs of children of migrant construction workers who come from drought-prone areas of the country to work in the cities. When work on one site is over, they move on to another with their families. Generally they live with only the most basic amenities, and schooling for the children is made very difficult by constant movement. Mobile Creches fits in with this nomadic lifestyle, the lifespan of each creche being the time it takes to complete a construction. The team move into any shed or unfinished part of a building that the contractor offers and soon turn it into a colourful schoolroom. Up to 150 children of all ages are cared for by a team of creche workers which includes teachers and supervisors, many of whom are from poor communities and are mostly also trained by Mobile Creches. Creative expression, too, is encouraged, and the children have become very accomplished at designing greetings cards which are then sold to help raise funds for the project. Lok

Doot is a theatre unit of Mobile Creches which gives monthly performances at creche sites.

Over 16,000 children have been reached through the 108 centres run by Mobile Creches in the last nine years. It is funded by contractors, the Indian Central Social Welfare Board, civic authorities, international agencies and individuals.

The Boston Children's Museum (USA) is unique. The working philosophy of Janet Kamein (Museum Developer) and her team is based on the understanding that insight comes through simple activities with interesting things. Now in its thirty-seventh year, the Museum is contemporary in outlook, bright, exciting and welcoming. Unusual projects are always going on. 'Exploring Work Experiences for the Future' is a scheme which enables children to have a glimpse of what it would be like to work in different environments – at the factory, in the supermarket or garage. There is an emphasis on 'Hands on' rather than the usual 'Please do not touch'. Volunteers are welcomed as unpaid professional staff. Nearly half the 5,000 museums in the United States are run by volunteers and a growing number of these are elderly people.

pARTner (Poland) is a group of artists who work with children in an exceptionally creative way. pARTner covers a wide range of art activities. Janusz Byszewksi, the founder, concentrates on the quieter elements of children's play – for example, 'The Book About' project. Children make blank books from stiff card with square pockets. They then fill the pockets according to the titles of the book: 'A Book About Me', 'A Book About Leaves'.

'Reconstructing Derelict Buildings' was an activity where the children painted on mock buildings the life that was there thirty to forty years before, giving them an insight into the lives of their parents and grandparents. pARTner also has a unique collection of international art games. Byszewski invited artists in different parts of the world to submit their own art games. He is now working on a new international idea, 'Every Man Is Different', collecting legends, sounds and different things that surround children through the world.

The Goran Workshop (Israel) is situated in a neighbourhood of Jerusalem where Jews and Arabs live together. Tamir Fogel and her colleagues organised integrated visual art activities for Jewish and Arab children. Again many of the activities took place in the community and involved the children in an attempt to improve their surroundings. The children decorated garbage cans with folk fairy stories from the different cultures.

Kreativ un Heim (Creativity in Homes) (Germany, FRG) had given a fresh perspective on life to residential homes. High-quality imaginative craft work is made by the residents from inexpensive or waste materials, such as wool, wood and industrial waste products. The work is exhibited in banks and other public places.

CREATIVITY IN PRISON

The work of Professor Siegfried Neuenhausen, a sculptor of plastic arts in Braunschweig (Germany, FRG), has influenced many students who worked on his projects. He has introduced sculpture, stonemasonry and other arts programmes in prisons, psychiatric hospitals and communities. Neuenhausen says: 'Art demands total involvement, giving these people a chance to fight against their denial of participation in the world.'

A Prison Mural Project (France) grew out of the cooperation between a team of three artists, a photographer, a video specialist and the departmental Board for Architecture Town Planning and Environment (CAUE). The artists worked with the inmates on the murals inside the prison, which were later exhibited to the general public through photographs and videos. From the outset the artists saw their role as technical advisers – the inmates were free to choose their own themes and develop their own ideas. The end products were of a very high quality. Some of the inmates discovered a new interest as well as a hidden talent and expressed a desire to carry on painting when they left the prison. For others painting represented an escape, for a few hours a day, from the confines of their imprisonment. Painting on the very walls that represent the limits of their freedom has enabled the inmates to find a way of communicating with the outside world.

The Community Arts Board (Australia) collaborated on a project to give women prisoners a means of expression as a way 'to develop and not to punish them'. A series of workshops started in 1983 at two women's prisons, Mulawa and Norma Parker. At Mulawa, a high-security prison, a team of women artists used slide-shows to introduce themes into these sessions. The first was 'labels', and the artists encouraged the women to describe the labels that applied to them, or those they used to describe themselves. An early – hostile – reference to the tutors as 'just your average bunch of housewives' allowed the label 'Housewife' to be explored and expressed through painting, collage and printmaking. As trust developed, more positive and confident statements emerged – 'I'm not bad . . . I'm just in gaol.'

Photography was a particularly popular medium, but circumstances within the prison made it impossible for the women to use camera or darkroom facilities. To overcome this the women 'directed' their tutors, constructing imaginative sets which were then photographed and printed by the artists to the prisoners' specifications.

The tutors themselves attribute the high quality and originality of the work to a number of factors – not least that the women had found a voice through which to express feelings hidden within themselves. Having never used these techniques before, they came to them without preconceptions.

A plea from the Chief Probation Officer for a volunteer to cope with the lack of creative facilities for long-term prisoners in a maximum-security prison prompted Carol Martys, a drama teacher, to start a drama and poetry group, *Prison Poems (UK)*. The following is an extract from a poem by one of her students which won the Koestler 1985 prize.

I Have Seen Red Skies that Cried a Nation

I have seen red skies that cried a nation
And heard sweet songs, from babies' lips
That swallowed sorrows lost ambitions
In scarlet whirlpool fading ships;

And yet I understand the wisdom of a fool,
Wrapped up in nightmare's clouded wool.

'Tis fate that casts life's lonely road
Across young faces tinged with hope;
Searching endless gold-sea reaches
On printed paper tied with rope;

And yet I understand the tireless hours,
That satisfy those scented flowers.
Let us not pretend we have not seen
The pretence of a foolish dream,
Shattered like a porcelain vase
And left us in a hopeless daze;

And yet I understand each time-felt year,
On wrinkled faces carved with tears.

And now the midnight of a winter moon
Tells us that the wake is soon

To spread beyond a timeless void
Where shoulders dance on celluloid;

And yet I understand why death is sweet
To lie with angels fast asleep.

DAVID MARTIN

DANCE, DRAMA, MUSIC

Theatre of the Senses (USA) has developed a form of theatre which utilises the sensitivity and perception of blind people. Some of this group's theatrical presentations, with both blind and sighted actors, require the audience to feel tactile sets, identify events by sounds, to smell or taste.

Atelier du Chandron (France) started life by working in psychiatric hospitals. Since then the company has moved away from workshops to explore the full potential of both disabled and able-bodied people working in the theatre. Many of the actors are severely physically disabled but this does not detract from the production. Denis Hirson, actor and coordinator, saw how the uniqueness of each actor's handicap deepened the quality of the character portrayed.

Tyst Theatre (Sweden) would like to spread the knowledge about sign language to people who can hear. Bo Andersson, a director of Tyst, who himself became deaf a few years ago, advocates a theatre which does not only concern itself with words. However, he also feels very strongly that '. . . it is not at all necessary that a theatre for the deaf devote itself primarily to showing what it is like to be deaf.' Tyst Theatre perform a wide variety of plays; from Chekhov to Beckett and Georges Feydeau – not only plays destined for deaf actors and audiences, but also for hearing audiences.

Hakan Englund, a director of Tyst, is not deaf. Although Englund feels that deaf people have the right to a culture of their own, to stay alive 'Silent Theatre' has to appeal to a wider audience. The goal, as he sees it, is stage performances which people can enjoy – regardless .

GARDENING

The PAM Assistance Center (USA) and *Horticultural Therapy (UK)* are two organisations concerned with gardening. The American *Pam Repeater, The Accessible Garden* and the British Society of Horticultural Therapy's magazine, *Growth Point*, give inspiration and practical advice to people with disabilities about discovering their green fingers. Remarkable, too, is the work of a gardening club in Golden Valley, Minnesota, for people who have suffered strokes. 'In the beginning of our project,' says one club member in *Stroke Connection*, 'it was difficult for many of us to understand the relationship between our plants and our own development. But as the weeks went by and we discussed the similarities, the relationship became more clear to us. Early therapy, structure in our life, support and friendships, along with basic understanding and caring, are all very important for our maintenance and in making us who and what we are.'

Horticultural Therapy's Gardening Advisory Service supports local groups throughout Britain with talks, demonstrations and information and helps individual disabled gardeners with their problems. One said: 'I had a serious stroke seven years ago and one of the things that enabled me to make a good recovery was gradually making a little "garden" round my council flat . . . On this lovely morning I can see roses, lavender, thyme, pansies, honeysuckle . . . it is such a joy!'

In both *Growth Point* and *The Accessible Garden* there are guides on correct posture for gardening, particularly from a sitting position – whether in a wheelchair or using a stool or bench. The correct tools for the job are vital to avoid straining and damaging the body, and many tools can be adapted to match a person's needs. For example, for easier gripping power, handlebar grips for bikes can be fitted over the ends of handles, as can foam rubber pipe insulation.

MUSIC

At *St John's School for the Deaf (Gambia)* John Jatta, the Principal, with the aid and encouragement of established deaf schools in Sweden and Sierra Leone, implemented a basic programme, including English, arithmetic, social studies, art and craft, physical education, metalwork, tailoring and music. The school introduced the 'talking drum' into its music sessions to help the students explore their talents and extend their appreciation of rhythm and melody. At first the children began playing the drums seemingly at random; then, Jatta says, 'Suddenly I realised that each child was trying to play a tune and from a cultural point of view the drum would be an ideal choice for any school interested in 'making music'; but in a school for the deaf it is of greater value because it is a way of communication and expression that is not reliant on the spoken word.'

The 'talking drum' is an integral part of African cultural life. Although today it is increasingly becoming a commercial form of entertainment, it is still an instrument of great religious and symbolic significance, played at all festivals, celebrations and communal gatherings. It is essential to the rituals of Muslim, Christian and animist religion. When the drums are played the whole community takes part, says Jatta, including 'the deaf, blind and mentally handicapped who can be seen amongst the crowd watching, dancing or listening.'

THE HEALING ROLE OF MUSIC

At the Rockefeller Foundation Conference in Italy (organised by HAI) on 'The Healing Role of the Arts' (European Perspective), Professor M. E. Fadli, a neuropsychiatrist from Cairo, presented a paper which described the experiments of Dr Nabila Mikhail, who has been researching into the effects of music on patients with psychosomatic disorders. Dr Mikhail presented the results of her work in a thesis submitted for her doctorate in music. Under the supervision of Professor Omar Shahein, a professor of psychiatry at Cairo University, she studied the effects of different types of music on a group of twenty patients, young and old, who were suffering from hypertension.

First, the music was classified in three distinct groups: 1 'Sad music – slow, repetitive, of low pitch and in a minor key, with simple instrumentation; 2 'Dance' music – fast rhythmic, of high pitch and in a major key, with a variety of instruments and singing; 3 'Quiet' music – naturalistic, slow, of low pitch and indefinite rhythm.

From the results of these experiments it was discovered that exposure to 1½ hours' continuous music of the 'quiet' type led to a marked decrease in blood pressure, especially amongst those aged under fifty; while an equal 'dose' of 'dance' music resulted in raised blood pressure, particularly in the older patients. Overall, Dr Mikhail found that the effect of 1½ hours of exposure to 'quiet' music is equal to six days of drug therapy.

Dr Mikhail and Professor Fadli both stress the potentially harmful effects of over-exposure to loud, extravagant music, and feel that the public should be made aware of its possible dangers.

The principal conclusion from this work is that doctors and psychiatrists should move away from their current over-reliance on drug treatments, to allow for more therapeutic use of music and the other arts. In many cultures music has been used for centuries as a treatment for mental illness, through traditional ceremonies which were believed to restore harmony and balance in troubled spirits.

ABOVE AND BELOW *Amici,* Silence. OPPOSITE *pARTner's 'Book About' project.*

TO JEST „KSIĄŻKA O...”

LEFT AND BELOW *'People of this World' puppets with disabilities.*

ABOVE RIGHT AND BELOW *The Polish artist Zbigniew Stec is a self-taught painter with muscular dystrophy – he has difficulty in lifting his hands.*

FASHION, CLOTHES

PRIDE is an organisation based in Connecticut, USA, which makes and adapts clothes for disabled and elderly people. Evelyn Kennedy, the executive director, first became aware of the difficulty in finding attractive, trendy clothes for disabled people when she broke her leg and was on crutches for three years.

Although great strides have been made in adapting architecture, jobs, transport and housing for disabled people, fashion has been ignored, supposedly because it is not considered a critical factor in people's lives. While this may be true, Kennedy argues that one of the most commonplace problems of disabled people is badly fitting clothes which can have severe psychological repercussions. Some physical and occupational therapists look on clothing as a rehabilitative tool. They have suggested that living in a dressing-gown for six months can be very depressing, and so dressing in an attractive garment can be a positive step towards adjustment to the world outside.

Today PRIDE is a thriving organisation, providing clothing consultancy services. Everything that PRIDE undertakes is geared towards self-help.

Ros Branson (Australia) has been doing similar work in Australia. She designs and makes clothes for disabled and elderly people, which she describes as 'nitty-gritty practical things', for people who do not fit the stereotypes or who have special needs. She specialises in loose-fitting easy clothes such as nighties, capes and kaftans, working with materials that do not need ironing.

SELF-HELP

Most of us would prefer to help ourselves rather than be helped. If the circumstances that surround you make it an extra daunting task to cope with life (which can be fairly daunting anyway), then it is encouraging to find you are not alone, and that there are others who have to meet similar problems. A number of self-help groups that made contact with Interlink are expressing their concerns through artistic mediums. Newsletters produced by self-help groups can reach out across nations and countries. The *Liberation Network (UK)* was formed to bring disabled artists and others together to achieve self-determination. They issue a magazine, *In from the Cold*.

Synskadade Konstnäver Konsthantverkares Forening (Sweden) (Association of Visually Handicapped Artists and Crafts People), Players Guide,

Media Office Employment and Disability (USA) and *Fair Play (UK)* are groups of artists with disabilities who ensure that they as artists are fairly represented.

Association Traumas, Association OSE and *Le Cheval Bleu (France)* are pressure groups formed by people who are or have been mentally ill. One of their many aims is to overcome their isolation through artistic mediums. Le Cheval Bleu set in motion a public enquiry about psychiatric practice in relation to cultural activities, aimed at encouraging a better understanding of people with mental illness. Association OSE introduces practical schemes to promote this understanding. For example, they arrange regular special evenings at the local cinema where patients from the St Jean de Dieu Hospital and the local community meet together after enjoying the movie.

Graeae Theatre (UK) and *Tose Sonke (Zimbabwe)* are groups of actors with physical disabilities. The Graeae Theatre Company works professionally, Tose Sonke is in the process of developing educational theatre. Both groups draw their audiences' attention to the problems and prejudices that disabled people have to face.

Frauenselbsthilfe Nach Krebs (Austria) is a support group for women who have or have had breast cancer. They issue a booklet, *What Happens Now?*, with information and activities available.

Ommekaar ('Let us care for each other') (Belgium) was a series of television programmes which featured different self-help groups.

Saravodaya Suwaseitha Sewa (Sri Lanka) endeavours to harmonise tradition with change and encourage under-privileged people to motivate themselves. They place an emphasis on creative activities. Sewa (awareness) is a movement which has developed out of a Buddhist philosophy.

ORD (Nicaragua) (The Organisation for Disabled Revolutionaries) campaigns for a recognition of their needs, which include creative opportunities.

These organisations are but a few examples of motivated people who work together to bring together.

GINA LEVETE

14
Training and Extra Support

Training opportunities vary from country to country, therefore this chapter makes practical suggestions about ways to train yourself.

DOES THE ARTIST NEED TO TRAIN?

The artist requires no further training in order to work in areas of disadvantage unless he or she wishes to become an artistic therapist. In that case there will be need for a further one to three years' training – the reason being that the work involves medical and therapeutic conclusions and treatment.

If you are working with students to communicate and teach your art form to them, perhaps what is first needed is a time of initiation. Should you find yourself a pioneer, with nobody else's approach to guide you, before starting spend some time with your would-be students in their own environment so that everyone becomes familiar with each other. Otherwise it is a good idea to observe and take part in someone else's sessions. If there is a coordinating service near, they will be able to tell you where this kind of work is taking place. Alternatively, contact local arts centres, hospitals, rehabilitation centres and special schools. Having established who is doing what and where, you can then attach yourself as a helper until you feel ready to branch out on your own. This working 'on site' is effective and will give you confidence.

In the late sixties when my colleagues and I began to work in prisons and hospitals, we had to find our own way. For most of us it was not a problem. Each group of students was just a 'new group' and their circumstances did not dominate or inhibit the way we worked. Obviously it was necessary to be sensitive to the various situations, and as we became more confident so the work became more challenging and stimulating for the students. Working with people in severely disadvantaged situations can be quite draining and you can find yourself beginning to identify with the problem rather than the creation. I feel it is important for artists to continue to develop and explore their own work, to keep up with what is going on. In this way you not only recharge yourself but bring a continued vitality to the students.

Never give a workshop without adequate helpers, be absolutely insistent on this. Make progress reports both for the benefit of yourself and future colleagues. Make use, too, of this book's Directory and correspond with people from other countries to share experiences. Doing this can open up new perspectives.

PROFESSIONAL STAFF: ARTS TRAINING

Perhaps you are a teacher, nurse, occupational or physical therapist interested in leading an arts workshop. You will need to have considerable experience and an enjoyment of the art form you wish to teach. Experience can be gained by attending evening or weekend classes at schools for the performing arts, arts centres, education institute polytechnics. If there is someone already working with your students on a short-term project, participate with him or her. Arrange for a local artist to run a course for staff. If this happens, ensure the course receives the maximum publicity so that others from surrounding areas can attend. If the concept is relatively new in your country, you may wish to invite a specialist from another part of the world. An international agency could be approached to provide a grant for this purpose.

It is surprising how much can be conveyed in a short space of time. Interlink was invited by a number of countries to give one- to two-week 'Creative Ideas' courses. Visiting artists worked with students of varying disabilities and disadvantages, and staff and local artists. Many new arts programmes have emerged as a result of those training weeks.

PROFESSIONAL TRAINING FOR PEOPLE WITH DISABILITIES

Schools and universities with performing arts courses should be encouraged to accept students with physical handicaps. The administrators frequently have understandable reservations, usually based on the practical difficulties. It is up to the people who are disabled, their families and the administrators themselves to suggest solutions. We have stressed before that there is nearly always a way to solve what may seem to be an insuperable problem.

Arts administration training is another area where people who are disabled have much to offer. Apart from their regular work they have the personal experience to provide a strong voice to help make the arts more accessible for others.

ARTS COURSES FOR THE AMATEUR

There are a number of ways to introduce courses. Arranging residential weekends where artists and craftspeople work with students of all kinds can be rewarding but they need a fair amount of planning and are somewhat costly. Non-residential weekend courses, perhaps held in a school which is empty at that time, are as a first step more practical. These are courses where parents, family and friends can participate with the students. This kind of participation is valuable and it can give the family a new insight into the creative potential of their child. For children there are summer schools (again held within a school) where able and disabled or abjectly poor people work together. I think that in some countries finding ways of integrating the latter group needs far more attention. Schools for the performing arts can be approached to see whether their final-year students could run courses during the vacation periods at the arts schools, thus enabling students to work in professional surroundings.

Some of the activities that are fun to explore are: clowning and basic circus skills, mask- and kite-making, creative make-up (the art of decorating your face), concrete sculpture (wonderful objects and shapes made together in the open air), murals, banners, photography (home-made cameras), designing jewellery or fashion design, making simple musical instruments, creative cookery, planning a garden (even if it never gets beyond that stage), animated films, strip cartoons, flower-arranging, story-telling, magic. Once you begin to arrange arts courses, you will discover people in your locality with unusual talents.

The previous chapters have shown how people with severe disadvantages can become part of the 'creative tree', and that the label attached by their circumstances is irrelevant in this context. None the less it will very often be necessary to provide extra support, and here are some suggestions to artists/staff leading workshops or arranging programmes.

PHYSICAL DISABILITY

If the activity arranged is to be held in a public place, ensure that the building is accessible and that ramps are provided if there are steps – long wooden planks will do as a makeshift if there is nothing else. Failing that, arrange for helpers for those people unable to walk. You will need adapted lavatories, or at least ones with room enough for a wheel chair. For transport you should have adapted mini-buses or helpers to lift people in and out. You need adapted work tools for people with severe disabilities; this applies for tools used in the plastic arts, craft, puppetry and music. Occupational therapists are very imaginative and resourceful at being able to adapt to individual needs. In dance sessions you should provide foam or soft mats (always with the staff's approval) for students who prefer to work from the floor.

VISUAL HANDICAP

An artist working wth these students should be aware that however proficient blind people are at finding their way around, this is a new activity which may be taking place in different surroundings. There may at first be a need for helpers.

Present the content of the workshop in a clear, colourful and descriptive way. Devise a programme that includes a tactile content. Use sounds to stimulate the imagination. For example, everyday noises can be recorded and played on a cassette – running water, tearing paper, glasses chinking, footsteps, door banging, bees humming, birds singing. Provide different smells – lavender, soap, spices; different textures – smooth, soft, silky, prickly. Gently blowing on an arm or tracing a part of the skin with water will indicate a shape or pattern; these sensations can be translated into brush strokes, shapes, sounds, words or movements.

HEARING HANDICAP

Some students prefer to lip read, others to work with sign language. It varies from place to place, country to country. A sign-language interpreter may be needed; failing that, speak clearly and face the students when doing so. If you are going to work with these students for some considerable time then it will be useful to learn a sign language. Learning to communicate with our faces, hands and bodies is something we should all do as a matter of course because so much expression can come through the body. If there were an international sign language that all of us learned from early childhood, we might be able to cross frontiers and understand each other better. It might even help the world be kinder to itself.

MENTAL HANDICAP

If students are taking part in a physical activity, ensure they have the right clothes – track suits or loose trousers, bare feet or light-weight shoes. All too often students arrive in inappropriate clothes – tight trousers, heavy shoes, short skirts or stockings inhibit their freedom of movement. No one wants to show their knickers. Invite a local clothing manufacturer to donate track suits or provide the money for buying

Interlink Training Courses.
OPPOSITE, ABOVE *Modelling session, Delhi workshop.*
OPPOSITE, BELOW *Deaf students making music, Calcutta workshop.*
RIGHT *St Giles Rehabilitation Centre workshop, Zimbabwe.*
BELOW *Modelling workshop, Sri Lanka.*

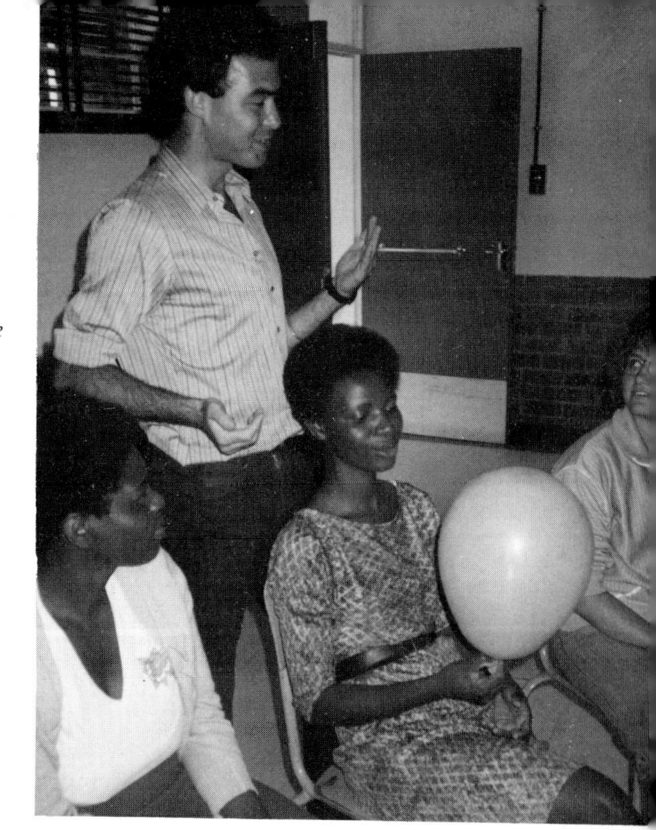

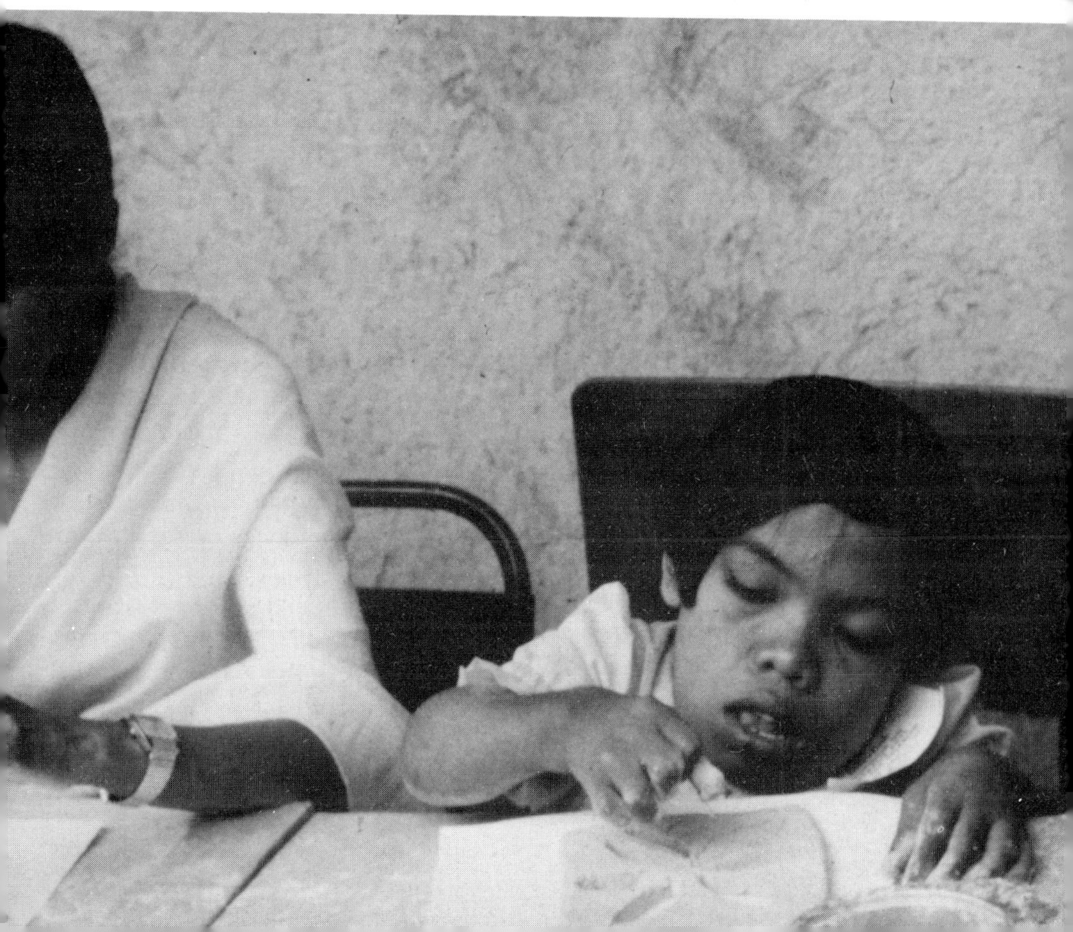

them. If you look the part, you feel the part; consequently your work is better.

Work with students on an equal footing. That means do not talk down or overpraise. You are there to stretch them to their full potential. Expect a high quality of work. Do not only ask them to copy, ask them to build on their own ideas, through shapes, sounds, words, movements. This does not necessarily mean you should exclude teaching a formal technique, for acquiring a technique lays down a foundation on which to build. Provide a clear framework to the workshop.

WORKING WITH OLDER PEOPLE

Older people in particular dislike being patronised or talked down to. On the contrary, we should realise it is our privilege to be able to work with them. Collecting forgotten recipes, stories or crafts helps older people realise the cultural contribution they still have to make through their years, rather than being demoralised because of their age. So invite students through a creative medium to share their past experiences or life styles with the younger generations. An example of how this can be done is shown through 'Games and Rhythms', a project that took place in Scotland. Helen Anderson, the coordinator, had the idea of restoring the 'lost games' that children had played at the beginning of this century. She met the older people in her community who recalled their childhood games. They then visited local schools to introduce the games to the children. Schools competed with each other at such events as 'whip and peerie', or 'gird and cheek' race and 'beds or peever'.

When providing art and craft materials for older students, if at all possible buy quality materials. Often a group of institutionalised older people can be seen sitting around a cramped table painting on small bits of sugar paper with watery poster paints. The Arts Centre at Charles Foix Hospital in France is an example of what can evolve if visual art is given a proper impetus. An art department was set up within the hospital and Bernard Colin-Cyvoct, a painter, used the place as his own studio. He left the studio doors open so that patients could come in when they wished to. From the first month onwards many residents began to attend on a regular basis. There was no instruction and any influence Colin-Cyvoct has had has been in the matter of materials (easels, oil paints, good brushes), not style. The art department has had the effect of opening the hospital to the public. Older people from the surrounding area come to work there as well and the result has been work of great variety and richness.

One general suggestion is to avoid showing that you think an activity (other than for medical reasons) is not suitable. The student's approach should be: if you are seventy and want to dance, then dance. If you have no previous musical ability and suddenly have a great desire to learn to play an instrument, go ahead. If you are not able to read or write but want to write a story, write it by speaking on to a tape, or let someone else do the writing for you. If you are bedridden and wish to model clay, then do so and forget about the possible mess. There is nearly always a way to solve a problem; through an individual's own effort it can go beyond what was imagined to be a limitation.

MENTAL ILLNESS

Understanding, sensitivity and encouragement are the support needed when dealing with people who are recovering from a mental illness. Everyday actions that most of us give little thought to may be hurdles to overcome. Using public transport, being away from the security of home, relating to other people, taking part in an arts activity, are all situations which after such an illness can cause tension. The workshop therefore needs to be planned at a pace which will allow time for relaxation. Start your session with calm breathing exercises and end with a rest period. Let your own schedule allow for individual informal conversation after the activity is over.

SOCIAL DISADVANTAGE

If a person is living under very disadvantaged circumstances, it will probably be that that situation overshadows any small wish to be creative. In this instance your openness and enthusiasm will be an encouragement. Suggest self-support groups that can work together. Try to involve groups in the planning and organisation of the programme. If possible arrange for the group to be able to work in an environment right away from their problem. In such situations people are more easily able to express themselves if, as well as the creative outline, they are given this moral support.

GINA LEVETE

RIGHT *Self portrait by Llinos Williams from Craig-y-Parc School, Cardiff for children with cerebral palsy. Part of a picture exchange with children in India.*
BELOW *Drama workshop, New Zealand; theme 'flowers'.*

An International Directory of Ideas

Since the inception of Interlink we have been receiving information about various arts projects throughout the world. Much of this data is included here. The Directory does not claim to be comprehensive and we are aware that there are many projects happening all over the world that we did not hear about. Nor has it been possible to include details of all the existing information Interlink received – and for this our sincere apologies. The main purpose of the Directory, therefore, is to describe the ideas: they may be the catalyst for a new independent intitiative.

There is a brief description of each project. Some of the information included dates as far back as 1983, and whilst most schemes are flourishing there will be others which have ceased. In the same way some contact names or addresses will have changed. Despite this, the reader will be able to connect up with many people across the world. The back of the Directory lists some of the places which offer artistic therapy training as well as contacts for marketing craft products. We have also included a very few names of international agencies who might provide readers with information or assistance relevant to this book.

GINA LEVETE

ARTS, COMMUNITY

Addison Road Community Centre
142 Addison Road, Marrickville, NSW 2204, **Australia**
The idea behind this centre is that different ethnic groups can rent a hut and use it to develop activities and services for their cultural group. Festival days like Australia Day and Carnival bring together the different groups as well as involving the local residents.

Art Reach
66 Albion Street, Surry Hills, NSW 2010, **Australia**
Aimed at fostering creative development among disabled people, particularly theatre and performance. Members include both able-bodied and disabled people.

Brown's Mart Community Arts Project
Smith Street, PO Box 2429, Darwin, NT 5794, **Australia**
A project involved with community music, dance, theatre events and celebrations. Its resource and information centre assists groups with funding applications, dissemination (including special needs).

Burwood Community Youth Support Scheme
18 Burleigh Street, Burwood, NSW, **Australia**
The Burwood CYSS provides a wide variety of courses and services for young unemployed people.

Community Arts Board, Australia Council
PO Box 302, N Sydney 2060, **Australia**
In New South Wales the prison authorities and local Arts Board have collaborated on a visual art project to give women prisoners a means of expression.

Community Arts Network (Tasmania)
77 Salamanca Place, Hobart, TAS 7000, **Australia**
Aims to advise and assist in all aspects of community-based arts activities and to initiate and promote arts activities in the community.

Cosmos Community Recreation Centre
245 New Town Road, New Town, TAS 7008, **Australia**

A community recreation centre providing for the recreational needs of handicapped people.

Network
66 Albion Street, Surry Hills, NSW 2010, **Australia**
The aim of this group is to promote and assert the value of community arts for development and enrichment. Produces and disseminates information for community arts workers and offers a resource pool of equipment, runs workshops and has mobile units for outreach programmes. Has an excellent newsletter featuring exciting projects and ideas. Recommended.

Network News
34 Liverpool Street, Sydney, NSW, **Australia**
The quarterly newspaper of the Community Activity Centres Network, whose ultimate aim is to assist institutions to become self-sufficient by providing arts activities as part of their normal programme.

Out-Reach
Foleys Road, PO Box 1223, North Wollongong, NSW 2500, **Australia**
Bill Johnstone established an outreach project by word of mouth for minority groups and disadvantaged adults. Examples of their work include a book of poetry by elderly patients; courses in languages, arts and crafts.

Active Retirement Association
4 Eblana Avenue, Dun Laoghaire, Dublin, **Eire**
Set up by retired people for retired people to participate in arts activities.

Actions Culturelles Contre les Exclusions et les Ségrégations
20 rue Soufflot, 75005 Paris, **France**
The aim of ACCES is to campaign against the exclusivity of the arts, especially the literary arts; there was a campaign about reading in the Bretigny and St Michel-sur-Orge region with games and storytelling from a mobile unit.

Centre d'Animation Rurale des Hauts Cantons
Faubourg Saint Roch, 34390 Olargues, **France**
CARHC is a group of 40 local organisations over a rural mountainous region with an isolated population. It aims to stimulate creative expression in the area through cultural activities for all social classes and age groups.

Centre de Recherche pour le Dévélopement Culturel
7 Chaussée de la Madeleine, 4400 Nantes, **France**
A regional arts body which aims to make arts activities available to a wider section of people and help in the development of cultural programmes, free of charge. It provides a national network of contacts involved in art activities, with emphasis on the theatre, and publishes a quarterly arts magazine, *Face B.*

Vieillesse Buissonnière
95 rue Rambuteau, 71000 Macon, **France**
Aims to bring together the isolated elderly and other groups in the community, especially through theatre; they have an annual theatre festival for the elderly.

Plainpied – GIHP (PH)
10 rue Georges de Porto Riche, 75014 Paris, **France**
GIHP was founded by young disabled people who wished to be responsible for their own lives. It now includes able-bodied people and issues a magazine, *Plainpied.*

CCPTAVARD
Room 5, St John's School, Bye Pass Road, Bulandshahr 203001, **India**
The Christian Council of Puppetry and Traditional Art Voluntary Agencies for Relief and Development is a combination of agencies for performing artists. It also aims to develop art and humanities for the disadvantaged, to entertain, and challenge people to see the world in new ways.

Nara Tanpopo no Kai
1527-4 Gojoyama, Rokujo-cho, Nara-shi, Nara-ten, **Japan**
A local community group to help the handicapped with activities such as pottery, arts etc., done with able-bodied voluntary groups.

Werkvereniging 'Zet je Schrap' [Brace Yourself]
Voorstraat 52, 3512 AR Utrecht, **Netherlands**
A self-help organisation in Rotterdam, set up for the young unemployed belonging to cultural minorities. Their cultural and ethnic backgrounds are the focus of activities involving music and dancing.

Artwork Studio
101 Federal Street, Auckland 1, **New Zealand**
Employs experienced visual and performing artists to work in the community on innovative art projects.

Asnes Commune
Kulturknotoret, 2270 Flisa, **Norway**
A local history project using people's experience of their environments between 1920 and 1940 is the basis of a theatrical production. Local people trained in all aspects of theatrical production. The project integrates the community's two linguistic groups who have maintained quite distinct identities.

pARTner
c/o Inst Wzorniotwa Przemylslowego, Swietojerska 5/7, 00-236 Warsaw, **Poland**
An independent private group of visual artists and designers who give workshops, organise exhibitions and design playgrounds. Although the focus of their work is with children, they invite the community, particularly elderly people and parents, to take part as well. Janusz Byszewski is also involved in an international mail-art scheme, where children in Poland exchange art with children in other countries. He is also collecting ideas for creative arts activities for children from all over the world in the project 'Arts Actions for/with Children'.

Seagull Group for Science & Arts
PO Box 368, Port Sudan, **Sudan**
A theatre project which involves artists and professionals interested in using theatre as a means of communication within the community.

Swedish Travelling Exhibitions
Riksutstallningar, Alsnogatan 7, S-11641 Stockholm, **Sweden**
One of three national state-supported cultural institutions which tour Sweden and help to disseminate culture nationwide. Organises art, craft, history and natural science exhibitions in collaboration with schools, adult education organisations etc. Provides advice and financial support to groups in producing their own exhibitions.

The Ark Drama Workshop for Mentally Handicapped People
South Hill Park Arts Centre, Bracknell, Berks RG12 4PA, **UK**
Runs integrated arts workshops for mentally disabled students. Also acts as information centre and coordinating service.

Artaction
c/o Mind, 44 Church Street, Stoke-on-Trent, North Staffs, **UK**
A voluntary group providing a variety of art activities for hospitals, long-stay hostels etc.

Artsreach
Jackson's Lane Community Centre, Jackson's Lane, London N6, **UK**
Runs workshops of arts activities for children with special needs; works closely with teachers who can learn new creative skills and continue the work.

Avenue Day Centre
10 Corsica Street, London N5, **UK**
Creative therapists work with people who have histories of psychiatric illness.

The Bakehouse
Queen Street, Bideford, North Devon, EX39 2JG, **UK**
A former warehouse has been converted into a craft centre, skills exchange, and activities centre by local unemployed people. It also provides premises for craft workers to train unemployed people.

The Barn Centre
Alexandra Road, Aberystwyth, Dyfed, **UK**
A community arts centre with studio space for resident artists. Projects have been established between resident artists and the mentally handicapped, who work with artists in their studios.

Belvoir Street, East Midlands Shape Community Project
27a Belvoir Street, Leicester, **UK**
East Midlands Shape set up a community project in an old boot factory employing 12 able-bodied and disabled people, providing an art service to hospitals etc., throughout the area.

The Blackie, Great George's Community Cultural Project
Great George Street, Liverpool 1, **UK**
A group of resident artists run a year-round programme. One of their projects was an animated cartoon called *Money Can't Buy You* made with groups of people with disabilities. Another was the film *Three Feary Tales*, a trilogy of responses to the questions: 'What are you most afraid of?' and 'How might you overcome your fear?'

Brass Tacks Recycling
18 Ashwin Street, London E18 3DL, **UK**
The project relies on donations of unwanted or broken household goods from the local community. The articles are then repaired or reconditioned and then distributed to local disadvantaged groups or

sold back to local people. All work is carried out by long-term unemployed.

Carousel
Rock Place Studios, 8 Rock Place, Brighton, Sussex, **UK**
Promotes the therapeutic use of creative arts for groups with special needs.

Camphill Village Trust
Delrow College, Hillfield Lane, Aldenham, Watford, Herts WD2 8DT, **UK**
The centre sprang from Camphill – founded by Rudolf Steiner to establish village communities where people, handicapped or otherwise, could live and work together.

CATS
St Catherine's Mill, Broad Lane, Bramley, Leeds LS13 2TD, **UK**
A club for the unemployed, housed in a converted mill, which provides facilities for people to find creative alternatives to paid employment.

The Cave
516 Moseley Road, Balsall Heath, Birmingham B12 9AH, **UK**
A Probation Service arts centre project with an emphasis on active participation from the local community.

Community Education Service
Ashcraig Secondary School, 100 Avenue End Road, Glasgow G33, **UK**
Available for groups and individuals evenings and weekends, the school is fully equipped for disabled people and includes theatre space, sports and craft facilities.

Creative Young People Together
21 Plover Close, East Wittering, Chichester PO20 8PW, **UK**
CRYPT creates small residential communities where young disabled persons can develop their creative skills without the pressures that can be discouraging in some institutions.

Crossover, The Volunteer Centre
29 Lower King's Road, Berkhamsted, Herts HP4 2AB, **UK**
Involvement in the fields of social welfare, environmental arts and the business world. The project aims to ease retirement transition by an introduction to voluntary work before retirement.

The Crypt
Agar Road, Truro, Cornwall, **UK**
Community centre run by and for the unemployed to help them keep in touch with the outside world, as people in rural areas can become isolated through unemployment. They are keen to establish links with unemployed groups to exchange ideas about crafts and lifestyles.

East Midland Shape Community Project
27a Belvoir Street, Leicester, **UK**
A scheme for unemployed people has focused its attention on design and manufacture of toys for children with special needs.

Hackney Pensioners Projects
287 Kingsland Road, Dalston, London E8 4DL, **UK**
A team of 8 people whose aim is to improve elderly people's awareness of their rights and opportunities. *Hackney Pensioners Press* is a free quarterly newspaper, planned and produced by 20 pensioners.

Handsworth Cultural Centre
Hamstead Road, Handsworth, Birmingham 21, **UK**
A culturally oriented recreational alternative for unemployed youth in the area.

Interchange Trust
15 Wilkin Street, London NW5 3NG, **UK**
Interchange Trust runs projects involving education and training. Make-it-yourself projects have given young people the opportunity to sample some of the processes involved in running a creative enterprise, such as producing and selling a record, books, calendars, magazines, etc.

Leisure and Advice Centre for the Elderly
Gourock Community Education Centre, 105 Dalrymple Street, Greenock, Scotland, **UK**
LACE is a club for elderly people with a focus on arts activities.

The Living Archive Project
Stantonbury Campus, Purbeck, Stantonbury, Milton Keynes MK14 6BN, **UK**
To further the use of local history as a resource for education and the arts, the community has been actively involved in interviewing, classifying material, writing, performing, creating music.

Multi-Cultural Arts Group
16 Ashton Way, Whitley Bay, Tyne & Wear NE26 3JH, **UK**
Formed to promote social and artistic interaction for women from ethnic minorities and women from the host community. Despite language difficulties the women have worked together creatively and through the medium of embroidery have been able to form friendships with each other.

New Perspectives Community Arts Centre
13 Curriers Lane, Ipswich, Suffolk, **UK**
A unique project for local unemployed, offering advice and tuition across a broad range of arts and crafts, from basic to advanced.

Oval House
54 Kennington Oval, London SE11 5SW, **UK**
A community centre running a wide range of arts workshops; it also operates as a club, with substantially reduced membership rates for the unemployed.

The Portobello Project
49-51 Porchester Road, London W2, **UK**
An arts and education centre, its main objective is to make information available to young people. It also runs workshops in cartoons, drama, writing, music.

Queen's Park Centre
Queen's Park Road, Aylesbury HP21 7RT, **UK**
A community arts craft centre, theatre and gallery, offering a wide range of tutored workshops.

Red Water Arts
Back Rough Farm, Coalclough Road, Todmorden, Lancs, **UK**
Established to provide a relaxing rural environment as well as a place for exploration and creative activity. It especially welcomes people from institutionalised settings.

Rotherhithe Theatre Workshop
107 Rotherhithe Street, London SE16, **UK**
Students from Dartington College started working with community groups in Rotherhithe and together they established a neighbourhood theatre programme.

Saints Youth Club
United Reformed Church, Lea Road, Penn Fields, Wolverhampton, W Midlands, **UK**
Workshops for the unemployed have been set up with young people themselves taking responsibility for the activities. The workshops include carpentry, metalwork etc., and the young people are involved in the entire manufacturing cycle from raw material to finished product.

Stoke & Newcastle Arts Project
19 Barracks Workshops, Newcastle-under-Lyme, Staffs ST5 1LG, **UK**
SNAP works with local community groups and trains artists to work with them.

The Summers Day Centre
High Street, West Moseley, Surrey, **UK**
'Conquest', The Society for Art for the Physically Handicapped, aims to encourage physically disabled people to participate actively in the creative arts.

Third Age Project
59 High Street, Totnes, Devon TQ9 59B, **UK**
Aims at providing creative opportunities for mature redundant workers: glass engraving, painting, enamelling, and weaving. A large number of activities are available at the 30 branches throughout Devon.

Arts for Elders
6816 N Villard Ave, Portland, Oregon 97217, **USA**
An umbrella organisation whose purpose is to encourage senior adults to become involved in the arts, especially drama and dance. Bonnie Vorenberg directs the Oregon Senior Theatre Ensemble. A very exciting project.

Iowa Arts Council
State Capitol Building, Des Moines, Iowa 50319, **USA**
Has sponsored a wide range of creative programmes for senior citizens.

Partners for Liveable Places
1429 21st Street NW, Washington DC 20036, **USA**
A network of organisations to promote better planning and design of business, cultural and recreational facilities. It also seeks to enlarge the arts presence in the community and believes that older people have an important role to play in this process.

Project 'Touch'
c/o Collage, National Council on the Aging, 600 Maryland Ave SW, Washington DC 20024, **USA**
To bring together elderly residents from convalescent centres and pupils from an inner city in New Haven, to share experiences and learn new skills together through artistic activities.

The Richmond Hill Senior Center
1243-8 Jamaica Avenue, Richmond Hill, NY 11418, **USA**
The centre has been serving hearing-impaired seniors for the past four years; it is the only centre serving both the hearing and impaired. It provides, amongst other things, art classes, captioned films, sculpture, dancing, exercise classes.

SCARP, Generations Together
600A Thackeray Hill, Pittsburgh Univ, Pittsburgh PA 15260, **USA**
Senior Citizens Artists Resource Program, to develop the arts in schools involving older (55+) volunteer artists.

ARTS, HOSPITAL

Leslie Edward Blaker
Concord Hospital, Hospital Road, Concord, NSW 2139, **Australia**
Co-founder Artreach; integrates arts activities for disabled and able-bodied people.

Niederosterreichisches Landeskrankenhaus for Psychiatrie und Neurologie
3400 Kloster Neuberg-Gugging, **Austria**
Dr Johann Feilacher, Dr Leo Navratil
A psychiatric hospital with an arts centre. Special renovation of a separate building for art work use facilitated a more concentrated working atmosphere. A gallery houses paintings for sale (profit going to patients). A collective of artistically active patients, a museum and gallery, and a meeting place.

Hospital Julio Diaz
Carr Wajay y Ave R, Boyerof, La Havana, **Cuba**

Creative sessions in visual and plastic arts were introduced into this rehabilitation hospital for children with severe physical handicaps, and have proved to be of great therapeutic importance.

Association Culturelle du Reims
23 rue des Moulins, 51100 Reims, **France**
This association has initiated a project 'Corps Accord' to establish links between the creative arts and hospitals, to encourage children and adults to express themselves about their bodies, health, illness and the hospital itself.

Bernard Colin-Cyvoct
Atelier de Peinture, Pavillion Loeper, Hôpital Charles Foix, 7 ave de la République, 94206 Ivry-sur-Seine, **France**
An artist set up a professional studio in this hospital. He left the door open and gradually the elderly patients began to do their own paintings. His role was to assist and advise. The project has produced some very beautiful work. The hospital now has a music centre as well.

Madeleine Lions
c/o Marionette et Thérapie, 14, rue Saint-Benoît, 75006 Paris, **France**
A puppeteer saw how lonely and boring hospital life could be for children. With a team of young helpers, she transformed wards into theatres for weekly puppet shows.

B.J. Medical College of Sassoon General Hospital
Pune, **India**
Dr Mohan Agashe, Associate Professor of Psychiatry
Arts activities have been introduced into this hospital for mental illness. Dr Deo introduced music as therapy, encouraging patients to play instruments in small groups. Dr Agashe has introduced patients to acting techniques.

Gajanan Ambulkar
Mahatma Gandhi Institute of Medical Sciences, Sevegram, MP 422 102, **India**
Gajanan Ambulkar is employed as a hospital artist in the Anatomy Department. His work includes making special drawings as teaching aids for medical students, and he has also created paintings for the hospital environment.

La Tinaia
c/o Ospedale Neuropsichiatrico, Via San Salvi 12, Florence, **Italy**

Massimo Mensi
An art and craft workshop run by a collective of artists in a psychiatric hospital in Florence. The programme is designed to help integration of those people who are inside the hospital, as well as out-patients. Its existence has helped to reduce the number of resident patients.

ZKP Stichting Ziekenhuis Kunstprogramme
Zuidlaan 16, 1861 G.t. Bergen, **Netherlands**
Dr D. Granaat
Dr Granaat (himself an artist) introduced a notebook to personalise hospital visits. Children and adults are given this book on admission and are encouraged to write their feelings, fears and questions. When visited by the consultant, patients could show the book and he would answer their questions and alleviate their fears. Dr Granaat also supervises a hospital decoration scheme of painting and sculpture, and an extension art therapy programme.

Porirua Hospital Recreation Department
Private Bag, Porirua, **New Zealand**
David Buller, Volunteer Coordinator Administrator
The recreation department organises ongoing creative activities for residents and arts festivals involving artists, staff and the general public, as well as artist-in-residence programmes.

Lillhagen Centre for Education Art and Recreation
Gothenburg, **Sweden**
Eva White, Head Administrator
A psychiatric hospital where patients attend courses in a variety of subjects, covering all the arts.

Centre for the Study of Psychopathological Expression
c/o Hôpital de Cery, CH-1008 Prilly, **Switzerland**
Dr A. Bader
Professor Christian Muller established a painting workshop and film studio in the hospital. Besides enabling the making of documentary films in the field of psychopathological expression, it provides patients with a new means of expression.

Artist in Residence Project
Leicester General Hospital Psychiatric Department, Gwendolen Road, Leicester, **UK**
Johan Benthin

Within the framework of an artist's exchange organised between Adult Education Institute in Hessen, West Germany, and the UK organisation East Midlands Shape, a Danish artist led a group of patients who decorated the cafeteria with a fresco/mural.

Bethnal Green Hospital
Cambridge Heath Road, London E2, **UK**
Michele Bacciotini
An art team of 30 unemployed people, set up by Shape, painted mural panels and created a recreation/physiotherapy garden, as well as becoming involved in design for the disabled and recreation therapy with geriatric patients.

Colchester District Hospital
c/o Eastword, Eastern Arts Association, 8/9 Bridge St., Cambridge CB2 1VA, **UK**
Roger Wollen, Editor
This new hospital has murals, photographs, paintings and sculptures installed throughout.

Egglomania Club
Cedars Villa, Rampton Hospital, Retford, Notts DN22 0PD, **UK**
Barry Atkinson, Charge Nurse
Many of the wards of this psychiatric hospital have hobbies sections and creative projects, 'Egglomania' for example. Patients blow and decorate eggs, much in the tradition of the jeweller Fabergé.

Help the Hospices Arts Advisory Group
BMA House, Tavistock Square, London WC1, **UK**
Provides short training courses for artists (not trained as therapists) to prepare them to work in hospices.

Hospital Arts Project
St Mary's Hospital, Hathersage Road, Manchester M13 0JH, **UK**
Peter Senior
Founded in 1973 by Peter Senior, visual artist/lecturer, this scheme was designed for the Manchester District Hospital Group. A team of full-time artists work within hospitals, health centres and clinics, providing a range of arts activities from mural painting to puppetry and the design of therapy aids. They also give workshops for staff, patients and visitors. This extremely successful scheme has been a model from which other hospital projects in the UK have emerged.

Memory Recall
Occupational Therapy Dept, Standen Hall, Lancaster Moor Hospital, Quernmore Road, Lancaster LA1 3JR, **UK**
Pamela Clark
A social worker and an occupational therapist used a 'recall' pack of reminiscence aids with a group of elderly people, using slides, music, sounds and descriptions of episodes between 1900 and 1980.

Northgate Arts Project
Northgate Hospital, Morpeth, Northumberland NE61 3BP, **UK**
Brian Scott, Coordinator
Set up in November 1982 to bring a range of creative activities to the 700 mentally handicapped residents and to form links with artists and arts organisations in the community.

St George's Volunteers
St George's Hospital, Stafford ST16 3AG, **UK**
Mrs. M. Hindle, Voluntary Services Officer
A branch of the Association of Health Services Volunteers, providing a forum for volunteers working in this psychiatric hospital. There is a Saturday morning art club, where local artists come and help patients. A team of occupational therapy aides use bell-ringing as therapy with patients, which has proved very popular. Professional artists have been engaged to train the occupational therapy staff in dramatherapy. A music appreciation group has been started and the chapel is being renovated to provide a centre for musical activities.

St Joseph's Hospice
Mare Street, Hackney, London E8 4SA, **UK**
Dr David Frampton
Creative arts projects: poetry, music and graphic arts are taken to patient's bedside.

For information on all UK Hospital Arts projects, consult The Arts in a Health District *by Peter Coles (DHSS, London, UK) or contact Peter Senior, Hospital Centre, Manchester.*

Art that Heals
Jonsson Comprehensive Cancer Center, Louis Factor Health Sciences Building, 10833 Le Conte Avenue 10-244, Los Angeles, California 90024, **USA**
Devra Breslow, Director for Special Programs

A comprehensive arts programme for all types of patients at the UCLA Medical Center and its affiliate Jonsson Comprehensive Cancer Center.

Arts in Hospice
Hospice Council of Vermont, 148 Main Street, Montpelier, VT 05602, **USA**
Virginia Fry
Arts programmes for dying persons and their families.

Duke University Medical Center
Box 3017, Durham, North Carolina 27701, **USA**
Janice Palmer, Cultural Services Programmer
A teaching hospital with a well-established, large, diversified arts programme.

Project Art
Iowa Hospital and Clinics, Iowa City, Iowa 52242, **USA**
Joyce Summerwill
A teaching hospital with a well-established comprehensive arts programme.

University of Washington Hospital
1959 NE Pacific, Seattle, Washington 98195, **USA**
Lynn Basa, Art Director
This hospital has a diversified arts programme.

ARTS, VISUAL

Arts for the Aged
PO Box 779 Murwillumbah, NSW 2484, **Australia**
Provides opportunities for older people in nursing homes to take up painting in a serious manner without any hint of patronage.

Arts Project
60 Illawarra Road, Hawthorn, VIC 3122, **Australia**
Formed with the intention of giving mentally handicapped people an opportunity to exhibit their artwork under conditions normally accorded to top artists. Working with teachers, students, artists and galleries, it also acts as an information and resource centre.

NECTA
PO Box 153, Balmain, NSW 2041, **Australia**
The Network for Exploring Creativity in Therapy through the Arts acts as a forum for workshops and ideas-sharing for all those involved in the creative arts as applied in therapy. It runs courses and publishes a quarterly newsletter.

Art en Marge
7 rue des Vierges, 1000 Brussels, **Belgium**
Functions as an art gallery for disabled and able-bodied artists. Emphasis on attracting a wide public to see the work.

Royal Museum for Art and History
Jubelpark 10, 1040 Brussels, **Belgium**
Has a 'Museum for the Blind'. One exhibition, 'The Cathedral', hoped to bring architecture as an art form to the visually impaired visitor.

Le Silex
rue Voot 82, 1200 Brussels, **Belgium**
A meeting place for mentally handicapped and able-bodied people. Programmes of creative arts workshops are held and over 100 mentally handicapped adults participate.

Canadian Folk Arts Council
263 Adelaide St West, Toronto, Ontario M5H 1Y2, **Canada**
Leon Kosser, Executive Director
Dedicated to the promotion and development of traditional heritage and folk arts in Canada. It provides an information service for groups active in folk arts, as well as carrying out research and studies.

Evelyn Roth
2705 West 2nd Avenue, Vancouver, BC, **Canada**
A multi-disciplinary artist has developed a variety of unique art activities in recycling, sculpture and dance. Recycling techniques are described in *The Evelyn Roth Recycling Book* (Talon, Vancouver). She formed a moving sculpture company and developed crocheted play environments which hold hundreds of children.

Expanding Human Horizons
Faculty of Fine Arts, University of Calgary, 2500 University Drive NW, Calgary, Alberta T2N 1N4, **Canada**
Organising an international perspective on the use of arts for, by and with special populations.

Art et Recherche
86 rue de la Croix Blanche, 33000 Bordeaux, **France**
Organises creative workshops with autistic children to study the relationships between artistic production and communication.

Atelier d'Art Originaire
Association ARTE, 45 rue de Montreuil, 75011 Paris, **France**
Jean Revol has been engaged in creative activity with mentally handicapped people and from this experience has developed a notion of original art. The objective is the establishment of an original art gallery.

Caue de Savoie
1 Place Metropole, 72000 Chambery, **France**
A mural project in the Chambery prison. Artists encouraged the inmates to choose their own themes and designs. The murals were intended to give the prisoners a means of self-expression through creativity.

Bundesministerium für Bildung und Wissenschaft
Postanfach 20 01 08, 5300 Bonn 2, **Germany FRG**
The Federal Ministry for Education and Science funds and organises projects and courses in which artists work with disabled and disadvantaged people in the community. Two artists, for instance, worked with apprentice painters and metalworkers to show that even their future work in industry need not be detached from creative activity. A sculptor/plasterer worked with a group of young people at an advice centre for drug addicts (none of whom had completed their work training) to construct something for the advice centre's canteen. Two members of the Freies Werkstatt Theatre, Cologne, worked on a three-month mixed media project with severely mentally disturbed women, including theatre make-up, costume-making, puppet-making etc. Two artists worked for five months with students aged 13-18 who had learning problems or suffered from epilepsy, to produce a picture book, each student being responsible for contributing three pages. Four actors from the Theatre of Rusellsheim worked for two weeks with backward children aged 10-16 creating a circus which performed to the public. Most of these projects lasted for 12 weeks.

Bundesvereiningung Lebenshilfe für Geistif Behinderte
Riaffeisenstrasse 18, 3550 Marburg 7, **Germany FRG**
The Society for the Mentally Handicapped's work includes organising exhibitions of paintings produced by mentally handicapped artists.

Haus 13
Allgemeines Krankenhaus, Ochsenzoll, Langenhorner Chaussée 560, 2000 Hamburg 62, **Germany FRG**
A number of art projects have been established involving musicians, actors and visual artists to help psychiatric patients release their creative abilities.

Kreinholz Community, Professor Siegfried Neuenhausen
Bertramsstrasse 4a, 3000 Hanover 1, **Germany FRG**
Professor Neuenhausen of the Braunschweig School of Arts is President of the Federation of German Artists. During 1979-83 he led four sculpture projects where residents of a prison, an old people's home and two psychiatric hospitals created their own sculptures and placed them in the grounds of their institutions. These ideas are now being put into practice at the Kreinholz Community of which he is a founder member.

Margit Schotschel
1296 Biesenthal Wullwinkel, Dahlienweg 20, **Germany GDR**
Sculpture and ceramic projects with groups of young mentally and physically handicapped people, including making life-size models of animals, and relief plaques intended as a tactile picture and given to blind people confined to bed.

Plastik zum Begreifen, Austellung für Blinde und Sehende
Petrikapelle, 18 Brandenburg, Burghof 3, **Germany GDR**
Dr Heinz Hoffman holds an annual summer tactile sculpture exhibition for blind and sighted people. The exhibition began as sculpture for blind people but has developed beyond that.

Gonen Vav Art Workshop
Taman Fogel, 12 Hapalmach St, Jerusalem, **Israel**
Situated in the Katamonim neighbourhood where Jews and Arabs live together, the Gonen workshop aims to integrate children through activity in all areas of the plastic arts.

Art Therapy Italiana
via Solenghi 4, 20145 Milan, **Italy**
Runs conferences, lectures and workshops; offers art therapy to many groups including psychiatric patients.

Associazione Disagio Esistenziale Giovanile (ADEG)
Corso Duca d'Aosta 19, 10119 Torino, **Italy**

A team of psychologists, social workers and artists collaborated on a programme combining relaxation techniques with art therapy. They work in schools with groups of children, some of whom have emotional or learning difficulties. The therapy is based on the theory that a person's physical self-image is reflected in his or her drawings.

Carcere e Comunita
Viale di Valle Aurelia 93/A, 00167 Rome, **Italy**
'Prisons and the Community' has organised exhibitions of paintings, weavings etc., produced by prisoners, with the works for sale and profits going to the prisoners' families.

Cooperative Porta Dipinta
via Porta Dipinta 10, 24100 Bergamo, **Italy**
The cooperatives had an 'Expressive Activities and Support Therapy Centre' where they offered a range of activities (clay-modelling, ceramics, graphic arts, animation, drama) to a mixed range of people with and without disabilities.

Society for the Study of Mental Illness through Creative Expression
Neuropsychiatric Research Inst. 912 Benten-cho, Shinjuku-ku, Tokyo 162, **Japan**
Annual congress with seminar on art therapy. Publishes Japanese *Bulletin of Art Therapy* with English summaries of the articles. Overseas researchers are invited to contribute.

Nutsateleir
Eerste Weteringplantsoen 6, 1017 SK Amsterdam, **Netherlands**
Art teachers who work in prisons.

Sterrenberg
Amersfoortseweg 56, 3712 BE Huis ter Heide, **Netherlands**
A community of mentally handicapped adults engaged in a programme of creativity development. Residents are encouraged to express themselves through pictorial media, believed by Max Timmerman, the project leader, to be an exciting way for mentally handicapped people to communicate.

Artists in Residence Scheme, Arts Council of New Zealand
110-16 Courtenay Place 1, PO Box 6040, Te Aro, Wellington, **New Zealand**
Artist in residence projects in various institutions. For instance, for one

month Te Aturangi Nepia Clamp lived and worked at the Pukeora Home for the Disabled. With the local Maori community he produced a panel carving and held bone-carving workshops which now continue on a regular basis.

Norwegian Art Therapy Association
Osthellinga 23, 1370 Asker, **Norway**
Borghild Bredeli Sandvik, a co-founder of the association, has published *Tegning, Faguttrykksmiddel-terapi* (Tiden Norsk, Oslo) about painting in schools and self-expression as therapy.

Pracownia Dziekanka
ul Krakowskie przedm 56, Warsaw, **Poland**
An exhibition and workshop centre devoted to alternative art activities. It is sponsored by the Ministry of Culture and the Art Academy in Warsaw and is responsible for organising events incorporating art and social issues.

Andrezej Renes
Bajana 34, 01-904 Warsaw, **Poland**
A sculptor who has designed Braille medals and a children's guidebook describing the Royal Castle at Warsaw in a tactile manner. His book *From a Little Grain of Corn to a Loaf* introduces pre-school children to the experience of feeling abstract art using relief illustrations moulded into thin plastic, and has an accompanying text in Braille. His next project is a 'dictionary of abstract art for blind people'. He would like to hear from other artists working in similar fields.

Zbigniew Stec
ul Bukowa 1, 87-800 Wloclawek, **Poland**
Surrealist painter suffers from muscular dystrophy.

Magdelena Tyszkiewicz
ul 3 Maja 17/7, 81-363 Gdynia, **Poland**
Runs a group for schizophrenic painters at the Gdynia Psychiatric Dispensary, and a writing and poetry group.

Zamek Krolewski w Warszawie
Plac Zamkowy 4, 00 277 Warsaw, **Poland**
Daniel Artymowski, Educational Dept.
The Royal Castle in Warsaw is one of the most important historical monuments in Poland. The Education Department is responsible for

developing programmes for disabled people. The outreach programme works with young offenders and the elderly. The department is particularly keen to exchange ideas with other museums.

Educational, Social and Cultural Organisation
26 Egodauyana, Moratuwa, **Sri Lanka**
Promotes arts programmes for the disabled and arts festivals.

Ulla Zimmerman
Björnasen, 52030 Ljung, **Sweden**
An art therapist working with severely mentally retarded women. She uses painting as a medium through which the women can 'talk' and 'read'.

Walter Zuber
Senseblickestrasse 4, 3174 Thorishaus, **Switzerland**
An artist who organised courses in drawing and painting for able-bodied and disabled people, young and old.

Conquest – The Society for Art for the Physically Handicapped
3 Beverley Close, East Ewell, Epsom, Surrey KT17 3HB, **UK**
Conquest aims to rehabilitate the physically disabled through active participation in the visual arts, providing teaching facilities, materials and information on art techniques and organising classes and exhibitions.

Mouth and Foot Painters
9 Inverness Place, London W2 3JF, **UK**
Partnership of severely disabled artists who market their work, particularly for calendars and cards.

Paintings in Hospitals
Nuffield Lodge, Regent's Park, London NW1 4RS, **UK**
Provides paintings to hang in hospitals.

Reach
1 Cricklade Street, Swindon, Wiltshire, **UK**
Works to enhance the quality of life of disadvantaged people using arts activities and working on a regular basis with special schools and centres.

Boston Children's Museum
Museum Wharf, 300 Congress Street, Boston, Mass 002210, **USA**
A bright, exciting place with a contemporary outlook and a policy of

activity and involvement, with the handling of exhibits encouraged. Special facilities are provided for disabled people, and able-bodied children are encouraged to experience some of the difficulties which disabled people face. There is a resource centre for parents which provides workshops and ideas for educational play activities.

Corcoran Gallery of Art
17th St & New York Avenue NW, Washington DC 2006, **USA**
Held an exhibition of Black folk art in America, focusing on the origins and sources. This theme could be translated into organising exhibitions of the paintings of older immigrants and their first impressions of a new country.

Form in Art
Programs for the Disabled, Philadelphia Museum of Art, Benjamin Franklin Parkway, Box 7646, Philadelphia PA 19101-7646, **USA**
An educational programme for blind and partially sighted people, FIA is a three-year course in art, the only qualification required being an interest in art.

Images of Aging
Kansas Arts Commission, Colombian Bldg, 112 West 6th St, Suite 401, Topeka, Kansas 66603, **USA**
Teams made up of a writer and an artist visited nursing homes where they interviewed and sketched residents, to encourage them to express feelings about their lives, past and present. The writer recorded this into a poem or oral history

Kinaesthetic Imagery Action Laboratories
1411 East Broadway, Columbia, Missouri 65201, **USA**
KI is a form of creative therapy using rooms with various large slide projections which can be made and manipulated by the participants themselves. Using handmade slides, sound and movement, it integrates play, art, music and movement. Workshops and demonstrations are given by the group.

Lions Gallery of the Senses
Wadsworth Atheneum, Hartford, Conn 06103, **USA**
Gallery aiming to make visual arts meaningful to blind people. Also have a special programme of exhibitions by artists with different handicaps which provide visitors with a setting to develop a new awareness of the abilities of each individual.

Metropolitan Museum of Art
Fifth Avenue at 82nd St, New York, NY 10028, **USA**
Holds free open evenings sponsored by corporate financing, issuing personal invitations which attract many first-time visitors; part of the museum's community programme. Senior volunteers guide people through the museum. Has a collection of programmes for the disabled.

National Museum of American Art
Smithsonian Institution, Washington DC 20560, **USA**
Margaret Cogswell, Chief of Special Services
Places particular emphasis on reaching disabled/disadvantaged areas of the community.

Pratt Institute Gallery
Brooklyn, NY 11205, **USA**
'Exhibition of Experience' where untutored older artists were invited to submit watercolour paintings. Their ages ranged between 61 and 91. Autobiographical experiences largely determined their choices of subject matter.

The BAT Workshop, National Gallery of Zimbabwe
PO Box 8155, Causeway, Harare, **Zimbabwe**
Established to develop the skills of young artists. The majority of the students have had no formal art training, with many unemployed. It is hoped that it will form the nucleus for a National Art School in the future.

National Gallery of Zimbabwe
PO Box 8155, Causeway, Harare, **Zimbabwe**
'Outreach' is a programme designed to reach groups in both the city and countryside, and enhances exhibitions with films, literature and workshops. 'Travelling Boxes' are packed with documentation and photographs of art pieces so that the gallery can reach even the most remote school. Children's workshops are held at the gallery.

COORDINATING/LINK SERVICES

Arts Access Society
17 St Andrew's Place, Melbourne 3002, **Australia**
Arts Access aims to make cultural activities more accessible to the

institutionalised and disadvantaged. It runs programmes aimed at developing the creative skills of participants at attendance centres, prisons, clinics, day centres, homes for the mentally handicapped and old people. 'Foster Grandparents' is one example, where retired people were invited to work with severely disabled children on a one-to-one basis in weekly drama sessions. A major project in 1982 was THEOREM, performed at the Melbourne Concert Hall. The first stage was a series of workshops organised by Aldo Gennaro, a Chilean dramatherapist, involving 800 people. The second stage involved the transfer of images and ideas developed in the workshops into a theatrical language. It was described in the *Melbourne Herald* as 'an unforgettable evening of shapes, colours and sound, put together by hundreds of disadvantaged people'.

Europe Contact
EREW Institute, Lessingstrasse 33, Postfach 10 02 49, 4060 Vienna 1, **Austria**
EREW has organised international meetings between disabled and able-bodied young people aged 16 to 26, along with their helpers. The goal is for the participants to try to get to know and understand each other through collective activities such as music, dance and discussions.

Osterreichischer Berufsverband der Musictherapeuten
Marc-Aurelstrasse 10/8, 1010 Vienna, **Austria**
The Austrian Association of Music Therapists has been set up to coordinate the diverse activities of music therapists. Its aim is to structure this work more effectively, acting as a centre for the exchange of idea and work opportunities.

Bureau for Action in Favour of Disabled People
Commission of the European Communities, rue de la Loi 200, B-1049 Brussels, **Belgium**
Pat Daunt
A permanent exchange of information between the bureau and disabled organisations.

Centre Creahm
Parc d'Avroy, 4000 Liège, **Belgium**
Creahm Tournai, rue de la Madeleine 22, 7500 Tournai; **Creahm Namur,** Univ Namur, Dept Psychologie, rue de Bruxelles 61, 5000 Namur; **Creahm Bruxelles,** rue Louis Zoenen 12, 1060 Brussels, **Belgium**
Provides a wide range of arts activities for mentally disabled children

and adults, information and courses for teachers, educationalists and parents. Organises exhibitions by disabled people. Centre Creahm also runs a café which provides financial support and which aims to avoid 'ghettoisation and to attract the general public'.

International Federation of Jeunesses Musicales
Palais des Beaux-Arts, rue Royale 10, 1000 Brussels, **Belgium**
FIJM is an organisation which aims to give young people from all over the world the opportunity to experience music of many different kinds. The section of Jeunesses Musicales in each country adapts its activities according to how music is structured in its own society.

Centro Nacional de Educacao Especial
Av Pasteur, 350-A-Urca, 22290 Rio de Janeiro, RJ, **Brazil**
Dr Francisco Jose da Costa Almeida
CENESP is part of the Brazilian Ministry for Education and Culture and its task is to plan and enhance facilities for gifted and disabled young people. It has two experimental centres, one where professional actors work with deaf students and one to bring together artists of all kinds and all disabilities from all over Brazil.

Arts Carousel
Box 342 Postal Station P, Toronto, Ontario M5S 2SB, **Canada**
Michael Seary
Arts Carousel exists to encourage participation in the arts by handicapped people. It provides and exchanges arts information, organises exhibitions, enables artists to go into homes of handicapped people to provide tuition. An exciting and informative project. Issues newsletter.

SENAME National Youth Service
Pedro de Valdivia No 4070, Casilla 6-A Carreo 22, Santiago, **Chile**
Maria Cecelia Milevcic Potin, National Director
A state body coordinating the work of institutions for disadvantaged children, including artistic programmes.

Grupo Latinamericano de Rehabilitacion Profesional
Carrera 6-A No 49-85 Piso 3, Apartado Aereo 56208, Bogota, **Colombia**
GLARP is an international organisation working in Latin America and the Caribbean, which offers technical assessment, promotes staff training courses, research etc. in the field of rehabilitation.

Asociacion Nacional de Ciego
Calle 76 No 29A 26 esq. a 29B, Municipio Playa, Havana, **Cuba**
Dr Carlos Olivares Sanchez, Director
The National Association for the Blind is an advocacy organisation for blind and visually impaired people with branches all over Cuba. They issue a newsletter, run a programme on the national radio, organise a national literacy competition for blind and sighted people, and support theatrical works by blind people.

Mrs Eva Klimova, Sr Officer, Dept of Social Security
Federal Ministry of Labour and Social Affairs, Prague, **Czechoslovakia**
The Ministry's officer with special responsibility for the disabled, Mrs Klimova has been involved in various artistic projects concerning severely handicapped people, such as the Conservatory of Music for Youth with Impaired Sight, which provides training for musicians, composers, teachers and piano tuners. Artistic programmes have been introduced into residential homes for those with severe physical and mental handicaps, and dance courses provided for physically and mentally handicapped youth.

AITA/IATA Secretariat
Vesterbrogade 175, DK-1800 Copenhagen V, **Denmark**
The International Amateur Theatre Association promotes dramatic art internationally by all theatrical groups devoted, without remuneration, to artistic and cultural aims. Coordinates its members' actions in their cultural and educative purposes.

Creative Activity for Everyone
31 North Frederick Street, Dublin 1, **Eire**
Dorothy Smith, Facilitator
CAFE was established in 1983 to coordinate and strengthen the efforts of all groups and individuals interested in the pursuit of creative activity for everyone

Union of Voluntary Organisations for the Handicapped
29 Eaton Square, Monkstown, Co Dublin, **Eire**
UVOH is a coordinating service for organisation of/for handicapped people, which has organised exhibitions and activities for disabled people to encourage their talents as artists.

Association Conseil Entreprise et Financier
7 rue Gilly, 06300 Nice, **France**

Coordinates creative workshops in theatre, visual arts with psychiatric patients, handicapped and elderly.

Association Culturelle du CHR de Reims
23 rue de Moulins, 51100 Reims, **France**
Artistic activities in hospital.

Centre de Liaison d'Information et de Recherche sur le Problème des Personnes, and **Centre Téchnique National d'Etudes et de Recherches sur les Handicaps et les Inadaptations**
27 Quai de la Tournelle, 75005 Paris, **France**
These organisations carried out a survey of existing creative initiatives in the area of Paris.

Centre d'Etudes et d'Action Sociales des Côtes du Nord
18 rue Abbé Vallée, 22000 Saint-Brieuc, **France**
CEAS is an organisation working as part of the 'handicap and culture' programme in the north of France. One project was 'Old People in the Country'; the aim of this was to help the elderly to discover their place in social life. They set up a working party of elderly people from five homes in the region, together with interested staff, to research into local history through the memories of people living there.

Centre Régional pour l'Enfance et l'Adolescence Inadaptée
Dept du Calvados, 88 Boulevard du Mal Lyautey, 14000 Caen, **France**
CREAI have initiated workshops in such varied subjects as music, computers, lace-making and expression in institutions for psychiatric patients and physically handicapped children and adults.

CREAI, Région Rhône-Alpes
46 rue du Président Herriot, 69002 Lyons, **France**
In conjunction with CRIAS, have organised creative programmes affecting 25 institutions in the area.

Culturothèque pour la Retraite
15 rue Chateaubriand, 75008 Lyons, **France**
A cultural information centre to meet the needs of institutionalised elderly and retired people. Holds resource information about existing services and how to set up activities.

Personimages
91 rue Vercingetorix, 75014 Paris, **France**
Denise Merle d'Aubigné

Set up to introduce artistic expression into the lives of mentally handicapped people of any age, by coordinating and promoting cultural activities in cities throughout France. It organises workshops in all art forms.

Sens Interdits
APASC de Saint Quentin en Yvelines, Centre des 7 Mares,
78310 Elancourt, **France**
Organises cultural projects/workshops for people with disabilities.

Intl Gesellschaft für Kunst Gestaltung u Therapie
Im Neuenheimer Feld 368, D-6900 Heidelberg 1, **Germany FRG**
Professor Wolfgang Jacob
The International Association for documentation and research in the field of art therapy publishes a monthly bulletin and coordinates international initiatives concerned with art and therapy.

Kölner Institut für Psychosoziale Entwicklung
Scheffelstrasse 52, 5000 Cologne 41, **Germany FRG**
A place of established research into the problems of psychosocial development, including investigation into the relationship between art and culture in connection with immigrant and disabled children.

Stephanusstiftung
Parkstrasse, 110 Berlin Weissensee, **Germany GDR**
Provides nursing homes, day centres, etc with craft work, weaving, pottery, leather work.

Felag Islenzkra Myndliwstarmanna
Freyjugotu 16, 101 Reykjavik, **Iceland**
This organisation, with the assistance of UNESCO, has organised experimental creative workshops for groups of staff from institutions for the disabled and for mixed groups of disabled and able-bodied people.

Art & Cultural Society of Bombay
Murar Nivas, Gokuloas Wadi, Gamdevi, Bombay 400 007, **India**
S. V. Gavankar
Art and cultural organisation specifically for the disabled.

Interlink Calcutta
14 Gurusaday Road, Tagore Hall, Calcutta 700 019, **India**
Mrs Savita Bhasin, Coordinator

A coordinating service that arranges for artists to work in hospitals, institutions etc. This local project began as a result of Interlink's work in India.

Israel Association of the Habilitation of the Mentally Handicapped
69 Herzlia Road, Tel Aviv 69410, **Israel**
AKIM is involved in social and cultural services for the mentally disabled. Regular drama activity is organised by students from the theatre department of Tel Aviv University. There are various group museum activities, including academic instruction and practical work.

The Lebanese Association for Mentally Handicapped Children
rue Mme Curie, Richani Bldg (nr Kraytem Mosque), Ras Beirut, **Lebanon**
Hala Hilmi
A parents' organisation seeking mainly to help the handicapped and their families and to promote public awareness. They hope to develop work in the expressive arts.

Interlink Hermosillo
Apremio, Campoy 808 Pitic, Hermosillo, Sonora, **Mexico**
Martha Peterson, Coordinator
Provides arts programmes for hospitals, centres and prisons. This project began as a result of Interlink's work in Mexico.

Vononteurope
Lindenlaan 20, 1405 AK Bussum, **Netherlands**
Liebje Hoekendijk
A committee whose purpose is to encourage cooperation on unpaid voluntary action.

Recreation for the Disabled
514 Great King Street, Dunedin, **New Zealand**
An organisation working in arts for the disabled. They coordinate arts projects and hold an annual Spring Arts Festival, gathering together artists, disabled people and community workers. There is a regular arts centre programme.

Nigerian National Advisory Council for the Deaf
PO Box 449, Yaba Lagos, **Nigeria**
Mrs Sarah Modupe George
The Council was founded to coordinate the activities of deaf societies and schools in Nigeria.

Instituto Panameno de Habilitacion Especial
Oficina de la Secretaria General de la OEA, AP 5039 Panama 5, **Panama**
Profesora Lideth Lia de Mejia, Subdirector General
The coordinating body for special education. Encourages aesthetic development of disabled children as part of a general policy for integration, through a wide range of arts programmes.

National Commission Concerning Disabled Persons
2nd Fl, Philsucomo Annex Bldg, North Ave, Diliman, Quezon City, **Philippines**
Loreto Y. Directo, Executive Director
Coordinates and organises projects on disability prevention and rehabilitation and equal opportunities. A data bank and information system provides comprehensive data on disability prevention and rehabilitation. Other projects include art and music festivals for young disabled artists.

Instituto Nacional de Servicios Sociales (INSERSO)
Ministerio de Trabajo, Sanidad y Seguridad Social, Maria de Guzman 52, Madrid 3, **Spain**
Introduces creative programmes for people with disabilities.

Interlink Sri Lanka
c/o Chitra Lane School, 45/3 Chitra Lane, Colombo 5, **Sri Lanka**
Hema Gnawardhana, Coordinator
A coordinating service that introduces artists of all kinds to institutions working with people who are disabled or disadvantaged. Set up with the help of Interlink.

Scandivaviska Institutet för Uttryckande Konst
Linneg 23, 413 04 Göteborg, **Sweden**
Phillip Speiser, Director
The Scandinavian Institute for Expressive Arts is an independent organisation functioning as a network centre for: facilitating the integration of the creative arts in all areas of society; providing training for professionals working in mental health and the educational system; establishing and maintaining professional standards and code of ethics for those professionals working with Expressive Therapy.

Focus
Case Postale 366, CH-1001 Lausanne, **Switzerland**
George Corner, Director

An organisation working to improve the quality of life for handicapped people internationally, as well as being concerned that handicapped people play a part in the artistic life of their environment.

Pro Infirmis Zentralsekretariat
Feldggstrasse 71, Postfach 129, 8032 Zurich, **Switzerland**
An organisation concerned with the social integration of handicapped people. Its affiliated body, Focus, is responsible for the creative and cultural expression and provides information about artistic activities in Switzerland, Denmark and Sweden.

Age Concern England
Head Office: 60 Pitcairn Road, Mitchum, Surrey CR4 3LL, **UK**
'Lifeskills' programme will provide grants for projects which use the skills of retired people, particularly where the usually dependent role of the elderly is reversed, so that older people are helping the young. Age Concern has a number of regional branches, many of which provide creative activities for elderly people. Information can be obtained from the head office.

Arts & Psychology
Hertfordshire College, 7 Hatfield Road, St Albans AL1 3RS, **UK**
Sue Ball, European Project Leader
A computer database held in thirty different categories relating to arts and disability (including therapy) throughout the European Community.

Artsline
5 Crowndale Road, London NW1 1TU, **UK**
A telephone advice service on the arts in Greater London for people with disabilities and special needs.

Council for Music in Hospitals
340 Lower Road, Little Bookham, Surrey KT23 4EF, **UK**
Arranges concerts by professional musicians in hospitals, homes and hospices throughout England.

Help the Aged Education Department
PO Box 460, 16 & 18 St James's Walk, London EC1R 0BE, **UK**
Produces educational materials which aim to encourage people of all ages, including older people, to question their attitudes and preconceptions about old age. One project is the 'Side by Side' scheme which aims to bring older people and the younger generation together.

Reach
1 Cricklade Street, Swindon, Wiltshire, **UK;** or The Arts Centre, Devizes Road, Swindon, Wiltshire, **UK**
See also under Arts, Visual.

Shape
1 Thorpe Close , London W10 5XL, **UK**

Shape is a coordinating arts organisation which creates opportunities for mentally and physically disabled, mentally ill, elderly and socially disadvantaged people to participate in arts activities. Much of its work takes the form of initiating regular arts workshops and organising performances using a wide range of professional artists and performers of all disciplines, in hospitals, day centres, homes, penal establishments and in the open community. The Shape network now includes 16 individual organisations, covering the whole of the UK (see below). It is recommended that readers write for further information, as the projects initiated by these organisations will provide many ideas.

Art Link
17a Hanover Street, Newcastle-under-Lyme, Staffordshire ST5 1HD
Lee Corner, Coordinator
Artlink for Lincolnshire and Humberside
Humberside Leisure Services, Central Library, Albion Street, Hull HU1 3TF
Sue Roberts, Coordinator
Artlink Edinburgh and Lothians
4 Forth Street, Edinburgh EH1 3LH
Thursa Sanderson, Administrator
Arts for Disabled People in Wales
Channel View Recreation and Community Centre, Jim Driscoll Way, The Marl, Grangetown, Cardiff
Phil Burton, Elizabeth Cheetham, Development Officers
Artshare South West
c/o South West Arts, Bradninch Place, Gandy Street, Exeter EX4 3LS, Devon
Pippa Warin, Coordinator
Arts Integration Merseyside
Merseyside Joint Council for the Disabled, Mount Vernon Green, Hall Lane, Liverpool L7 8TF
John McGrath, Coordinator

Shape Network (cont:)

Committee for Arts – Scottish Council on Disability
Princes House, 5 Shandwick Place, Edinburgh EH2 4RG
Fiona Bonas
East Midlands Shape
New Farm, Walton by Kimcote, Leicestershire LE17 5RL
Anne Peaker, Director
Northern Shape
18/20 Dean Street, Newcastle upon Tyne NE1 1PG
Colin Langton, Director
North West Shape
Back of Shawgrove School, Cavendish Road, Manchester M20 8JR
Hazel Roy, Director
North West Shape
4 Hawkswood, Eccleston, Chorley, Lancashire PR7 5RW
Joyce Morris, Director
Projectability
c/o Elly Sinclair Hall, 27 Hyndland Road, Glasgow G12
Shape East
c/o Eastern Arts, 8/9 Bridge Street, Cambridge CB2 1UA
Pat Coleman, Coordinator
Shape Up North
191 Bellevue Road, Leeds LS3 1HG
Cynth Hopkins, Coordinator
Solent Artlink
Hornpipe Community Arts Centre, 143 Kingston Road, Portsmouth
Peter Taylor, Coordinator
Southern Artlink
The Studio, 81 Langley Close, Headington, Oxford OX3 7DB
Piers Benn, Coordinator

Inter-Action Centre
Royal Victoria Dock, London E16 1BT, **UK**
Aims to foster an exchange of ideas and resources between youth workers, youth clubs, and young people themselves. Amongst other activities they introduce workshops to develop creative skills. Inter-Action works internationally with advice and training in arts technology.

Alliance for Arts Education
JFK Center for the Performing Arts, Washington DC 20566, **USA**
Network coordinating projects designed to encourage and strengthen the role of the arts in education, issuing the newsletter *Interchange*.

American Association of Disability Communicators
2100 Pennsylvania Ave NW, Suite 232, Washington DC 20037, **USA**
Robert H. Ruffner, President
Exists to promote a positive image of disabled people through all aspects of the media. Encourages job opportunities for disabled people in the media.

American Association of Retired Persons
1909 K St NW, Washington DC 20049, **USA**
Mary Jo Gibson, Senior Program Specialist
AARP exists to secure better treatment for members of the 50-plus generation who are employed or retired. It publishes a bi-monthly magazine, *Modern Maturity*.

Artreach, Milwaukee
161 W Wisconsin Ave, Suite 7011, Milwaukee, WI 53203, **USA**
Brings handicapped, institutionalised and elderly people to the arts and arts to them.

Arts International
Bacon House Mews, 1801 F St NW, Washington DC 20006, **USA**
Pamela D. Walker, Executive Director
Aims to provide more opportunities for American art and artists to be seen in other nations and that of other countries to be seen in the USA by providing assistance and finding new sources of financial and administrative support for arts exchange.

Arts with the Handicapped
1385 Hancock Street, Quincy, Boston, Mass 02169, **USA**
Training artists and workers in cultural fields to develop programmes for disabled children and their families.

Bread and Roses Cultural Project Inc.
330 West 42nd Street, New York, NY 10036, **USA**
Moe Foner, Executive Director
Trade union cultural programme: theatre, photography, books, posters etc.

Bread and Roses
78 Throckmorton Avenue, Mill Valley, CA 94941, **USA**
Lana Severn, Associate Director
Arranges performances and workshops in institutions. Not to be confused with preceding.

Brookdale Center on Aging
425 East 25th Street, New York, NY 10010, **USA**
Promotes educational and cultural opportunities for elderly people. Publishes a newsletter, *Elder Arts.*

Center for Intergenerational Learning
Temple Univ Inst on Aging, 1601 N Broad Street, Philadelphia, PA 19122, **USA**
Dr Nancy Henkin
Committed to fostering cooperation and exchange among people of different generations. A variety of programmes exist involving young and elderly.

Connecticut Network: Arts for the Handicapped
600 Main Street, Hartford, Conn 06103, **USA**
An important part of the Network's programme are the Very Special Arts Festivals.

Cultural Survival
11 Divinity Avenue, Cambridge, MA 02138, **USA**
Supports projects on five continents to help indigenous peoples survive both physically and culturally. Project evaluations, research and dissemination of information are part of their work.

HAI (Hospital Audiences Inc)
220 West 42nd Street, New York, NY 10036, **USA**
Michael Spencer, Director
An agency that takes the arts to all areas of disability and organises outside events where wheelchair and even bedridden people can take part. HAI has enabled many thousands of people to participate in the mainstream entertainment life of New York. There are affiliated branches throughout the States. It is recommended that readers write for further information as the projects initiated by this organisation will provide many ideas.

International Federation on Aging
1909 K St NW, Washington DC 20049, **USA**

The IFA facilitates the exchange and dissemination of information which is of use to elderly people and to practitioners in the field of aging.

Kansas Council of Disabled Persons
2021 N, Old Manor, PO Box 8217, Wichita, KS 67208, **USA**
To further education, housing, employment and cultural opportunities for disabled people.

Massachusetts Committee Arts with the Handicapped
Dept of Education, 1385 Hancock Street, Quincy, Mass 02169, **USA**
Dan Weiner, Coordinator
Trains artists/workers in cultural fields to develop programmes for disabled children and their families.

Media Office of the California Foundation on Employment and Disability
156 San Vicente Building 32, Santa Monica, CA 90402, **USA**
Alan Toy
Functions as the liaison between the disability community and the entertainment/media industry. In 1985 over 150 TV and film roles were portrayed by performers with disabilities as a direct result of their services. They also provide guidance to individuals with disabilities in pursuit of careers in media.

Mobility International USA
PO Box 3551, Eugene, Oregon 97403, **USA**
MIUSA is made up of disabled and able-bodied people involved in expanding opportunities in travel, leisure and educational exchange programmes in the USA and abroad.

National Council on the Aging
600 Maryland Ave SW, West Wing 1001, Washington DC 20024, **USA**
Coordinating group involved in community education; intergenerational arts programmes. Publishes the newsletter *Collage – Cultural Enrichment and Older Adults.*

National Educational Council of Creative Therapy (NECCT)
20 Rip Road, Hanover, NH 03755-1699, **USA**
Connie E. Naitove, President
A network of creative therapists. Issues newsletter, information. Provides training and workshops.

The Ohio Very Special Arts Network
512 Milford Avenue, Columbus, Ohio 43202, **USA**
Arts for special groups include training senior citizens as puppeteers to perform for disabled schoolchildren.

Rehabilitation International
25 East 21st Street, New York, NY 10010, **USA**
A federation of 122 organisations in 79 countries conducting programmes to assist people with disabilities and all who work for prevention, rehabilitation and integration. Publishes *International Rehabilitation Review*

Senior Citizens Artists Resource Programme Generations Together
600 Thackeray Hall, Univ of Pittsburgh, Pittsburgh, PA 15260, **USA**
Dr Sally Newman
A programme designed to bring older volunteer artists into schools.

Very Special Arts
JFK Center for the Performing Arts, Washington DC 20566, **USA**
Joanne Grady, Director of International Programs
Aims to make the arts an integral part of the education of handicapped young people. Provides information and resources. Publishes a monthly newsletter. Established the Very Special Arts Festival Programs nationally and internationally.

Very Special Arts Hawaii
PO Box 88277, Honolulu, Hawaii 96815, **USA**
Organises projects and an annual festival.

All Russia Association of the Blind
Central House of Culture, 14 Novaya Place, Moscow, **USSR**
Mrs Olga Bogdanova, Head of International Department
The main focal point for creative activities of the blind. There are affiliated clubs throughout Russia. The centre provides opportunities for acquiring skills in all the arts. There is a special music library for blind students. The families of the visually impaired are encouraged to make use of the centre

CELART
Asturias 1435, Montevideo, **Uruguay**
Professor Saloman Azur, Senior Director

A centre of studies in research and documentation of expressive/ creative activities. Promotes arts projects for handicapped children, with a particular focus on integration with non-handicapped young people.

Instituto Interamericano del Niño
Av 8 de Octubre 2904, Montevideo, **Uruguay**
Dr Rodrigo Crespo Toral, Director General
A specialised body of the Organisation of American States which encourages the study of problems affecting children and families. They have a computerised information centre which provides information in response to requests from all over the American continent.

Fundacion para el Desarrollo de la Educacion Especial
Edificio de Educacion, Piso 12, Esquina de Salas, Caracas 101, **Venezuela**
Consuelo Briceno Canelon, President
Coordinates recreational and cultural programmes for disabled people: setting up creative workshops across 20 suburbs; arranging for receiving artists to perform in schools.

Artists/Hospital Link Project
Zimbabwe National Association for Mental Health, PO Box A196, Avondale, Harare, **Zimbabwe**
The project puts local artists into the psychiatric unit of the Parirenyatwa Hospital.

National Association of Societies for the Care of the Handicapped
PO Box UA 504, Union Avenue, Harare, **Zimbabwe**
Bob Stumbles, Chair
NASCOH is an umbrella organisation which coordinates agencies providing services for the disabled.

Zimbabwe Integration Through the Arts (ZITA)
c/o Zimnamh, 58 2nd St, Harare, **Zimbabwe;**
c/o DPI, 1 Trust House, Bulawayo, **Zimbabwe**
ZITA is two coordinating arts services established with the help of Interlink as a result of its work in Zimbabwe. The schemes introduce local artists to areas of disadvantage and disability to give workshops. They also arrange creative arts courses for staff working in the caring professions.

UNESCO (United Nations Educational, Scientific & Cultural Organisation)

UNESCO
7 Place de Fontenoy, 75700 Paris, **France**
Madeleine Gobeil, Head of the Sector of Artistic Creation, Division of Cultural Development; M. Makagiansar, Assistant Director General, Cultural Sector, Division for the Promotion and Circulation of Information; Lena Saleh, Special Education Section, Division of Structures, Content, Methods and Techniques of Education; Cooperative Action Programme, Public Liaison Division.

UNESCO
1 rue Miollis, 75015 Paris, **France**
Secretary General, International Theatre Institute; Secretary General, Association Internationale des Arts Plastiques; Secretary General, International Music Council.

International Fund for the Promotion of Culture
c/o UNESCO, 31 rue François, Bonvin, 75015 Paris, **France**
Director, Juan Carlos Langlois.

CRAFT/CRAFT TRAINING SCHEMES

Australian Forum for Textile Arts
PO Box 77, Univ of Queensland, St Lucia, Brisbane, Queensland 4067, **Australia**
Information on several textile craft projects for disabled people, including a children's play structure, clothes designs, and adapted spinning and weaving equipment.

Angela Bornman
PO Box 890, Broome, WA 6725, **Australia**
Angela Bornman taught textile skills to a community of unemployed black people, mainly women, in South Africa. Although the group started with very little money and old sewing machines, not only did individuals respond but their standard of living improved as well. She would like to hear from anyone doing similar work in Australia.

Craft Council of Queensland
109 Edward St, City, Brisbane 4000, Queensland, **Australia**
All activity therapy centres in Queensland were invited to take part in a group rug-making project. Patients were asked to paint pictures based on a theme. Then selected ones were sent to the craft council and the centre received back a kit of hooked rug backing with the cartoon of the original picture on it, to be made by the patients. A final large piece was assembled by joining the separate pieces.

Ernabella Arts Inc
Ernabella, via Alice Springs, NT 5751, **Australia**
Winifred M. Hilliard, Handcraft Adviser
As part of a move to develop and encourage traditional aboriginal arts and crafts, Ernabella aims to use traditional skills in new ways; there is a focus on giving work to unemployed women.

Forest Community Arts Centre
c/o Network, 66 Albion Street, Surry Hills, NSW 2010, **Australia**
A project which trains unemployed people in tapestry weaving.

Interarts
10 Cumberland St, Eaglemont, Melbourne, VIC 3084, **Australia**
Agency run by a visual arts administrator, Thomas McCullough, and his wife, Roma, who teaches art and craft to mentally handicapped adults. Tom has worked for many years organising contemporary sculpture festivals and ethnic crafts exhibitions.

Topfer und Webstube Ateliers
Galerie Wickenburg, Wickenburg 4, 1080 Vienna, **Austria**
Workshops attached to the gallery, where disabled people are given the opportunity to practise pottery.

The Able Disabled, The Guild for Arts and Crafts
170 The Donway West, Suite 122, Don Mills, Ontario M3C 2G3, **Canada**
Bruno J. Kuemin, Coordinator
Develops interest and talent among disabled in arts and crafts.

Le Fil d'Ariane
250 Place d'Youville, Montreal H2Y 2B6, Quebec, **Canada**
Suzanne B. Truidel, President
Louise Cimon Annet, an art teacher at a school for retarded children, started a workshop where students could use their artistic skills.

Success came rapidly because of the quality of the artwork. This is now a centre of experimental art, producing colourful wall hangings and weavings.

Cyprus Rehabilitation Centre for Disabled People
Strovolos, Nicosia, **Cyprus**
Cleanthis Karageorghiades, Director
Children and adolescents up to the age of 18 are trained in a range of traditional craft skills. On leaving, if the students wish to work independently at the craft they have learned, they receive a small government grant to help buy materials and set up a business.

The Ramses Wissa Wassef School
Harrania, Cairo, **Egypt**
Rames Wissa Wassef, an architect, started a school of weaving in 1951. The weavers were drawn from the poorest areas. The present generation produce high-quality work which is sold and exhibited worldwide.

Kreativ im Heim
Landesversorgungsamt, Hessen-Aussenstelle, Adickesallee 36, 6 Frankfurt, **Germany FRG**
Kreativ im Heim is a craft project sponsored by the state of Hessen which has given a fresh perspective on life in residential homes for the elderly. National exhibitions display imaginative craft work produced from inexpensive materials.

National Vocational Centre for the Deaf
PO Box 34, Bechem B/A, **Ghana**
The only school offering courses for the deaf in Ghana, this centre caters for 200 students offering crafts training in joinery, carpentry and metalwork. The VSO carpentry instructor has been training his students to produce chairs and tables, hasps and locks using scrap metal, brazier stoves and metal trunks.

Grenada National Institute of Handicrafts
Carnegie, St George, **Grenada**
Gallery which exhibits high-quality crafts and jewellery made by disabled people.

The Prabha Institute
C807 Curzon Road Apartments, New Delhi 110 001, **India**
A craft centre founded by the father of Prabha Shah, a well-known

visual artist who is herself deaf. This centre teaches craft skills to local disabled people in order that they may lead an independent life.

Somali Women's Handicraft Training Centre
c/o Oxfam, Mogadishu, PO Box 2808, **Somalia**
Cooperative training centre giving a basic 6-month training course in one of the following skills: block-printing, hand-printing silk scarves, screen-printing, tie-dying, tailoring.

Kontaktwerkstatt
Eichstrasse 11, 8604 Volketswil, **Switzerland**
Contact Workshop offers classes in all kinds of crafts and arts for handicapped and able-bodied artists, architects and craftspeople. There are now Contact Workshops in Berne and Poschiavo and in different studios in Zurich.

The Barton Spinner
Barton Lodge, Radlett, Herts, **UK**
A. F. Llewellin
The Barton Spinner is a tabletop machine containing all the components equivalent to those in a conventional treadle spinner, designed so that it can be used by disabled people. As well as being operated by a foot switch, it can be placed on the thigh and operated by the forearm, or by body weight alone. Available within the UK at £135 (1985).

Aid to Artisans Inc
64 Fairgreen Place, Chestnut Hill, Mass 02167, **USA**
James S. Plaut, President
This is a non-profit organisation aiming to help needy craftsmen and craft communities in developing countries and the USA. It does this by encouraging the making and marketing of crafts, and trying to increase income and employment potential for craftsmen everywhere.

Camphill Village USA Inc
Copake, NY 12516, **USA**
A non-profit-making volunteer community of about 200 people, half of whom are mentally disabled. It is one of about 50 related establishments in Europe and Africa. Each villager undertakes a task which he or she is capable of doing, the wide range of industries include copperware, enamelling, toy-making and weaving. Their work has been exhibited across the USA and they won national acclaim with an exhibition of textiles in Washington's Textile Museum.

Isla Negra and Santiago Women (Chile)
610 Long Way, Ashland, Oregon 97520, **USA**
Chilean women have adopted the traditional craft of embroidery to provide employment and self-expression. Santiago women interpret the political and economic reality in their work and in rural Isla Negra they take images from folk art. Information on these craft projects has been gathered by writer and painter Betty La Duke.

Senior Potters
Northwest Center for Older Adults, Germantown, Philadelphia, Pa, **USA**
Glenda Frye
Pottery workshops with amateur potters aged 65-84, eventually making a mural with tiles to be installed at a local hospital.

Bulawayo Home Industries
Box 2034, Bulawayo, **Zimbabwe**
Mrs Joan Gumpo
This is a self-supporting scheme which enables needy families and young unemployed people to work, by adapting traditional skills to make articles of clothing and ornaments for sale overseas.

The Gatehouse Training and Rehabilitation Centre
PO Box 454, Marondera, **Zimbabwe**
Mrs Lyn Hall
Established to enable unskilled single women to support themselves and their dependents by making carpets which are then sold in retail outlets. A wide range of carpets are made, such as Persian-type rugs and those with traditional designs.

Larkhill Handweavers
Larkhill Estate, PO Box 23, Marondera, **Zimbabwe**
Pat MacIlwaine founded Larkhill Handweavers in the 1960s. There are now about 70 women weavers, who also rear angora goats, geese and silkworms. Plant dyes are used for the wool, giving subtle colours.

Mzilikazi Art and Craft Centre
PO Box 2034, Bulawayo, **Zimbabwe**
The centre has a pottery and an art school, offering training in pottery, painting and sculpture. Free training is given to school leavers with no qualifications. Provision is also made for people with disabilities, local schoolchildren and factory and shop workers.

CREATIVE WRITING/POETRY

Résidence Ary Geoffray Villereversure
01250 Ceyzeriat, **France**
Reminiscence workshops: Marie-Claude Para transcribes the elderly people's memories and their stories and reflections form the basis of a quarterly publication.

Artist in Residence Poetry Project
c/o Dist Recreation Coord for the Disabled, 514 Great King Street, Dunedin, **New Zealand**
Maggie Belcher, Recreation Coordinator
Poetry workshops for disabled people, some so severely disabled that they could only communicate by pointing at symbols.

Philip and Mette Newth
Paal Bergsvei 74, 1349 Rykkinn, **Norway**
These professional writers/illustrators of children's books have produced adapted books for handicapped children, including several for blind children.

Cinder Dip for Breakfast
c/o Artlink, 17A Hanover Street, Newcastle-under-Lyme, Staffordshire ST5 1HD, **UK**
A writer held a series of workshops for people aged 74-86. Joyce Cheeseman, the writer, compiled a fascinating booklet of the students' memories.

Games and Rhymes
Community Education Service, Craigbank School, 36 Damshot Road, Glasgow G53, **UK**
To record and publish old games and rhymes which may be in danger of being lost to future generations. Volunteers from local pensioners' clubs went into local primary schools for a few hours a week to teach children the games which they played in their childhood.

Carol Martys Independent Arts
The Meadow, Yafford, nr Shorwell, Newport, Isle of Wight PO30 3LH, **UK**
Drama teacher runs drama and poetry projects in prisons.

The Windows Project
22 Roseheath Drive, Liverpool, **UK**
To promote the acceptance of literature and to increase interest in and knowledge of the language by stimulating creative writing and reading, especially among young people. It has a reputation for the success of its unique work with children.

Writers and Journalists Workshop
69 De Burgh Street, Riverside, Cardiff, S. Glamorgan, **UK**
Designed for the participation of disabled and able-bodied people.

Creative Writing Workshop
New Mexico State University, c/o *Collage*, National Council on the Aging, 600 Maryland Ave SW, West Wing 100, Washington DC 20024, **USA**
Students, whose average age is 70, meet to write and discuss their work.

Kaleidoscope
United Cerebral Palsy Services for the Handicapped, 326 Locust Street, Akron, Ohio 44302, **USA**
An arts magazine which gives artists and writers with a disability a place for artistic expression.

Time Capsule Inc
GPO Box 1185, New York, NY 10016, **USA**
This company compiled an anthology of creative writing by disabled people.

Writing and Story-telling
University of Nebraska, Div of Continuing Studies, Lincoln, Nebraska, **USA**
An annual writing and story-telling festival which has given many older adults the opportunity to write.

DANCE

Estudio de Danzas Contemporaneas
Calle Callao 289, 20 Piso, 1022 Buenos Aires, **Argentina**
Maria Fux, a dance therapist, works with disabled and able-bodied adults and children. She published a book about her work, *First*

Encounter with Dance Therapy. In her work with psychiatric patients and deaf children she uses colour as a theme for improvisation, projecting slides of a primary colour, or black with white lines, on to a wall, and finds that her students lose their timidity and fear of movement.

Sun Ergos
2205/700 9th Street SW, Calgary, Alberta T2P 2B5, **Canada**
A theatre dance group which performs in a wide variety of settings such as schools, community centres, hospitals and shopping malls.

Cuban National Ballet
Calzada 509, Vedado, Havana, **Cuba;** or, Hospital Psiquiatrico de la Habana, Dept de Psicoballet, **Cuba**
Professor Maria Victoria Gutierrez
Teachers of the ballet company and school work with psychiatrists and teachers and have developed a dance therapy course call 'Psicoballet' for children suffering from disabilities or emotional or physical handicaps.

Federal Committee of the Union of Invalids
Karlinske namesti 12, 186 03 Prague 8, **Czechoslovakia**
Czechoslovakia has eleven theatre/pantomime groups for deaf actors. The standard and professionalism of these groups is very high. Every second year there is an international pantomime festival of the deaf in Brno.

Association Danse Education Culture
Siège Social, 19 rue des Gravilliers, 75003 Paris, **France**
ADEC promotes dance as an educational and cultural activity. The project has been taken to schools, centres for handicapped children and dance institutions.

Ki Productions
20 rue de Staël, 75015 Paris, **France**
Kitsou Dubois is a choreographer who has initiated dance workshops (held at a dance centre) for psychiatric patients at the CHS de Ville Evrard.

Frankfurt Tanzkreis
Walter Rietig Strasse 48, 6070 Langen, **Germany FRG**
The Frankfurt Dance Circle is an information resource centre concerning dance; it places teachers in jobs and offers training courses for people involved in dance in education.

Institut für Spiel u Theaterpädagogik, Hochschule der Kunste
Fachbereich 10, Malteserstr. 74-100, 1000 Berlin 46, **Germany FRG**
Young deaf and non-deaf people are taught dance and movement.

Rhytmik u Tanz für Horgeschedigte u Horende
Haussmanstrasse 143c, 7000 Stuttgart, **Germany FRG**
Telos is a dance group, led by Ursula Bischiff-Musshake, which offers training for both hearing and hearing-impaired people. It has achieved a professional standard.

Nalanda Dance Research Centre
Plot A-7/1, NS Road no 10, JVPD Scheme, Vile Parle (West), Bombay 400 049, **India**
A post-doctoral institute with a research department called 'Department of Asian Studies in Fine Art and Human Development'. One of their most ambitious projects is research into dance therapy, analysing the movements of Indian classical dance as related to body kinetics and their utilisation for therapy and rehabilitation.

Hademama Dance Group
Hoffburger ORT Vocational High School for the Deaf, 25 Hamarcha Street, 33 Tel Aviv 0907, **Israel**
Hademama (The Silence) is a group of dancers who are deaf and use modern dance to attain confidence and broaden their outlook in order to cope with living and working as ordinary individuals.

Kol Demama Dance Company
23 Petach Tikva Road, Tel Aviv 66182, **Israel**
Kol Demama (Sound and Silence) is a professional group of hearing and deaf dancers who use ballet, modern dance and mime. Dance cues are transmitted via 'rhythmic circles', a unique system combining body language and vibrations.

Dance Therapy Centre
c/o Charlotte Querido, Koningstraat 5, 7315 HR Apeldoorn, **Netherlands**
The centre was established by Charlotte Querido and is open to everyone regardless of age, sex or disability. Attendance is usually for one year.

Dutch Wheelchair Dancing Association
Praam 63, 1186 TB Amstelveen, **Netherlands**

Corrie van Hugten has pioneered wheelchair dancing. The association aims to expand the possibilities for wheelchair dancing through liaising with ballroom dancing associations and international associations. Training is also now available to qualify people to teach wheelchair dancing.

Dr Hannah Rylke
Institute of Educational Research, Department of Psychology, Gorczewska 8, 01-180 Warsaw, **Poland**
Working with colleagues and people with mental illness, using different forms of dance movement under the label of 'body experience'.

Centro de Reabilitacao de Paralisia Cerebral Calouste Gulbenkian
Ave Rainha D Amelia'Lumiar, 1600 Lisbon, **Portugal**
The Calouste Gulbenkian Cerebral Palsy Rehabilitation Centre has initiated a programme of dance practice.

Marlene Claire Foster da Cunha Esteves
Avenida Marconi 16-3-E, 1000 Lisbon, **Portugal**
A professional dancer working with mentally and physically disabled children.

Maite Leon Escuela de Psico Ballet
Jorge Juan 127, Madrid 4, **Spain**
This school uses science and art to help impaired children reach physical rehabilitation through performing arts, dance, body expression and mime.

Samson and Pemsiri Silva
Chitra Lane School, 45/3, Chitra Lane, Colombo 5, **Sri Lanka**
A professional actor and dancer work extensively with disabled adults and children.

Amici
Wolfgang Stange, 68 Baron's Court, London W14, **UK**
A company of disabled and able-bodied dance students which started as an evening class in creative dance. Founder Wolfgang Stange has created a company with visually and mentally handicapped and able-bodied performers. They have had two successful productions in a London theatre.

Body Torque
9 Tyrwhitt Road, Brockley, London SE4 1QD, **UK**
A dance, movement, health and fitness group which works with the unemployed, people with disabilities, and women with young children.

Maria Bullard
8 Royal Parade, Blackheath Village, London SE3, **UK**
A qualified yoga teacher who works with people with disabilities and runs training courses for teachers.

Bulmershe Resource Centre for the Handicapped
Bulmershe Court, Woodlands Avenue, Earley, Reading RG6 1HY, **UK**
An advisory board on dance and drama for both hearing and hearing-impaired people. Bulmershe has promoted performances by the 'Three D' group, composed of deaf and hearing dancers and actors.

Dance for Everyone
6 Milverton Road, London NW6, **UK**
Introduces dance to schoolchildren and works with disabled children.

Invitation to the Ballet
Royal Opera House, Covent Garden, London WC2E 9DD, **UK**
Dancers from the Royal Ballet tour hospitals and hospices. They begin by explaining some of their exercises and then, accompanied by a pianist, perform an excerpt from classical repertoire in full costume. This is followed by a question time.

Ludus Dance Company
Owen House, 6 Thurnham Street, Lancaster LA1 1YD, **UK**
A professional dance company which initiates projects with special audiences and aims to involve the general public and groups with special needs.

Wheelchair Dance Association
15 Knightsbridge Road, Dechmont, West Lothian, **UK**
Wheelchair dancing for the cerebral palsied developed from lessons devised to assist new wheelchair users. The emphasis has changed from dancing as therapy to an enjoyable activity in its own right. The association was founded in 1974.

American Dance Therapy Association
Suite 230, 2000 Century Plaza, Columbia, Maryland 21044, **USA**
Open to everyone professionally involved in dance therapy.

Dance Project for Blind and Visually Impaired Students
Alvin Ailey Dance Theatre, 1515 Broadway, New York, NY 10036, **USA**
This two-year project enabled ten NYC students to participate in a specially devised dance programme away from school. This model project is designed to be repeated all over the country.

Dancers of the Third Age
Dance Exchange, PO Box 40909, Washington DC 20016, **USA**
A performance company of older people give dance classes and workshops at local institutions and perform. Dance Exchange is composed of professional dancers who tour combining dance with realistic imagery and political/social commentary.

Robert Joffrey Ballet School
434 Avenue of the Americas, New York, NY 10001, **USA**
The Joffrey Ballet has a 'Dance for Deaf Children' programme. Children are selected from local deaf schools, stick figures are used to illustrate ballet postures, rhythm is taught by beats and music is quadraphonically amplified.

Whistlestop Improvisational Dance Company
PO Box 20801, Seattle, WA 98102, **USA**
Whistlestop is composed of dancers and musicians and has developed methods to enable disabled people to benefit from the experience of dance.

DRAMA/THEATRE

Access Arts Inc
PO Box 24, Brisbane, Queensland 4000, **Australia**
A theatre troupe of disabled and able-bodied artists; they were the first disabled theatre company to tour Australia.

Australia Theatre Club
c/o Australia Council, PO Box 302, North Sydney, NSW 2060, **Australia**
A theatre club where a 'friend' is available to meet and accompany the member to the theatre. A large proportion are disabled, though the club makes no distinction. A very successful venture which integrates people without labelling their problems.

Drama Programmes in WA Prisons
Adreso House, 1004 Hay Street, West Perth, Western **Australia**
WA prisons run drama workshops and productions as part of a general education programme.

Grass Roots Theatre Company
PO Box 752, Bunbury, WA 6230, **Australia**
A group of intellectually disabled adults who hope to illustrate the changes that can take place by the use of movement and drama education.

New South Wales Theatre for the Deaf
153 Dowling Street, Potts Point, NSW 2011, **Australia**
Professional theatre group playing to deaf and hearing audiences in schools, community theatres and mainstream theatres.

Playback Theatre Company
c/o Deborah Pearson, 153 Park Street, Subiaco, WA 6008, **Australia**
A form of community theatre of able-bodied actors and musicians. Unlike traditional theatre, the audience recount their experiences for the actors and musicians to play back using movement, mime, sound and dialogue. Prior to a performance, the company researches the interests of the audience.

Theatre of Difference
GPO Box K759, Perth, WA 6001, **Australia**
Provides theatrical experiences for all sectors of the community and includes professional performers, disabled and able-bodied members.

Der Blaue Kompressor
Postfach 637, 1011 Vienna, **Austria**
The Blue Compressor (floating and stomping company) is a group of artists concerned with expansive arts for the disabled.

Ich Bin OK [I'm OK]
Haidgasse 4/27, A-1020 Vienna, **Austria**
A cooperative troupe of severely physically handicapped and non-disabled artists using theatre and creative movement to help performers gain recognition for their individual talents.

Smile Theatre Company
427 Bloor St West, Toronto, Ontario M5S 1X7, **Canada**
A professional company performing only to isolated audiences and people in institutions.

Project Roger
Instituto Andrea Jimenez, 1145 Avenue 11C 17B, San Jose, **Costa Rica**
The Colina Theatre and the Andrea Jimenez Institute aimed to arouse the interest of disabled children in the theatre, both as spectators and participants. Professional actors also lead theatrical games in Special Education Centres.

Doves Teater
Kastelsvej 58, 2100 Copenhagen O, **Denmark**
One of the largest deaf theatre groups in Denmark, much of their work is based on old folk legends. The group uses sign language and if necessary a narrator for hearing people.

International Amateur Theatre Association
Vesterbrogade 175, DK-1800 Copenhagen V, **Denmark**
Promotes dramatic art internationally by all theatrical groups devoted, without remuneration, to artistic and cultural aims. Coordinates its members' actions in their cultural and educative purposes.

Ciotog Community Theatre Group
The Grove, Rockenham, Waterford, **Eire**
This group works in theatre-in-education to develop the awareness of young people about a variety of subjects, including disability.

Theatre Omnibus
4-5 Creagh Lane, Limerick, **Eire**
Dance and mime company performing and giving workshops, classes and shows in schools, special schools, hospices, etc.

Association Atelier d'Art et d'Echanges
27 rue Mazarine, 75006 Paris, **France**
Worked with Beaubourg Children's Workshop, aiming to bring handicapped and able-bodied children together in creative projects.

Atelier du Chaudron
Cartoucherie, Route du Champ de Manoeuvre, 75012 Paris, **France**
The atelier began working on a theatre project at the request of patients aged between 25 and 65, all with severe cerebral-motor handicaps. Three of the original group, now actors in their own right, and three actors from Atelier du Chaudron perform professionally.

Nancy Breitenbach
7 rue Pecquay, Paris 75004, **France**
A combination of drama and creative make-up has proved to be an

outlet for self-expression for disabled and able-bodied children. Exploring the face through the use of stage make-up is fun as well as helping withdrawn children to feel more positive.

Compagnie de l'Oiseau Mouche
136-8 rue Pierre de Roubaix, 59100 Roubaix, **France**
This company, composed of 20 professional actors with mental disabilities, has the specific aim of creating and performing a primarily gestural theatre.

International Visual Theatre
Centre Socio-Culturel des Sourds, Tour de Village, Château de Vincennes, 9300 Vincennes, **France**
Alfredo Corrado established IVT, composed of deaf actors. Its goal is to search for a new visual theatrical language based on a world-view shared by the deaf.

Lucernaire
53 Notre Dame de Champs, 75006 Paris, **France**
A community workshop which, although dealing principally with theatre, also offers other arts activities to people with psychiatric illnesses.

Les Magiciens du Trottoir
28 avenue Daumesnil, 75012 Paris, **France**
P.A. Gradry, an actor, with other actors, retired and elderly people, set up a new theatre venue for performance art and other activities, aiming to encourage meetings between different generations.

Théâtre de l'Arche
51 rue de Mouzaia, 75019 Paris, **France**
Runs creative projects and theatrical activities for children, adolescents and adults suffering from mental disabilities.

Théâtre et Thérapie
Centre International de Recherche sur l'Utilisation Thérapeutique du Travail Théâtral, Université Lyon, 69500 Lyon Bron, **France**
Research into the relationships between practical theatre, the body and illness.

Viellesse Buissonière
95 rue Rombuteau, 71000 Macon, **France**

A theatre association whose aim is to bring together isolated elderly and other groups in the community. This centre is at the café-theatre La Buissonière Bleue.

Ag Spiel und Theater
Nordrhein Westfalen eV, Klarastrasse 9, 4350 Recklinghausen, **Germany FRG**
Runs a theatre centre for unemployed young people, and also works with disabled people, deprived children, immigrant workers and prisoners.

Clown Chiko
Sagestrasse 26, 8952 Schlieren, **Germany FRG**
Participatory performances for able-bodied and disabled children, Chiko feels that working alongside therapists is increasingly important.

Professor Ernst J. Kiphard
Einheimer Stadtweg 119, D6000 Frankfurt 50, **Germany FRG**
Professor Kiphard has Chair of Preventative Treatment and Rehabilitation through Exercise and Sport. He trained as a teacher of physical education, then did a doctoral thesis on handicap and movement. He is also E. J. Kiphard the Clown, who visits centres for physically handicapped children.

Munchner Cruppel Cabaret
Mehringdam 51, 1000 Berlin 61, **Germany FRG**
A group of handicapped performers who have put on a cabaret showing clearly what life is like when you are handicapped.

Theatre That Moves
Atelier Roonstr. 78 eV, 5000 Cologne 1, **Germany FRG**
Mehmet Fistik, a Turkish pantomime artist, is the founder of the company, an ensemble of 8 handicapped and able-bodied pantomime artists.

Solheimar I Grimsnesi
801 Selfoss, **Iceland**
A small community for mentally retarded adults which has a theatre group performing traditional plays. Drama has been used as a therapy and mime especially has been chosen.

Children's Little Theatre
Aban Mahal, Gariahat Road, Calcutta 700 029, **India**

Provides a children's theatre and workshop for able-bodied and disabled in a deprived area.

Jagran Theatre of the Oppressed
E-7/10-8 Vasant Viher, New Delhi 110057, **India**
A group of mime artists who form a small travelling theatre unit. Jagran work in the 'slum colonies' of Delhi and also take their shows into the rural areas. Jagran seek to provide greater awareness of the problems of the poor and to galvanise audiences into action on their behalf.

Light Up Your Life
Oral School for Deaf Children, 4b Short Street, Calcutta 700 016, **India**
Zarim Choudhuri, an actress, and Dhun Adenewalla, a teacher, founded 'Light Up Your Life', a mime theatre club whose students have now reached a professional level of performance.

National School of Drama
Bahawalpur House, Bhagwandas Road, New Dehli 110 001, **India**
The school is interested in researching into new ways to make greater use of the arts with disabled people.

Habib Tanvir
Naya Theatre, 1-15 DDA Staff Quarters, Berer Sarai, New Delhi 110 016, **India**
Theatre group composed of local people who perform traditional Indian theatre and educational plays.

Theatre Action Group and Tag's Remedial Drama Unit
The Okhla Centre for Mentally Retarded Children, Okhla Marg, New Delhi 110 025, **India**
Organise educational tours and creative workshops.

Jamaica School of Drama
Cultural Training Centre, 1 Arthur Wint Drive, Kingston 5, **Jamaica**
The school includes courses in special education and is anxious to encourage greater artistic opportunities for disabled and disadvantaged people and those in prison.

Sistren Theatre Collective
100 Hope Road, Kingston 6, **Jamaica**
Established by a group of working-class women, using drama to analyse and help solve local community issues.

Japanese National Theatre of the Deaf
Daisan-Hayama Bldg, 3-21-25 Nishi-Azabu, Minato-Ku, Tokyo 106, **Japan**
This group is widely acclaimed and bases many of its performances on the classical Noh theatre, using sign language and voice.

Bemiddelings Buro Dans en Drama
L. Meyer, Passeerdersgracht 32, 1016 XH Amsterdam, **Netherlands**
A theatre group working in hospitals.

Stichting Visueel Theater en Doven-Communicatie
Postbus 15 641, 1001 NC Amsterdam, **Netherlands**
The foundation is actively concerned with teaching and workshops that are relevant to the problems faced by deaf people wanting to join in the world of theatre. They start with the premise that such people do not develop motor cognitive skills as quickly as hearing people and suggest that schools should include drama sessions in their curriculum.

Snowball Theatrix
c/o IHC, Box 7111, Newsome, **New Zealand**
Amateur performers with disabilities. Jane Venis, recreation officer for the Nelson Crippled Children Society, would like to establish a permanent Nelson theatre school for disabled people.

Theatre Corporate
14 Galatos Street, Auckland 1; Box 68422, Newton, **New Zealand**
Community Theatre Company is the educational branch which aims to bring performances and workshops both to children in schools and to those who are unable to experience live theatre – such as those in homes and hospitals.

Olsztynska Pantomima Taubentheater Olsztyn
Wojewodski, dom Kultury, Olsztyn 10-233U L, Barkowa 1, **Poland**
Grounded in the rich tradition of workers' theatre in Poland, this is a highly professional group using deaf artists in elaborate and spectacular mime performances.

Drama Outreach Project
4 Virginia Ave, Vredehoek, Cape Town 8001, **South Africa**
Part of the 'People's Space Theatre', the project is organised by Arthur Benjamin and offers workshops in drama, music, mime and movement for able-bodied and disabled people.

Pion Jarteaterensemblen
c/o Riksteatern, Rasundavagen 150, S-171 30 Solna, **Sweden**
The Pioneers tour prisons and psychiatric institutions, giving performances of established drama with a 'message'.

Tyst Teater [Silent Theatre]
Swedish National Theatre Centre, Svenka Riksteatern, Rasundavagen 150, S-171 30 Solna, **Sweden**
A professional theatre company acting in sign language, the company has three deaf actors who tour both classical plays and plays related to deaf people. Tyst Teater would like to spread knowledge about sign language among people who can hear.

The Wheel Theatre
Hornsgatan 137, S-117 28 Stockholm, **Sweden**
A theatre company composed of 7 severely physically handicapped people. Half the production side are professionals, all the actors are amateur. They perform plays about universal issues in various settings in Sweden and also overseas. The theatre is funded by government grants and is housed within the Labour Union.

Taipei Theater of the Deaf
41 Jen-Ai Road, Taipei 10018, **Taiwan**
Founded in 1977 after the College Students' Deaf Association began to sponsor activities, including the first sign-language classes for hearing people. Joined by Wang Chi-mei, Associate Professor at the National Institute of the Arts and Chairperson of the Deaf Sign Language Research Association of the Republic of China. Their performances are acclaimed nationally.

Age Exchange Theatre Company
15 Camden Road, Blackheath, London SE3 0QA, **UK**
A theatre and publishing company producing shows and publications based on the recollections and current concerns of older people in London. The elderly are involved as fully as possible in the creative process leading to performance.

The Ark Project
The Media Centre, South Hill Park, Bracknell RG12 1BR,**UK**
A small drama studio concerned with providing mentally handicapped students and their staff with opportunities to develop their own ideas and creativity within an informal environment.

A39 Theatre Group
3a Penlee Villas, Playing Place, Truro, Cornwall, **UK**
A theatre group of formerly unemployed people who work with hospitals, homes and employment centres in Cornwall.

Bedside Manners
51 Chalcot Road, London NW1 8LY, **UK**
A touring theatre company performing for the elderly in hospitals and day centres. Shows are based on music of the '20s to '40s written to provoke communication.

Double Exposure Theatre Company
72 Ansell Road, London SW17 7LT, **UK**
Seeks to promote integrated theatre, with the emphasis on giving performers with disabilities the opportunity to work in productions which may have no direct theme of disability.

Gog Theatre Cooperative
Assembly Rooms, High Street, Glastonbury, Somerset, **UK**
A theatre-in-education group offering 'life and social skills' sessions to all youth training schemes.

The Graeae Theatre Company
The Diorama, 14 Peto Place, London NW1, **UK**
A professional company composed of actors with physical disabilities.

Greenwich Young People's Theatre Project
Burrage Road, London SE18, **UK**
Theatre project for students with mental disabilities.

Interim Theatre Company
67 Tower Bridge Road, London SE1, **UK**
The company has six actors, three of whom are deaf. It does not make handicap a feature; there is complete integration within the cast.

Intriplicate Mime Company
7 Birchington Road, London N8, **UK**
Mime-drama in performances and workshops. The company works with mixed ability and handicapped children and adults in schools, hospitals, community centres.

Mimika
26 Highbury Terrace, Leeds LS6 4ET, **UK**
A two-person professional touring company creating highly visual and

exciting theatre. All shows are non-verbal and involve an audience across a wide ability range.

Myriad Theatre Company
167 Beaumont Road, Bournville, Birmingham 30, **UK**
A theatre-in-education group whose shows are aimed at children of primary school age, particularly those with learning difficulties.

Newham International Festival of Theatre in Education
Monega Arts & Drama Centre, Monega Road, London E12 6TT, **UK**
NIFTIE is an international festival hosted each year by the London Borough of Newham. It exists to bring together the best exponents of theatre in an educational setting.

St Albans Players
St Albans Day Centre, Penrose Street, Walworth, London SE5, **UK**
A group of elderly people performing productions with a musical bias based on their experiences and reminiscences.

The '66 Club
857 Hertford Road, Freezywater, Enfield, Middlesex EN3 6UH, **UK**
Working with hearing-impaired adults to provide an opportunity for young deaf people to develop their skills in drama, mime, dance, etc. The National Youth Theatre of the Deaf aims to explore the potential of sign theatre as an artistic form in its own right.

Strathcona Theatre Company
Strathcona Road, Wembley, Middlesex, **UK**
Based at and part of a social education centre, this company of actors who have mental disabilities are students at the centre. Their ability and quality of performance has made a considerable impact on their audiences.

Theatro Technis
26 Crowndale Road, London NW1 1TT, **UK**
Founded for Greek Cypriots living in London, it has two theatre groups: the Community Theatre Group and the Young People's Theatre. In both, about 80% of the performers are unemployed or elderly; some are professional actors.

Time and Talents
Rotherhithe Theatre Workshop, 107 Rotherhithe Street, London SE16, **UK**

'Young in Heart' is a drama club run by a neighbourhood centre. Elderly people perform their plays and cabarets for schools, day centres and homes.

Access Theatre
2428 Chapala Street, Santa Barbara, CA 93015, **USA**
A totally accessible theatre encouraging the integration of physically disabled, deaf, able-bodied performers, adults and children, in its productions and workshops.

American Theatre Association
Wright State University, Dayton, Ohio 45435, **USA**
A computerised data bank listing individuals and programmes in the USA and Cananda working in theatre with disabled people. A resource guide is published as an annotated version of the data bank.

Boston Theatre of the Deaf
Box 804, Back Bay Annex, Boston, MA 02117, **USA**
Its purpose is to foster and utilise the art of Visual Language Theatre as a means of enhancing communication and fellowship among deaf and hearing people. It works with hearing and deaf actors, who explore the art of visual language.

Bread and Roses
78 Throckmorton Avenue, Mill Valley, CA 94941, **USA**
Free shows by amateur and professional artists to audiences in institutions, hospitals, prisons, special schools etc. (See also under Coordinating Link Services.)

Centre for Advanced Study of Theatre Arts
Graduate School and Univ Centre, New York Univ, 33 W. 42nd St, New York, NY 10036, **USA**
CASTA has organised conference on the utility and availability of drama in prisons. Its publication *The Arts in Prisons* contains details of creative activities in prisons around the world.

Alysa B. Chadow
40-01 Little Neck Parkway, Little Neck, NY 11363, **USA**
A graduate student in the field of special education who deals in her work with the experience of being disabled.

Children's Theatre Company
2400 Third Avenue South, Minneapolis, MN 55404, **USA**

Written by blind actress Leslye Orr, *Hand in Hand* is based on Helen Keller and Anne Sullivan. Intended for both sighted and blind audiences, it presents an aural portrait using effects such as sound recordings, the smell of cigar smoke to suggest after-dinner conversation, and costume fabrics passed round the audience, to encourage people to use their inner mind's eye. Leslye also trains blind and sighted people in movement.

Creative Alternatives of New York Inc
1 Gustave Levy Place, Annenburg 20-210, New York, NY 10029, **USA**
A theatre programme serving psychiatric patients in the NY area, based at Mount Sinai Hospital. Patients are referred to workshops by their doctors. To join the programme, artists have to undergo a nine-month training course.

Elders Share the Arts
c/o Collage, National Council on Aging, 600 Maryland Ave SW, Washington DC 20024, **USA**
Runs a 'Living History Theatre' workshop for elderly people, focusing on transforming their personal reminiscences into performances.

Fairmount Theatre of the Deaf
11206 Euclid Avenue, Cleveland, Ohio 44106, **USA**
FTD was selected to represent America at the Pantomime Festival of the Deaf in Czechoslovakia with their show *Smircus – A Sign Mime Circus.*

Geese Theatre Company
667 West Cornelia, Chicago, Illinois 60657, **USA**
A national touring group providing live performances, workshops and residences in prisons throughout the USA.

The Human Tree Players
Delaware County Association of Retarded Citizens, Muncie, Delaware, **USA**
A drama group composed of mentally disabled people who develop and produce a touring show.

Living Stage Theatre Company
6th and Maine Avenue SW, Washington DC 20024, **USA**
The company performs for many groups; projects include performance workshops with disabled children, deprived youth and prison inmates.

Loon and Heron Theatre
194 Boylston Street, Lincoln School, Brookline, MA 03246, **USA**

Seeks to provide the highest quality performing art experiences possible for children, adults and people with special needs. The Theatre of the Senses takes the emphasis from visual impact by the use of a tactile set as well as sound, smell, taste and distorted visuals, to create a new theatre that requires participation. Loon and Heron work with both sighted and blind artists.

National Theatre of the Deaf
Hazel E. Stark Center, Chester, Conn 06412,**USA**
Professional theatre group from which many other deaf actors and theatre groups have received training.

National Theatre of the Deaf
325 Spring Street, New York, NY 10013, **USA**
The company consists of five actors, three deaf. The theatre speaks with two voices: one for the ear, another for the eye. Blending the spoken word with sign language has created a new dual-language theatre.

National Theatre Workshop of the Handicapped
106 West 56th Street, New York, NY 10019, **USA**
Founded by Rick Curry, the NTWH exists to train disabled actors and press for their employment in mainstream theatre, TV and film.

New York Pantomime Theatre/Training Centre
242 West 27th Street, New York, NY 10001, **USA**
A highly trained mime company which trains people from all over the world in mime technique. It has special courses for children and a programme in which mime is used as a therapeutic tool for work with handicapped people.

One Nighters Theatre
Drama and Dance of Older Adults and Special Populations,
6816 N Villard Avenue, Portland, Oregon 97217, **USA**
A senior theatre group (One Nighters Senior Theatre Ensemble) run by Bonnie Vorenberg, which incorporates dance as well as drama. They perform at community centres and schools, including singing and dance routines. Performances have been widely acclaimed.

Stop-Gap
PO Box 484, Laguna Beach, CA 92652, **USA**
A professional theatre company that uses theatre to build communication between generations. The drama therapists and actors represent a wide age span.

Theatre News
American Theatre Association, 1010 Wisconsin Avenue NW, Washington DC 20007, **USA**
Magaret Rockwell, herself blind, helped develop a theatre project for visually impaired people: an audio description using volunteer commentators to provide verbal descriptions of a play for audience members equipped with FM headsets.

Theatre Patrons Association
University of Maryland, College Park, Maryland 20742, **USA**
Have installed wireless earphones for the broadcast of audio descriptions to make their productions richer for visually impaired people.

Theatre Unlimited
San Francisco Center for the Handicapped, 207 Skyline Boulevard, San Francisco, CA 94132, **USA**
Herb Felsenfeld, Managing Director
Ensemble company of actors/dancers, half of whom have developmental/physical disabilities.

Tose Sonke Theatre Group
c/o DPI, 1 Trust House, Bulawayo, **Zimbabwe**
A drama club and performing group of 15 physically disabled and 10 able-bodied members and students from Hillside Teachers' College. Founded in 1985 by Interlink and the National Council of Disabled Persons of Zimbabwe, it aims to perform plays which focus on integration between disabled and able-bodied people, and it integrates the four languages: Shona, Sindebele, English and sign language. Tose Sonke is a combination of words from the national languages of Zimbabwe, meaning 'all of us together'.

MISCELLANEOUS

CHESS

Network
5th Floor, 34 Liverpool Street, Sydney 2000, **Australia**
John Roarty is a former New South Wales chess champion who now works for the Handicapped Persons Alliance. He says : 'Chess is

classless. You don't have to be physically fit. You can be totally disabled. Each square has a name so you can ask someone to move the pieces for you. And the best thing about chess? You know you've won because you've won, not because they've let you.'

FASHION

Ros Branson
c/o *Link* Newspaper, GPO Box 909, Adelaide 5001, **Australia**
Ros Branson designs and makes clothes for disabled people, on order for people in nursing homes or in private homes.

FLOWER-ARRANGING

Marie Freestun
108 Ninth Avenue, St Lucia 4067, **Australia**
An artist who teaches severely disabled and ill people flower-arranging. This project set out to broaden recreational opportunities and enhance manipulative skills.

LEISURE

Tuesday Night Club
38 First Avenue, Blacktown, NSW 2148, **Australia**
Club for intellectually disabled people, largely run by themselves.

CREATIVE HOLIDAYS

Handicapped/Able-Bodied Summer Camps
Heimgasse 8, 1238 Vienna, **Austria**
Sigrid Schmidt
An organisation which runs summer camps for handicapped and able-bodied young people, aged 17-25, from England and Austria. Various creative and leisure activities are offered.

COMPUTERS

Arts Carousel
Box 342, Postal Station P, Toronto, Ontario M5S 2S8, **Canada**
Held symposium on computer art for physically disabled people. The machine acts as a medium betwen conception and realisation. Report available.

MAGIC

Peter the Great
c/o Arts Carousel, Arts with the Handicapped Foundation, Box 342, Postal Station P, Toronto, Ontario M5S 2S8, **Canada**

Peter Galashan is a magician who has cerebral palsy. His 'Project Magic' is a therapy programme for disabled youth to help them use the hands through learning and performing magic.

ZOO THERAPY

Alberta Arts Therapy Association
Box 957, Station G, Calgary, Alberta T3A 0E0, **Canada**
Zoo therapy has been highly successful with children who have been battered and sexually abused. The children are put into a programme where they adopt an animal, anything from a lizard to a horse, and are taught the proper care of an animal. This experience builds self-respect.

PLAYGROUNDS/GARDENS

Jiri Kastak
Smeralova Street NL 11, 170 00 Prague 7, **Czechoslovakia**
Designer of special playgrounds for people with disabilities.

FUNDING

Inspektion for Specialundervisningen
V. Voldgade 117, 152 Copenhagen V, **Denmark**
Disabled people wishing to take part in creative activities may rely on the Special Education Section of the Ministry of Education, who will meet the costs for the event and oblige schools to provide suitable accommodation. The only restriction is that groups consist of at least five people and one instructor.

COOKERY

Savoir Culinaire, Pratiques Alimentaires et Personnes Agées
Fed Laique et d'Education Permanente, 20 ave Bujanet, 79005 Niort, **France**
M. Jean Lavault, Coordinator
The Federation initiated a cultural project around the theme of food because elderly people leaving their independent way of life to settle in institutions are often cut off from an essential feature of their existence – their culinary routine.

GARDENING

Jardin d'Animation à Bourges
Ville de Bourges, Hotel de Ville, 18000 Bourges, **France**
M. Marceron, Service Technique de la Ville
A garden managed and maintained by physically handicapped people.

The garden has been adapted and includes an open-air theatre. The gardeners are responsible for the events which take place there.

MEDIA TRAINING

Xavier Institute of Communication,
St Xavier's College, Bombay 400 001, **India**
Aims to bring about change in India by using the media in a constructive and enlightened way. The institute is primarily a teaching establishment giving its students various media-related programmes.

TYPEWRITER ART

Japanese Society for Rehabilitation of the Disabled
3-13-15 Higashi Ikebukuro, Toshima-Ku, Tokyo 170, **Japan**
Have been running an annual art competition since 1961. The organisers decided to add typewriter art to the existing categories of painting and calligraphy in order to allow participation by those who cannot hold a pen or a brush. The works of art produced have been beautiful and exciting.

DIRECTORY

Arts Council of New Zealand
Alexander House, 131-5 Lambton Quay, Private Bag, Wellington, **New Zealand**
Jenny Rouse, Senior Research Officer
The Arts Council have complied a resource kit, *Arts and the Disabled,* which provides a directory of arts and disabled organisations, artistic residence programmes and other useful information.

HOLIDAY HOUSE-SWAPS

Disabled Persons Assembly
424 Jackson Street, Petone, **New Zealand**
Alexia Pickering is collating ideas about the feasibility of holiday home-swaps in New Zealand.

RECYCLING

The Product Life Institute
5 rue Pedro Meylan, CH-1208 Geneva, **Switzerland**
The Institute can be contracted by any company or organisation to do consultancy work in the field of product life of goods and services. It researches into the field of wealth creation and welfare development by finding opportunities for new services or goods that are based on wasted resources such a people, buildings, land, discarded goods.

ACCESS

Arts Access
336 Brixton Road, London SW9 7AA, **UK**
Offers guidance and architectural advice to managers of venues regarding access to the arts.

CULINARY ARTS

Applejacks Café
The Camden Society for Mentally Handicapped People,
245 Royal College Street, London NW 9LT, **UK**
A training project where trainees are selected from people with a mental disability. They receive training in a variety of jobs, from serving to cooking food. The café is open to the public 5 days a week.

FASHION

Fashion Services for the Disabled
B270-B320 Saltaire Workshops, Ashley Lane, Shipley, Yorks BD17 7SR, **UK**
Mrs Nellie Thornton, Project Director
A research project looking at the clothing needs of people with disabilities and ways of producing individually designed garments at reasonable cost. Also runs a training centre and workshop.

GARDENING

Gardens for the Disabled
Headcorn Manor, Headcorn, Kent TN27 9HP, **UK**
Founded to help encourage the building of special gardens. The Garden Club gives help and advice with gardening for disabled people living at home.

The Harington Scheme
Furnival House, Cholmeley Park, Highgate, London N6, **UK**
A horticultural training project for young people with disabilities. The two-year course covers a wide range of practical gardening skills, with classes in life and social skills and basic computing.

Horticultural Therapy
Goulds Ground, Vallis Way, Frome, Somerset BA11 3DW, **UK**
Offers a wide range of practical services to help disabled people enjoy and benefit from gardening, horticulture and agriculture.

Screened Garden
Occupational Therapy Dept, Southend Hospital, Prittlewell Chase, Westcliff-on-Sea, Essex SS0 0RY, **UK**
Spare space close to the occupational therapy department has been provided as a garden for the patients, enabling a wide range of therapy projects associated with gardening. The occupational therapy logo was used to design wrought-iron gates and screens, sections of which were constructed by patients

SKILLS EXCHANGE

Age Concern
Lewisham Skills Centre, 15 Brownhill Road, Catford, London SE6, **UK**
A scheme where elderly people teach their skills to local schoolchildren.

FASHION

PRIDE Foundation Inc
1159 Poquonnock Road, Groton, Conn 06340, **USA**
Evelyn S. Kennedy, Executive Director
Consulting services are provided and resources are available for the adaptation of garments so that everyone can wear fashionable, comfortable clothes. Custom-designed patterns are provided for individual needs.

GARDENING

Gardens for All
180 Flynn Avenue, Burlington, Vermont 05401, **USA**
The USA National Association of Gardening researched a book on tools and techniques for disabled gardeners.

LIBRARIES

Arizona State Library for the Blind and Physically Handicapped
1030 N 32nd St, Phoenix, Arizona 85008, **USA**
As well as an extensive talking book service this library offers taped programme notes on radio opera broadcasts.

RESOURCES

The PAM Assistance Center
601 W. Maple Street, Lansing, MI 48906, **USA**
A resource and information support centre offering advice and practical help for people with disabilities – from fashion to gardening. Issues a newsletter *The PAM Repeater*. Recommended.

MUSIC

Australia Music Therapy Association (New South Wales Branch)
83 Bland Street, Ashfield 2131, NSW, **Australia**
Miriam McFarlene
Australia Music Therapy Association (Victoria Branch)
8 Haigh Street, Deepdene 3103, Victoria, **Australia**
Mrs Margaret Evans
This association, with branches in every state, is for everyone in Australia interested in using music to help handicapped people achieve their potential. AMTA is interested in helping, advising, and learning from individuals using music in this way.

Caroline Chisholm Special School
Napoli St, Padstow 2211, Sydney, **Australia**
Bain Painter
Sound Playground Project; the aim is to enable handicapped children to explore sound and music through an atmosphere of play, whilst developing initiative.

Sound Playgrounds
Temple Park, Gold Street, Brunswick, Melbourne, **Australia**
Ros Brandt
A sound playground set up by Brandt in a disadvantaged area of Melbourne. Simple wooden and metal instruments installed in frames adjoining the normal play area. A sound experience combined with the traditional idea of a playground.

Hochshule für Musik und Darstellende Kunst
'Mozarteum', Sonderabteilung Orff-Institute, Frohnburgweg 55, A-50-20 Salzburg, **Austria**
Shirley Salmon, Music Teacher
Musical education based on the Carl Orff method. It is applied as music therapy to children with various disabilities.

Christine Jones
Kuntskanzlei-interart, Riemergasse 14/29, 1010 Vienna, **Austria**
A jazz singer who has developed her own technique for combining

music and visual art for deprived children. Christine works with groups of students, singing to them whilst they paint the sounds conveyed by her songs.

Berta Klement
Musische Arbeitgemeinschaft, Buchengasse 1700, 1100 Vienna, **Austria**
A music workshop group concerned with the creative development of mentally disturbed and emotionally handicapped people.

'No Problem Orchestra', Jugend am Werk
Kartnerstrasse 25, 8020 Graz, **Austria**
An organisation whose aim is to integrate disabled people into the community; Josef Schorkmayr, a music therapist, uses electronic percussion instruments for therapy. He leads the No Problem Orchestra, made up of 7 disabled musicians.

Osterreichischer Berufsverband der Musictherapeuten e.V.
Marc-Aurelstrasse 10/8, 1010 Vienna, **Austria**
The Austrian Association of Music Therapists coordinates the diverse activities of music therapists. Its aim is to structure this work more effectively, acting as a centre for the exchange of ideas and work opportunities.

CEDE
Rua Tenente Negrao 188, Sao Paulo, **Brazil**
Nancy Derwood Mills Costa
A 'teaching dynamics centre' developing musical activities with psychotic children.

Professor M.E. Fadli
5 Hassan Mousa, El-Akkad, Heliopolis, Cairo, **Egypt**
Professsor Fadli, a neuropsychiatrist at Ain-Shams University in Cairo, has been exploring the uses of music as an alternative to drug therapy in the treatment of patients with psychosomatic disorders. They have discovered that quiet music has a marked effect in reducing tension and blood pressure, and that loud rhythmic music can have potentially harmful effects.

L'Amarch le Kinnor
48 rue Davy, 75017 Paris, **France**
Jean Claude L'Hotel, President
The Association for Music and Aid for Community Re-education of

Handicapped People utilises music in all its forms to bring about human and spiritual development with a concern for the whole community.

Assoc pour le Développement des Ateliers de Créativité pour Personnes Agées
11 rue Erard, 75012 Paris, **France**
Réné la Forestrie
ADACPA is helping to set up workshops in creative activities for institutionalised elderly people. One of these is a music studio at Charles Foix Hospital in Ivry.

Claire Joie, Association des Infirmes Moteurs Cérébraux
Fonds d'Intervention Culturelle, 14 rue Notre Dame des Victoires, 75002 Paris, **France**
Patients and staff from hospitals in the Bourg en Bresse region of France have formed a choir known as 'Claire Joie', one of several projects set up by the Centre for Psychotherapy at L'Ain.

Groupe de Musique Expérimentale de Marseille
44 rue des Dominicaines, 13001 Marseille, **France**
Nadine Mistretta, Group Coordinator
This circle of 7 composers devotes part of its activity to a weekly music workshop for young people with intellectual and physical handicaps, using electro-acoustic music suited to individual needs created by the various handicaps.

C. Pheline and M. Lemercier
c/o Art et Thérapie, 34 rue Alain Gerbault, 4100 Blois, **France**
C. Pheline, a neurosurgeon, and M. Lemercier, a music therapist, worked together on treatment of coma sufferers, using simple sounds and rhythm as a tool for bringing the patients to an awareness of their environment.

Sound Sculptures
11 rue Jean de Beauvais, 75005 Paris, **France**
Vincent Baschet
The Baschet sound structures were designed to introduce children to the world of sound. Exhibitions of the sound structures in other countries made the Baschets aware that children's interest in the instrumentarium should be cultivated for education and therapy. The Baschets hold long-term workshops.

St. John's School for the Deaf
PO Box 2409, Serrekunda, **Gambia**
John Jatta, Principal
The 'Talking Drums Project' was introduced to help students explore their talents and extend their appreciation of rhythm and melody. An integral part of African cultural life, the talking drum is played at all festivals. One of the school's pupils won a disco dancing competition, able to feel the vibrations of the music through the drums.

Silke Jochims
Stolzingstrasse 10, 8000 Munich 81, **Germany FRG**
A music therapist who has worked with cancer patients, in particular breast-amputated women who seem to see their bodies as mutilated and tend to neglect them. The most important objective is to give these women a sensation of being in possession of their bodies through dance and responding to different moods of music.

Joseph Rommel
St Vincent School for the Blind, Music Department, Petionville, **Haiti**
Joseph Rommel, the Director of Music, is a blind musician who studied violin at the University of Cincinnati and with the Boston Symphony. The School also has a handbell choir.

Gandharva Mahavidyhalaya
Vishnu Digamber Marg, New Delhi 110 002, **India**
Vinaya Chandra Mandgalya, Principal
One of India's most celebrated music academies, teaching Indian classical music and dance, with a commitment to bringing classical music to the masses, and encouraging blind people to become students at the school.

Indian Gospel Singers
Old Town, A.P., Tanuku 534 211, **S India**
N. Bhanumurthy, Executive Director
A choir who perform in hospitals, prisons, as well as on television, radio, with the aim of spreading the Christian message.

Karaoke Club
Japan Sun Industries, Kamegawa, Beppe, Oita 874-01, **Japan**
Kazuo Morita
The club was introduced at Japan Sun Industries (a group of commercial firms and sheltered workshops employing people with physical

disabilities). Karaoke literally means singing to a taped instrumental accompaniment, preferably in front of an audience, and is very popular throughout Japan. Club members meet to practice and learn from a professional singer.

Wataboshi Concert
Japan Youth Volunteer Kyokai, c/o NYC, 3-1 Kamizono-cho, Yoyogi, Shibuya-Ku, Tokyo, **Japan**
Wataboshi is Japanese for dandelion. A group of parents who had children with disabilities sought to help their children become part of the mainstream of life. The first Wataboshi Festival was held in 1975 with the hope that, like a dandelion flower, it would spread all over the country – which it has.

International Society for Music Education
School of Music, Univ of Canterbury, Private Bag, Christchurch 1, **New Zealand**
John Ritchie, Secretary General
ISME is an organisation which can provide international information and addresses.

'The Sign Singers' Independent Theatre of the Deaf
2/115a Landscape Road, Mount Eden, Auckland, **New Zealand**
Dulcie McKie, Coordinator
A group of deaf performers whose show is a mixture of mime, sketches and sign singing. By performing to hearing and deaf audiences alike, they bring a greater understanding of deafness to hearing people.

NOMUS
Toftesgate 69, N-0552 Oslo 5, **Norway**
The Committee for Nordic Musical Cooperation is the joint musical organisation within the framework of cultural cooperation between Denmark, Finland, Iceland, Norway and Sweden. The capital of each country has a music information centre. It promotes and disseminates information about musical life and musical cooperation in Scandinavia, covering the whole area of Nordic musical life: composition, improvisation, performance, teaching, both professional and amateur activities.

The Singing Medics
Mindanao Sanatorium and Hospital, Iligan City, **Philippines**
Peter Donton, Administrator

A group of doctors, nurses and orderlies who tour wards to sing patients' requests. Another facet of this 'music recovery programme' is the piping of quiet taped music to all the wards daily. The programme has spread to six hospitals in the Philippines

Boras Free Music School
Rikskonserter, Box 1225, S-111 82 Stockholm, **Sweden**
The Municipal Arts Committee and adult education association have cooperated to initiate a cultural policy and develop the Boras Free Music School. It is free and open to all. As well as giving instruction at the school, it sends teachers to secondary schools.

Svenska Förbundet för Musikterapi
Kungliga Musikaliska Akadmein, Blasieholmstorg 8, 111 48 Stockholm, **Sweden**
Ing Colding, President
Music therapy association.

Swedish State Academy of Music (Musikhögskolan)
Valhallavägen 103-109, S-115 37 Stockholm, **Sweden**
Kurt Lindgren, Lektor
State music high school with large-scale therapy activities.

Bristol Music Therapy Centre
Brentry Hospital, Charlton Road, Bristol BS10 6JH, **UK**
Leslie Blunt, Director
Music therapy for physically and mentally handicapped and mentally ill people.

Dartington Music Foundation for the Handicapped
Dartington Hall, Totnes, Devon TQ9 6EJ, **UK**
David Ward, Principal Officer
An associated activity of the Dartington Hall Trust and College of Arts, its aims are to provide access to music for handicapped individuals and to develop a collection of instruments, music, special equipment and other resources for the use of musicians who visit handicapped people.

Echo City Sonic Playgrounds
Flat 1, 12 Highbury Grange, London N5 2PX, **UK**
Group of musicians who design and create sound playgrounds for able-bodied and disabled children. Have completed one for visually handicapped children.

English Sinfonia
72 St James's Street, Nottingham NG1 6FJ, **UK**
Stuart Bruce, Education and Community Officer
Educational schemes in junior schools and pioneering schemes in special schools, through instrumental workshops, orchestral musicians and electronic workshops.

The Firebird Trust
38 Lodge Road, Newthorpe, Eastwood, Nottingham NG16 2AZ, **UK**
The trust aims to make music part of everyone's experience, and to be of benefit to all sections of the community, especially disadvantaged groups, through performances, workshops and visits to a wide range of community-based locations.

Hayward Handicapped Adventure Playground
Market Road Gardens, Market Road, London N7, **UK**
Laura Browning, Senior Playleader
Interlink arranged for a team of musical instrument makers to design and build sound structures tailored to the needs of children with disabilities. Creations like aluminium frameworks holding marbles which make a sound like the sea, an octagonal fibrephone producing a booming noise, are some of the percussive instruments at the playground.

Music Advisory Service
Disabled Living Foundation, 380-4 Harrow Road, London W9 2HU, **UK**
Gives advice and answers questions on every aspect of music, both amateur and professional, for disabled people and those working or living with them. Recommended.

Music for the Physically Disabled
Morley College, 61 Westminster Bridge Road, London SE1 7HT, **UK**
Audrey Podmore, Organiser
A class of players of orchestral and other instruments combining instrumental teaching, ear training and group playing.

Music Performance Skills Project
Guildhall School, Barbican, London EC1, **UK**
Peter Renshaw, Project Director
This project is designed to broaden the performance scope of 3rd and 4th year music students by equipping them with skills and insights needed to communicate with different audiences such as mentally and

physically handicapped children, hospital patients and prisoners. Before each performance the students visit the venue.

Tibble Trust
Lodge Farm, Babraham Road, Fulbourn, Cambridge CB1 5HV, **UK**
Bert Santilly, Director
Short courses on music for those working in hospitals and residential homes.

Music Education for the Handicapped
Box 454, Summit, New Jersey 07901, **USA**
Meg Peterson, Executive Director
MEH's primary purpose is to train elementary classroom and music teachers to help provide musical experience for handicapped children.

National Association for Music Therapy
1133 15th St NW, Suite 1000, Washington DC 20005, **USA**
E. L. Norwood, Executive Director
NAMT was founded to promote the progressive development of therapeutic use of music. It certifies registered music therapists only if they have completed college courses in music therapy or master's degrees approved by the association. Publishes a newsletter highlighting academic research.

PUBLICATIONS

Billedterapenter
Norwegian Association of Art Therapists, Osthellinga 23, 1370 Asker, **Norway**
Borghild Bredeli, editor
The journal of the Norwegian Association of Art Therapists.

Arts and Disabled People [The Attenborough Report]
c/o Carnegie UK Trust, Comely Park House, Dunfermline,
Fife KY12 7EJ, **UK**
Geoffrey Lord, Secretary and Treasurer
A report containing wide-ranging recommendations to involve more people in the arts. Published by Bedford Square Press, NCVO, London 1985 (£5·75). Available from Macdonald and Evans Distribution Services Ltd, Plymouth PL6 7PZ.

Arts for Everyone **(Anne Pearson)**
c/o Centre on Environment for the Handicapped, 126 Albert Street, London NW1 7NF, **UK**
A book published by the Carnegie United Kingdom Trust which provides information for people working in the arts.

Clothes for Wheelchair Users
Disabled Living Foundation, 380-4 Harrow Road, London W9 2HU, **UK**
An information/training pack consisting of slides and lecture notes together with illustrated sewing hints on useful adaptations, alterations to paper patterns, and a list of names and addresses of suppliers of clothing made specifically for wheelchair users.

Clothes Sense for Disabled People of All Ages **(P. Turnbull and R. Rushton)**
Disabled Living Foundation (Sales) Ltd, Book House, 45 East Hill, Wandsworth, London SW18 2OZ, **UK**
This book discusses all aspects of clothing and dressing, such as choosing suitable fabrics and styles, dressing techniques and aids, reinforcements, and how to adapt existing clothes.

Creative Alternatives: Participation in the Arts for Young People with Severe Mental Handicaps
Carousel, Rock Place Studios, 8 Rock Place, Brighton, East Sussex, **UK**
A Carousel Conference publication, published at £2 .

Cue & Review Recording Service for the Blind and Visually Handicapped
Lendale Lane, Bishopbriggs, Glasgow G64 3LL, Scotland, **UK**
The first national newspaper of its kind in the UK. It reaches 5,000 visually handicapped young people throughout the UK.

Gavarnie Publications
41 Legion Way, East Wittering, Chichester, West Sussex PO20 8PP, **UK**
A small publishing house which has been set up to encourage the talent of young artists and writers from disadvantaged groups.

Guidance for Funding Organisation and Applicants
Carnegie UK Trust, Comely Park House, Dunfermline, Fife KY12 7EJ, **UK**
Geoffrey Lord, Secretary and Treasurer
Outlines the variety of work which receives and awaits support, and suggests some of the considerations that should be given to applications for funding.

Please Touch **(Dr Peter Cole)**
c/o Carnegie UK Trust and Centre on Environment for the Handicapped, 126 Albert Street, London NW1 7NF, **UK**
An evaluative study of a tactile exhibition of sculpture at the British Museum. Dr Cole considers that museums and galleries can do a great deal to encourage those with a visual handicap to enjoy their facilities.

The Accessible Garden [PAM Repeater No 29]
PAM Assistance Centre, 601 W Maple St, Lansing, MI 48906, **USA**
This special number of the *PAM Repeater* is a very good guide to gardening for people with disabilities because it gives inspiration and practical advice.

Companeras **(Betty La Duke)**
City Lights Mail Order, 261 Columbus Ave, San Francisco, CA 94133, **USA**
Companeras brings together the personal stories of women in the Caribbean and Central and South America, showing how both urban and rural women are using crafts and fine art to express themselves in the face of rapid social/political change.

Museum Opportunities for Older Persons
Institute of Lifetime Learning, American Association of Retired Persons, 1909 K Street NW, Washington DC 020049, **USA**
A booklet designed to help elderly people learn more about the opportunities that exist to do voluntary work in museums.

The National Arts Jobbank
Western States Arts Foundation, 141 East Palacee, Sante Fe, NM,**USA**
A publication providing job openings and other opportunities in the visual and performing arts for disabled and able-bodied people.

Resource Guide to People, Places and Programs in Arts and Aging
National Council on the Aging, 600 Maryland Ave SW, West Wing 100, Washington DC 20024, **USA**
The guide aims to facilitate networking between projects and programmes working with and for the elderly.

With Wings: An Anthology of Literature and Visual Art
The Feminist Press, Box 334, Old Westbury, NY 11568, **USA**
Confronts the issues and prejudices facing disabled women as artists and writers.

PUPPETRY

Famous People Players
301 Lansdowne Avenue, Toronto, Ontario M6K 2W5, **Canada**
Diane Dupuy
A highly skilled and internationally renowned puppet theatre with the majority of the performers being people with mental disabilities.

Théâtre de l'Avant Pays
550 Avenue Atwater, Montreal, Quebec H4C 2G6, **Canada**
Diana Bouchard
A puppet theatre company which recently presented *Les Enfants de ma Rue*, a French-Canadian version of *The Kids on the Block*. The work has the aim of encouraging integration of handicapped children in able-bodied classes. The puppeteers also give workshops and introduction to puppet manipulation.

Marionette et Thérapie
14 rue Saint-Benôit, 75006 Paris, **France**
Gladys Laugerin
A national organisation which promotes puppetry as a means of therapy. They offer courses in puppetry with the opportunity to study for the Diploma of Animators (for doctors, psychiatrists, therapists etc.). Experimental workshops and performances of puppetry in hospitals.

Théâtre du Fust
19 rue P. Julien, Hôtel Dieu, 26200 Montélimar, **France**
Corinne Destombes
A professional puppet theatre which develops puppet performances for adult audiences, including special groups.

Tous Vents
Institut Scolaire Educatif et Professionel, rue de Capitaine Favré, 16000 Angoulême, **France**
Claude Micard, Bernard Demoulin
The ISEP offers training and education to boys who have behavioural difficulties leading to problems. The Institute runs puppetry workshops to approach the boys' problems in a different way.

Calcutta Puppet Theatre
20 Ballyganj Kasba Flyover, Calcutta 700 019, **India**
Suresh Datta, Director
A group of puppeteers who are internationally acclaimed for their unique and attractive style. They present puppetry to all types of audience including the disabled and severely deprived.

Christian Council of Puppetry and Traditional Art
Voluntary Agencies for Relief and Development (CCPTAVA),
Room no. 5, St John's School, Bye Bass Road, Bulandshahr 203 001, **India**
Tour and give performances; made up of disabled and disadvantaged performers.

UTSAH – 'People of this World'
2 Sunrise Park Tenements, Thaltej Road, Ahmedabad 3800 54, **India**
Established by Krina Patel, with the help of Interlink, UTSAH uses puppetry and drama as a means by which young disabled people can express themselves creatively. The performing group 'People of this World', established with the help of Interlink, use large puppets that have been made with disabilities.

Deaf Puppet Theatre Hitomi
Foundations Modern Puppet Center, 869 Ida Nakahara-Ku,
Kawasaki, **Japan**
Yutaka Ohsugi
Founded by Yutaka Ohsugi; the main focus of the centre is to create a workplace for modern puppetry, where professional deaf puppeteers invite amateurs to work at the centre. They reach out to schoolchildren as well as performing nationally. A highly professional and artistic company.

Ursula Tappolet
CH-1246 Corsier Port, **Switzerland**
An art therapist working with puppet performances. The puppet theatre for her is a way of investigating specific needs of patients; she believes that a puppet, a marionette character, can influence people's attitudes, behaviour and psychological state.

Dandelion Puppets
Cwm Meigan, Boncath, Dyfed, Wales, **UK**

Involved in puppetry project in Sudan. This group specialises in puppetry as an educational medium for ecology. Their 4-year Sudan project is to help establish tree-planting to counteract the encroaching desert.

Little Angel Marionette Theatre
14 Dagmar Passage, Cross Street, Islington, London N1, **UK**
London's only theatre constructed solely for the presentation of puppetry in all its forms. Courses for people involved in the different aspects of puppet therapy are held at the theatre. The prinicipal tutor, Caroline Astell-Burt, a performer and creator of puppets, specialises in work with the mentally handicapped.

Piccolo Puppet Company
11a Walpole Gardens, Strawberry Hill, Twickenham, Middlesex TW2 5SL, **UK**
Angie Passmore
Piccolo introduces children to the experience and enjoyment of theatre.

Polka Children's Theatre
240 The Broadway, London SW19 1SB, **UK**
A puppet centre for able-bodied and disabled. Its puppetry workshops have been particularly successful as a medium for disabled children. The practical aim is to make shadow or 'junk' puppets. Excellent performances.

Jacqueline Michlin
59 Hampshire Drive, Rochester, NY 14618, **USA**
An art therapist uses puppet-making as the focal point for group art session with the elderly. Soft sculptured foam puppets are made because of their attractive textures and expressive quality.

The Ohio Very Special Arts Network
512 Milford Avenue, Columbus, Ohio 43202, **USA**
Darryl Bojanowski
Trains senior citizens so that they can provide arts experience, via puppetry to disabled children in schools.

Nancy Renfro Studios
1117 West 9th St, Austin, Texas 78703, **USA**
Author of several books on puppetry, and particularly concerned with its applications for disabled children. Her company designs and produces puppets for classroom and library use.

SELF-HELP GROUPS

Verein Frauenselbsthilfe nach Krebs
Wiener Urania, Uraniastrasse 1, 1010 Vienna, **Austria**
Frau Martha Fruhwirt
The Self-Help Association for women who have suffered from cancer aims to look after women who have had a breast operation. If the patient wishes, hospital visits can be arranged and access to other practical pieces of information. Events are organised by the association, including exercise and movement classes.

Manic and Depressive Self-Help Group
41 Ilka Street, Lilyfield 2040, NSW, **Australia**
Started by Meg Smith. People often write, paint, draw, etc, while manic and then no longer do this when depressed. Meg Smith also runs a welfare course in arts, creativity and therapy. Issues quarterly newsletter. Highly recommended.

Association OSE
Centre Culturel Communal Boris Vian, 8 rue Gaspard Picard, 69200 Venissieux, **France**
Group of people who have been mentally ill at the Saint Jean de Dieu Hospital wishing to reintegrate those who are still unwell and need the support of the group. Reintegration organised through arts activities including making use of local cinema with other members of the community for debates and discussion.

Le Cheval Bleu
66 rue Claude Bernard, 75005 Paris, **France**
The aim is to set in motion a public inquiry into madness and psychiatric practice in relation to cultural and artistic activities, and to encourage a better public understanding of psychiatric institutions.

Self-Help Association of Paraplegics (Soweto)
PO Box 303, Orlando 1804, **South Africa**
SHAP was set up by Friday Mandla Mavuso, a paraplegic. The centre serves as a base for its rehabilitation programmes. All facilities are open on a multi-racial basis.

Motivation for Underprivileged
Sarvodaya Suwasetha Sewa, 55 De Soysa Road, Moratuwa, **Sri Lanka**
Sarvodaya (awareness) tries to harmonise traditions with change, and encourages and helps underprivileged people in villages to motivate themselves to self-help. People are encouraged to be creative and develop their skills.

Association of Visually Handicapped Artists and Craftspeople
Blamesvägen 3, S-731 42 Köping, **Sweden**
An alliance of visually handicapped artists and craftspeople to look after its members' interests and to stimulate further professional activity.

Swiss Association of Self-Help for Handicapped and Sick People
Effingerstrasse 55, 3008 Berne, **Switzerland**
ASKIO was formed so that self-help groups for disabled people might join together as an umbrella organisation to enable groups to exchange ideas and to promote their interests

Disabled Action
30 Benson Road, London SE23 3RJ, **UK**
A pressure group on behalf of disabled actors set up by Bill Ward, himself a disabled actor.

Fair Play Campaign for Equal Opportunities in the Arts
9 Fitzroy Square, London W1P 6AE, **UK**
A pressure group for all people with disabilities who are involved in the arts. Its aims are to promote equal training and employment opportunities and campaign for accurate representation of and by the disabled.

Greater London Association for the Disabled
336 Brixton Road, London SW9 7AA, **UK**
GLAD, a pressure group and advocating body, carries out research into the needs of people with disabilities. Produces information sheets including a listing of theatres, cinemas, places of worship and meeting halls with systems for hearing impaired people. Campaigns to make London's entertainment facilities more accessible.

Liberation Network
Micheline Mason, Flat 4, 188 Ramsdon Road, London SW12 8RE, **UK**
Formed with the aim of bringing disabled people together so they can promote and publicise their needs and achieve self-determination. The network publishes *In from the Cold*. Recommended.

Creative Aging
700 West End Avenue, New York, NY 10025, **USA**
An organisation devoted to changing the quality and image of aging through arts activities and entertainment.

People First of Washington State
PO Box 381, Tacoma, Washington 98401, **USA**
A self-advocacy group of mentally handicapped people.

Players Guide
c/o NCAH Education Office, JFK Center for the Performing Arts, Washington DC 20566, **USA**
An advocacy group has been set up at America's National Theatre for the Deaf, for job opportunities for deaf arts. Publishes a *Players Guide.*

TRAINING/REHABILITATION/EDUCATION

Aboriginal Training and Cultural Institute
14 Jane Street, Balmain, NSW 2041, **Australia**
Organisation run by Aborigines to help train Aboriginal people throughout Australia. It offers training projects including craft work and provides consultancy services for Aboriginal community organisations.

The Bindi Centre Activity Therapy Centre
Alice Springs, **Australia**
One establishment in a network of activity therapy centres throughout Australia. Mentally disabled people are engaged in silkscreen and woodwork training.

Cumberland College Foundation
PO Box 170, Lidcombe, NSW 2141, **Australia**
L. D. Crow, Secretary
Helps extend the activities of the college into a range of community services. The foundation aims to integrate disabled people in regular community services. Sponsorship of the national disability awareness programme in 1981 using the 'Kids on the Block' disabled puppets. Regular training programmes for those working with the disabled,

including people from Pakistan, Singapore, Indonesia, Thailand and Malaysia.

Minda Special School
South Australian Education Department for Mentally Handicapped People, Brighton, **Australia**
Students from 6 to 20, grouped according to age or ability, learn crafts such as printing, papier-mâché, batik, weaving, woodwork, spinning, embroidery and painting

Ngeringa
PO Box 390, Williams Road, Mount Barker 5251, SA, **Australia**
Noela Simpson, Libbi Turner
A social therapy centre for young people with physical and mental handicaps who come in for a programme of training and therapeutic activities. Work is in the kitchen, on the farm, in the garden, building or craft work. Ngeringa is a member of the Australian Association for Rudolf Steiner Curative Education and Social Therapy.

Western Australian Paraplegic Quadriplegic Association Activity Therapy Centre
Selby Street, Shenton Park, WA 6008, **Australia;**
PO Box 257, Subiaco, 6008, **Australia**
The ATC offers a wide range of programmes, from puppetry to creative writing, with physically handicapped people.

Arbeitsgemeinschaft für Rehabilitation
Nonntaler Hauptstrasse 110, 5020 Salzburg, **Austria**
To prepare and promote social intregration. The association runs training courses such as painting, carpentry, metalwork, cooking, home economics and clothes-making.

Centro de Dinamica de Ensino
Rua Tenente negrao 1088-Itaim, 04530 Sao Paulo SP, **Brazil**
Mrs Nancy Derwood Mill Costa, Director; Dr Izelinda Garcia de Barros, Supervisor
Offers diverse specialised programmes to disabled and psychotic children. Children take part in arts activities as well as the normal curriculum.

Oficinas Pedagogicas da Sociedade Pestalozzi do Brasil
Rua Visconde de Viteroi, 1450 S. Cristovao, Rio de Janeiro, **Brazil**
Professor Olivia Pereira

Institution concerned with the needs of people with mental disabilities. Working with young and old, the centre runs a programme of 'Education through Art', offering a wide range of creative activities.

Education Dept, Glenrose School Hospital
10230 111 Avenue, Edmonton, Alberta T5G 0B7, **Canada**
Centre for physically and emotionally handicapped students. The industrial arts programme and the arts activities of the occupational therapy and recreation departments place great emphasis on development through art.

Corporacion de Ayuda al Niño Limitado (COANIL)
Julio Prado 1761, Santiago, **Chile**
Gloria Cristi de Herrera, Executive Director
The Corporation to Help the Disabled Child focuses on integral care for mentally handicapped children. It places an emphasis on arts activities.

Departmento de Educacio Especial
Centro de Perfeccionamiento, Experimentacion e Investigaciones Pedagogicas, Ministerio de Educacion, Casilla 16162 Correo 9, Providencia, Santiago, **Chile**
Professor Adriana Pena Donoso, Head
The Department of Special Education seeks to integrate disabled people and sees the various art forms as an important part of its policies.

El Comite Regional de Rehabilitacion de Antioquia
Calle 65 no 49-4, AA 50867 Medellin, **Colombia**
Elena Maria Molina
The Regional Committee for Rehabilitation offers services in special education and social promotion and runs educational programmes for parents.

Institut Psycho-Pédagogique de Brazzaville
La Sécretaire Génèral de la Commission Natl Congolaise pour l'UNESCO, BP 493 Brazzaville, **Congo**
A rehabilitation centre for children of school age with learning difficulties, some of whom have associated physical and sensory disabilities. Its aim is to integrate these children through creative expression. It offers an exceptional range of artistic activities.

St Barnabas School for the Blind
POB 3511, Nicosia, **Cyprus**
The school provides primary and secondary education as well as

technical and vocational training. Music, drama, crafts and pottery are important parts of the education programme.

Matej Kruml, Union of Invalids in CSSR
Karlinske Nemesti 12, PO Box 25, 186 03 Prague, **Czechoslovakia**
Information and educational body dealing with problems of disability. Sets up projects, festivals, competitions, enabling disabled people to have contact with the arts.

Hojskolen i Spaniensgade
Spaniensgade 15, 2300 Copenhagen 5, **Denmark**
Jorgen Molballe, Head Teacher
Takes severely mentally retarded young adults on a one-year course. The emphasis is on discussion as a means of learning to think and deal with problems, and on visual and dramatic expression. Molballe managed to get a studio fully equipped with television cameras. Since the students are not readers, other media need to be used. The students create their own shows and have travelled in Europe with these performances.

Samariteranstalten
124 Furstenwalde, August-Bebel Strasse 1-4, **Germany GDR**
Bruder Ernst J. Utermark
A church training centre working alongside specialists and parents. Individual programmes are drawn up for children, which include creative occupational therapy.

Mundo Nuevo (New World) Special School
Manuel Vega 8-38, Cuenca, **Ecuador**
Esperanca Duran de Estrella, Director
Established by the initiative of parents and the Association for the Education of Mentally Retarded People. Emphasis is placed on arts activities.

Dr Mohamed Lotfy El-Sayed
University of Helwan, Cairo, **Egypt**
The university participates in the promotion of the arts with the handicapped population in various fields, along with several other organisations. Activities include the plastic arts, role-playing and simple plays.

Théâtre Ecole Créativité
21 rue des Filles du Calvaire, 75003 Paris, **France**

This project represents a new approach to drug addiction, to give young people coming off drugs the means of reintegration through creative activity. Opened a centre run with the participation of young drug addicts who are not receiving medical treatment. The centre acts as a meeting place, a cultural centre, a support/advice unit.

Asociacion Guatemalteca de Rehabilitacion de Lisiados
6a Avenida A 36-01, Zona 11, Guatemala City, **Guatemala**
Silvia de Rivera
Aims towards the rehabilitation of physically and mentally disabled people. The support programme workshop makes artificial limbs and orthopaedic shoes for people of limited resources. Workshops in shoemaking, tailoring, dressmaking and carpentry.

Association Haitienne pour la Réhabilitation des Handicapés
St Vincent School, Petionville, **Haiti**
Sister Joan Margaret, Director
This association between a group of educational institutions for disabled students has developed arts programmes, recognising their importance as a means of self-expression and self-fulfilment.

The Hong Kong Association for the Mentally Handicapped
705 Duke of Windsor Social Service Bldg, Room 705, 15 Hennessy Road, **Hong Kong**
Debra M. N. Chow, General Secretary
Started by a group of parents, the association now runs 11 schools. They participate actively in cultural activities.

Alakendu Bodh Niketan Residential P11/4/11
CIT Scheme VII-M, VIP Road, Kankurgachi, Calcutta 700054, **India**
Dr B. N. Roy, Director
The vocational training centre includes a varied crafts programme.

Blind Boys Academy
Ramakrishna Mission, PO Narendrapur, Pin 743508, 24 Parganas, West Bengal, **India**
Blind youths train to become professional musicians. Students have been taking university exams in music.

Department of Special Education, PVDT College of Education for Women
Sir Vihaldas Vidyavihar Juha Road, Santa Cruz (W), Bombay 400 049, **India**

Dr Yashu Mehta, Head of Special Education Department
A 'Creative Ideas' training course, led by Interlink for students of the college, concentrated on a new approach to ways of communicating the creative arts to disabled students. Students now develop ideas from the course within their practical work.

Fellowship of the Physically Handicapped
FPH Bldg, Lala Lajpatrai Marg, Bombay 400 034, **India**
A. J. Joglekar, Hon. General Secretary
FPH started an industrial workshop/training centre in such skills as printing, carpentry, metalwork, bookbinding and weaving.

Manovikas Kendra (Abhinav Bharati)
11 Pretoria Street, Calcutta 700 071, **India**
Anjana Guha, Director
A school for mentally disabled children. Pre-vocational training includes sewing, embroidery, knitting, painting, carpentry and cooking. A quarterly magazine is produced to encourage children to sharpen their writing talents.

Mobile Creches Bombay
2nd Floor, Oxford House, Apollo Bunder, Bombay 400 039, **India**
Dr Indu Balagopal
Started as a response to the needs of children of migrant construction workers. Mobile Creches fit in with this nomadic lifestyle, the lifespan of each creche being the time it takes to complete a construction. Creche workers will move into any shed and turn it into a colourful schoolroom. Creative expression is encouraged. 'Lok Doot' is the theatre unit of Mobile Creches. Volunteers from the staff present shows on educational themes.

Okhla Centre for Mentally Retarded Children
Okhla Marg, New Delhi 110 025, **India**
Yasho Karan Singh, President
Following an Interlink Creative Ideas Training Course, there is an established arts centre programme of varied activities. The Theatre Action Group, a handicapped children's drama group, is open to all children in the city.

Remedial Education Assessment Counselling for the Handicapped
241 Jodhpur Park, Calcutta 700 068, **India**
REACH started a Special Child Development Centre for children who are physically or mentally handicapped or emotionally disturbed.

The Spastic Society of India
Upper Colaba Road, opp Afghan Church, Bombay 400 005, **India**
Trains young multi-handicapped people in various trades: office-file-making, woodwork, printing, textile printing and ceramics.

Angela Bragato
C SO Sebastopoli 57, 10134 Torino, **Italy**
A teacher working with children aged 3-6 years. The school employs a method of teaching through 'animation' – dramatic performance. This method is based on an extensive use of the body as a natural alternative means of communication.

Cooperative Porta Dipinta
24100 Bergamo, Via Porta Dipinta 10, **Italy**
Centre of expressive activities and support therapy for mentally ill and able-bodied. Work with clay, ceramics, graphic arts and drama.

Thika Variety Village Vocational Training Centre
Salvation Army Territorial HQ, PO Box 40575, Nairobi, **Kenya**
A vocational training centre which has a sign-writing department where young physically disabled people can learn this art.

Centro de Estudios de Psicologia Humana
Universidad Nacional Autonoma de Mexico, Mexico DF, **Mexico**
This centre is dedicated to special education. Their work is geared towards making the student self-sufficient in all areas and to stimulate creativity through art workshops.

The Pargos Group
Morelos No 128 Pte, Mazatlan, Sinaloa, **Mexico**
Teresa de Paez, Coordinator
A project which rehabilitates children and teenagers with physical disabilities. The policy of the group is to finance itself by organising collective activities undertaken by parents and members of the group. Emphasis is placed on creative activities: art, dance, music and traditional art. Art exhibitions are held twice a year and the proceeds used to buy materials.

(DOKT) Akadamie voor Edukatieve Arbeid de Jelburg
Regentesselaan 5, Postbus 249, 3704 AE Baarn, **Netherlands**
Social academy with creative therapy department.

(DOKT) Akadamie voor Edukatieve Arbeid de Kopse Hof
Hugo de Grootstraat, Postbus 9029, 6500 JK Nijmegen, **Netherlands**

A training establishment for the higher education of residential workers, tutors and creative therapists in a number of fields, including music.

Akademie voor Expressie Door Woorden en Gebaar
Postbus 407, 3500 AK Utrecht, **Netherlands**
Joseph Nothuis
The Academy for Expression by Word and Gesture is a teachers' college offering students a four-year programme in which they are trained as professional dramatists, specialising in the creative handling of drama and audiovisual media and working with the deaf.

Aktiviteitencentrum Wychen
Huisstede 14-03, 6606 HA Wychen, **Netherlands**
A project for people with physical handicaps. Participants follow individually devised activity programmes including art, crafts, drama, music, wheelchair dancing and rhythm.

Nederlandse Vereniging voor Kreatieve Therapie
Centraal Sekretariaat NVKT, Postbus 236, 1200 AE Hilversum, Postgiro 2144180, **Netherlands**
J. Boomsluiter
The association is divided into three sections: art therapy, drama therapy and music therapy.

Sterrenberg
Amersfootseweg 56, 3712 BE Huis ter Heide, **Netherlands**
A community of mentally disabled adults. A programme 'Creativity Development' allows students to work with professional artists, choosing their own art form. Apart from enriching the quality of life for the residents, projects like this are invaluable to all those working with disabled students. A slide and video presentation of the artists and their work is available.

Stichtung Artistieke Schuit
Kreaftif Centrum voor 'S Hertogenbosch ED,
St Joristraat 133, 'S Hertogenbosch, **Netherlands**
An establishment for mentally disabled people whose staff are all trained in arts and media, film, video, theatre or puppetry. The students do all the work as well as the research.

Werkenrode
Nijmesgen 9, 6561 ke Groesbeek, **Netherlands**

A national residental centre open to young physically handicapped people between 16 and 25 from all over the Netherlands. In addition to training it provides a full programme of leisure activities including the arts.

Centro Rehabilitacion Gaspar Garcia Laviana
INSSBI, Aptdo Postal No 1649, Managua, **Nicaragua**
Maria Auxilladora de Perez Alonso
Set up in response to the numbers of people wounded or disabled in the fighting and thus open to all political factions. As part of a wide programme of rehabilitation the centre runs an art workshop.

Asociacion Talleres Protegidos Monterrico
Urb El Vivero, Manz, B, Lote 2, Surco, Lima, **Peru**
Vilma Cavero de Castro
Offers training and work opportunities to young people over 14 with a mental or physical handicap. There are workshops in cooking, confectionery, weaving, dressmaking and carpentry.

Centro de Rehabilitacion para Ciegos de Lima 'Cercil'
Avenida Pardo 669, Lima 18, **Peru**
Fernando Barrenechea
The Rehabilitation Centre for Blind People combines skills training in factory work and programmes of vocational guidance and job allocation.

Centro de Rehabilitacion Profesional
Industrias Peruanas de Buena Voluntad, Manuel Miota no 247, San Antonio, Miraflores, Lima, **Peru**
Emilia Ramond Tejada, Executive Director
Private charitable institution with the aim of rehabilitating the physically and mentally disabled. They take anyone over the age of 15. Training includes arts and crafts programmes.

Departamento de Educacion Inicial y Especial
Ministerio de Educacion, Parque Universitario, Lima, **Peru**
Dra. Nelly Victoria Alva Cabanillas, Director General
Art for disabled people is coordinated by the Special Education Department. Programmes are organised through schools. Peruvian crafts and folklore are included.

Instituto de Educacion Especial Santea Magdalena Sofia Barat
Guillermo Prescott 337, San Isidro, Lima, **Peru**

An organisation whose goal is the education of children with language, learning and emotional difficulties. The Special Occupational Centre teaches bookbinding and other crafts.

Central Organisation for the Disabled
PO Box 05, Bandarawela, **Sri Lanka**
R. Senadeera Marasingha, President
A national umbrella organisation run by people with disabilities, COD has four workshops in different parts of the country. Wood-carved designs are produced which are exported. This income pays the wages of the workers with disabilities, and purchases raw materials.

Chitra Lane School for the Special Child
45/3 Chitra Lane, Colombo 5, **Sri Lanka**
Mrs Delysia Gunewardene, School Director
Lays great emphasis on providing opportunities for students to participate in arts activities. The philosophy is that the creative arts are an integral part of any educational programme.

The Disabled Are Also People
Foundation for Disabled's Independence, PO Box 5, Bandarawela, **Sri Lanka**
R. Senadeera Marasinghe, President
For the training and rehabilitation of disabled people. Its objective is encouraging independence by offering training in various trades and crafts.

Lillhagen Centre for Education, Art and Recreation
Göteborg, **Sweden**
Eva White, Head Administrator
A psychiatric hospital where the majority of the patients attend arts courses. An imaginative project.

Goeran Muhlert
Galeasgatan 30, 421, 71 Västra, Frolunda, **Sweden**
A blind musician who teaches pre-school children. He uses his disability in the design of a number of educational games which teach the children about the problems of being blind.

SIVUS Project
Swedish National Board of Health and Welfare, Division for Services for the Handicapped, Linnegatan 87, S-106 30 Stockholm, **Sweden**
Sophian Walujo

A programme of support for mentally retarded people. Activities include a wide range of arts and crafts. A very interesting project.

La Castalie
Centre Médico-Educatif Cantonal, CH-1870 Monthey, **Switzerland**
Mme S. Reichenbach, Director
A residential and day centre for children, adolescents and young adults who are severely mentally or multi-handicapped. There is therapy, including music therapy. It encourages the broadening of ideas, individual choice and creativity.

Special Education Division
Dept of General Education, Ministry of Education, Bangkok 10300, **Thailand**
There are special education programmes for groups of children with special needs. In the programme for the deaf, emphasis is put on vocational skills such as dressmaking, weaving, typing, hairdressing and woodwork. At present there are no post-secondary education programmes for the disabled. Thailand welcomes technical assistance from developed countries in the form of fellowships for training and study tours.

Buckhaven Parish Church Agency
St Michael's House, East Lawrence Street, Buckhaven KY8 1BQ, Scotland, **UK**
Members of the church have tackled some of the problems of local unemployment by converting two former church buildings into places that provide facilities for a wide range of creative/community projects, in all employing more than 500 people. Craft workshops include candle-making, bookbinding, painting, carpentry, costume and theatre design.

Lupus Street Mental Health Centre
66 Lupus Street, London SW1, **UK**
The philosophy behind this drop-in centre is that mental and physical well-being concerns us all, not just those who have problems at a particular time. There is a workshop, and counselling and meeting rooms. Regular workshops are held on music, gardening, woodwork, sports, drama and dance, photography.

The Mill
Oxford Mental Health Association, 125 Walton Street, Oxford, **UK**
Jane Hope, Day Care Development Officer

This community centre for young people suffering chronic mental illness is a place where they can meet in a relaxed atmosphere and participate in creative activities and in running the centre.

The Old Brewery
Culm Valley Activities Centre, High Street, Uffculme, Cullompton, Devon, **UK**
In a converted six-floor building, with fully equipped woodwork and metalwork workshops, a sewing room, pottery workshop, darkroom, artroom and handicrafts space. The centre also liaises with homes for the mentally handicapped and community psychiatric services.

Project Fullemploy
120 Clerkenwell Workshops, 31 Clerkenwell Close, London EC1, **UK**
There are nine 'Fullemploy' schemes in the UK. This one is unique in that it is concerned with training for self-employment. The project takes people who are motivated and have a skill or an idea that can be turned into self-employment – anything from picture framing, jewellery, sign-writing, to fashion design. The course is full time, running for 15 weeks, after which there is an optional 3-month day-release course. Students return for one day each week to seek advice on practical problems encountered in their new business.

Stamford Secure Unit
206 Goldhawk Road, London W12, **UK**
Stamford House is a remand and assessment unit in West London. Workshop activities have been held in conjunction with the local Riverside Arts Centre. The boys attend two sessions a week. One is a theatre workshop, the other is devoted to specialist sessions with visiting artists.

Upper Springland Flats for the Physically Handicapped
Isla Road, Perth PH2 7HQ, Scotland, **UK**
24 flatlets for adults with cerebral palsy. The new recreation centre includes a specially designed theatre. Drama in its widest application is practised.

Gallaudet College
Kendall Green, Washington DC 20002, **USA**
A college for people with hearing difficulties. Activities include a travelling modern dance group which tours worldwide and the Deaf Awareness Troupe, who perform in American sign language.

Grandparent 'Read to Me'
1470 Victoria, Lakewood, Ohio 44107, **USA**
The programme combines the needs of senior citizens and pre-school children, in which local volunteers read to children with delayed development on a one-to-one basis. It has benefited both age groups for there has been an increase in interest and development among the children.

The Interrelated Arts Program
1258 Greenly Drive, Silver Spring, Maryland 20906, **USA**
The programme is working on projects using all art forms with all kinds of children, using the arts to reinforce basic skills.

Magic Movers
University of Montana School of Fine Arts, Drama/Dance Department, Fine Arts Building, Missoula, MT 59812, **USA**
Develop materials, strategies and training for parents. The programme promotes art-based activities with young children at home.

Project Projimo (Mexico)
The Hesperian Foundation, PO Box 1692, Palo Alto, CA 94302, **USA**
David Werner, Director
A rural rehabilitation programme in western Mexico run by local villagers, most of whom are disabled. The creative activities are directed towards rehabilitation and integration. Local schoolchildren helped to build a playground which is full of ideas about how to make therapy fun, like special swings for children who cannot support themselves. They educate local people by means of theatre skits performed by the workers and some of the patients.

Senior Citizens Humanities Enrichment Project
Services to Senior Citizens, Chicago Public Library,
425 North Michigan Ave, Chicago, Illinois 60611, **USA**
Jim Pletz, Coordinator
Part of the library's services to senior citizens, it is designed to provide easier access to study for elderly people.

Avepane Art Workshops
6sa Transversal no 21-7, Altamira, Caracas, **Venezuela**
In three Avepane educational institutions for the mentally retarded, interdisciplinary teams of professionals run arts workshops, conceived as educational reinforcement.

VIDEO/PHOTOGRAPHY/CINEMA/RADIO

'Ommekaar'
Belgische Radio en Televisie, A. Reyerslaan 52, 1040 Brussels, **Belgium**
'Ommekaar' ('Let's care for each other') was the title of a self-help programme on TV produced by Belgische Radio en Televisie. One programme featured a play by 5 ex-psychiatric patients.

Atelier Audiovisuel pour Jeunes en Difficulté
Association Les Amis du Centre Familial de Vitry, 1 rue de 11 Novembre, 92120 Montrouge, **France**
The association produces videos made by young people at the Centre.

Bureau de Documentation Audovisuelle sur les Handicapés (BDH)
40 rue Pascal, 75013 Paris, **France**
Jacques-Daniel Vernon
Holds information on video projects.

Crayons de Couleurs – Horus
31 rue de la Cérisale, 75004 Paris, **France**
Jacques Sapiega
One of the projects of the Association for Audiovisual Research and Creation was a film, *Horus*, made with deaf actors.

Hors les Murs [Outside the Walls]
Agences pour la Communication et l'Enseignement des Téchniques (ACET), 14 rue Edouard Lockroy, 75011 Paris, **France**
Hors les Murs is a documentary film about alternative practices in the field of psychiatric treatment.

Starcam Production
29 rue de Pont, 92200 Neuilly-sur-Seine, **France**
Umberto Vidali
Starcam have made several video documentaries around the theme of handicap and social integration, taking stories from the real lives of handicapped people who have sucessfully found a way into normal and active life. Videotapes can be bought from Starcam or rented from Laboratoire de Recherche B. Frybourg, Conservatoire National des Arts et Métiers, 292 rue Saint Martin, 75141 Paris.

Studio of Creative Video
Hospital of Saint Jean de Dieu, 290 rue de Vienne, 69009 Lyons, **France**
M. Lebesson, Animateur Audio Visuel
A small group of staff and patients (mainly psychiatric) work together using video and have produced several fictional pieces. The workshop also produces a video information magazine for the hospital.

Vidéotheque Européenne pour l'Intégration Sociale des Personnes Handicapés
Conservatoire National des Arts et Métiers, Laboratoire Brigitte Fribourg, 292 rue Saint Martin, 75141 Paris, **France**
Producing videos on the theme of disability, the Brigitte Laboratory is now working to establish an inter-European video library.

'Pathways', Path Resource Centre
6 Courtney Drive, Kingston 10, **Jamaica**
Dr M. J. Thorburn
A weekly radio programme for people with disabilities. The centre intends to reach more disabled people in Jamaica and the Caribbean, and to extend its work, which provides information, training and public education on all aspects of disability.

'Future Indicative'
Radio New Zealand, PO Box 2092, Wellington, **New Zealand**
Helen McConnochie's weekly national radio programme about disability carries interviews and features on what is happening concerning disability in New Zealand and overseas.

Disability or Capability
Valley and Vale Community Arts Ltd, Blaengarw Working Men's Hall, Blaengarw Road, Blaengarw, nr Bridgend, Mid Glamorgan, **UK**
A community video project. Once a week disabled people share a day centre with a group of mentally ill adults. The combination of varying experiences, attitudes and abilities has produced some stimulating material around the issues of disability or capability.

Liz Hare
29 Gladstone Terrace, Bulk Road, Lancaster, Lancs, **UK**
Please Leave This Gate Open is a video about working in drama with mentally handicapped people. The tape is VHS colour lasting 30 minutes and accompanied by an explanatory booklet outlining how the material can be used as a springboard for further work. Cost £20.

Interface Productions
22 Pinetree Avenue, Noctorum, Birkenhead, Merseyside
L43 9RX, **UK**
Chris Davies
A film and television company of 15 disabled and able-bodied people. It aims to produce television programmes.

Photography for the Disabled
190 Secrett House, Ham Close, Ham, Richmond, Surrey, **UK**
Arthur Scrase, President
Provides advice, instruction and adapted equipment to disabled people to enable them to enjoy photography. Each year a competition is held.

Self-Image Photography Project
c/o Chrisi and Sara Bailey, 144 Teg Down Meads, Winchester, **UK**
A 4-week project for young people with or without experience of photographic techniques. It looks through photographs at the way we perceive ourselves, and at the different kinds of images produced by different types of photograph.

Southern Arts Association
19 Southgate Street, Winchester, Hampshire SO23 9DQ, **UK**
Bill Dalton, Director
A project at Portsmouth College of Art and Design has given disabled and able-bodied young people a chance to be involved in film and video, photography and animation. Professionals in these fields regularly offer their expertise

Town and Country Productions
21 Cheyne Row, London SW3 5HP, **UK**
Produced a number of films and videos concerned with disabled people. The films can be hired on 16mm or video.

Viper Television
Countess of Chester Hospital, Liverpool Road,
Chester CH1 3ST, **UK**
Alan Gaunt, Production Supervisor
A cable television station based at the hospital, its policy is to provide a service for patients in the psychiatric wards by making entertaining programmes of community interest inside and outside the hospital.

Rehabfilm Directories, RIUSA
1123 Broadway, New York, NY 10010, **USA**

The film division of Rehabilitation International has produced films and videotapes covering all aspects of rehabilitation and integration of people with disabilities.

Corporation on Disabilities and Telecommunications
PO Box 27573, Los Angeles, CA 90027, **USA**
Neil Goldstein
Superfest 12 is an internationally recognised film festival in California, with films for and about people with disabilities.

Doug Blandy, School of Art
Bowling Green, Ohio, 43403-0211, **USA**
The Division of Art Education/Art Therapy at the Bowling Green State Univeristy, Ohio, has set up a programme focusing on the community-based art practice and theory. Both theory and practice are thought to encourage understanding of needs in the multicultural education. The emphasis is placed on the relationship between art and politics, art and economics, art and mental health, as well as the functions and purposes of art establishments in society. Students develop sensitivity to the values of particular communities and learn to recognise, encourage and expand those values. One of the more successful methods to achieve such an understanding is through the use of social documentary photography.

ART THERAPY TRAINING COURSES

A.K.T. Forum
Volkarstrasse 16, 8000 Munich, **Germany FRG**
4-year part-time course leading to a diploma in art therapy.

Dartington College of Arts
Totnes, Devon TQ9 6EJ, **UK**
Diploma in higher education – art and design in social contexts. 2-year degree course.

Hertfordshire College of Art & Design
Division of Art and Psychology, 7 Hatfield Rd, St. Albans, Hertfordshire AL1 3RS, **UK**
Postgraduate diploma in art therapy.

University of London Goldsmiths' College
Art Therapy Unit, 27 Albury Street, London SE8 3PT, **UK**
Postgraduate diploma in art therapy. 1 year full-time. 2 years part-time.

Art Therapy Program
Vermont College, Norwich University, Montpelier, VT 05602, **USA**
A 15-month Master of Arts in art therapy course.

The George Washington University
Graduate School of Arts & Sciences, 801 22nd Street NW, Washington, DC 20052, **USA**
2-year full-time Master of Arts degree in art therapy.

Loyola Marymount University
Graduate Division, Loyola Blvd. at W 80th Street, Los Angeles, California 90045, **USA**
2-year full-time course leading to a Master of Arts degree in clinical art therapy.

New York University
Dept of Art & Art Education, 735 East Building, 239 Greene Street, New York, NY 10003, **USA**
1-year master degree in art therapy.

ORGANISATIONS FOR INFORMATION ON ART THERAPY TRAINING

The Alberta Arts Therapy Association
Box 957, Station G, Calgary, Alberta T3A 3G2, **Canada**

International Society for Art, Creation, Therapy
c/o Abteilung fur Arbeits u. Sozialhygiene Klinikum der Universitat Heidelberg Im Neuenheimerfeld 368, 6900 Heidelberg 1, **Germany FRG**

Israel Association for Creative Art in Therapy
32 Hatayassin Street, Jerusalem, **Israel**

The Norwegian Art Therapy Association
Osthelinga 23, 1370 Asker, **Norway**

Scandinavksa Institutet Uttryckande Konst
Linneg. 23, 413 04 Goteborg, **Sweden**

British Association of Art Therapists
13c Northwood Road, London N6 5TL, **UK**

American Art Therapy Association
4822 South 9th, Apt. C-Z, Arlington, Virginia 22206, **USA**

GENERAL CREATIVE THERAPIES TRAINING COURSES

Aboriginal Training and Cultural Institute
14 Jane Street, Balmain, NSW 2041, **Australia**
Training community programmes in art and management.

Cumberland College Foundation Limited
PO Box 170, East Street, Lidcombe, NSW 2141, **Australia**

Lebenshielfe Wien Gesellschaft fur Entwicklungs Behinderte
Ebendorferstrasse 10, 1010 Vienna, **Austria**

Cemea
12 Rue Monthyon BP 1112, 97482 Saint Denis, Ile de la Reunion, **France**

The Israeli Association of Creative and Expressive Art Therapies (ICET)
32 Hatyassim Street, Jerusalem 92509, **Israel**

De Jelburg Instelling voor Hoger Beroepsonderwijs
r. van Rozenburglaan 4, Postbus 249, 3740 AE Baarn, **Netherlands**
Diploma in Creative Education/Social and Cultural Studies.

Nederlandse Vereniging voor Kreatieve Therapie
Central Sekretariaat NVKT, Postbus 236, 1200 AE Hilversum;
Nederlandse Vereniging voor Kreatieve Therapie,
Sektie Muziektherapie, Kastanjelaan 36, 1214 LJ Hilversum, **Netherlands**

Social Pedagogische Opleidingen Middeloo
Hooglanseweg, 3813 Amersfoort, **Netherlands**
Diploma full-time course in Creative Therapy

Arts and Disabled People: A European Training Initiative
Hertfordshire College of Art & Design, Division of Arts & Psychology, 7 Hatfield Road, St Albans, Herts AL1 3RS, **UK**
Postgraduate courses in Art Therapy and Drama Therapy for EEC residents. Scholarships available.

Edgar Wood Centre
Faculty of Art & Design, Manchester Polytechnic, Daisy Bank Road, Manchester M14 5GH, **UK**
1 year full-time or 2 years part-time course leading to a Certificate in Recreational Arts for the Community.

Hahnemann University Graduate School
The Creative Arts in Therapy Program, Broad & Vine Streets, Philadelphia, PA 19102 – 1192, **USA**
2-year programme leading to a Master of Creative Arts in Therapy Degree.

Lesley College Graduate School
Institute for the Arts and Human Development Division, 29 Everett Street, Cambridge, MA 02238, **USA**
Postgraduate 1-year MA course in areas related to the arts in education.

National Educational Council of Creative Therapies (NECCT)
20 Rip Road, Hanover, New Hampshire 03755 1699, **USA**

University of Louisville
Expressive Therapies Dept., Louisville, Kentucky 40292, **USA**
2-year programme in Expressive Therapies leading to MA. Students can specialise in visual art, music, drama, dance, puppetry.

DANCE THERAPY TRAINING COURSES

Nalanda Dance Research Centre
Plot A-7/1, NS Road no 10, JVPD Scheme, Vile Parle (West), Bombay, **India**
Research and propagation of Indian Classical Dance. BA, MA, PhD courses in Dance. (See also under Dance.)

Dance in the Community
The Laban Centre for Movement and Dance, University of London, Goldsmiths' College, London SE14 6NW, **UK**
1-year full-time course. 2-year part-time leading to the Laban Centre Certificate.

Dance-Special Education
The Laban Centre for Movement and Dance, University of London, Goldsmiths' College, London, SE14 6NW, **UK**

The Laban Centre for Movement and Dance:
University of London, Goldsmiths' College, London SE14 6NW, **UK**

University of Surrey
Dance Studies Office, Guildford, Surrey GU2 5XH, **UK**
4-year course leading to BA (Hons) Degree in Dance in Society.

Antioch/New England Graduate School
Rosbury Street, Keene, New Hampshire 03431, **USA**
2-year full-time training graduating as qualified Dance Therapist.

Colombia College, Chicago
600 South Michigan Ave, Chicago, IL 60605-1996, **USA**
MA programme in Dance Therapy, 2 years.

Dance Centre of Colombia College
4730 North Sheridan Road, Chicago, IL 60640, **USA**
4-year BA degree in the Fine, Performing and Media arts, majoring in Dance.

Hunter College
City University of New York, Dept. of Health & Physical Education, Dance Therapy Masters Program, 440 East 26th Street, New York 10010, **USA**
2-year Master's programme in Dance Therapy.

DRAMA THERAPY COURSES

Hand Dance Studios
R.R. #5 S-11 C-16, Kelowna, BC VIX 4K4, **Canada**

Hertfordshire College of Art & Design
7 Hatfield Road, St Albans, Herts AL1 3RS, **UK**
2-year part-time course for those employed in a therapeutic institution.

The Rose Bruford College of Speech & Drama
Lamborbey Park, Sidcup, Kent DA15 9DF, **UK**
3-year diploma course in Community Theatre Arts.

Kingsway-Princeton College
Dept. of Creative & Vocational Studies, Hugh Maddleton Centre, Sans Walk, Rosoman Street, London EC1R 0AS, **UK**
1-year course in Drama and Movement in Therapy leading to Kingsway-Sesame Joint Certificate.

PUPPETRY TRAINING COURSES

The Little Angel Marionette Theatre
14 Dagmar Passage, Cross Street, London N1, **UK**
Courses of different types and lengths to suit the varying needs of students.

Marionette et Therapie
14 rue Saint Benoît, 75006 Paris, **France**
Offers courses in puppetry which can result in a Diploma of Animators.

Katharina Sommer
The German Association for Therapeutic Puppetry, Parcusstrasse 13, 6100 Dramstadt, **Germany FRG**
Runs short courses (minimum 3 days with 5 consecutive seminars). Association covers general information on all aspects of this field including details of training courses in Germany.

MUSIC THERAPY TRAINING COURSES

Facultad de Musicoterapia
School of Paramedical Disciplines, San Salvador University, Buenos Aires, **Argentina**
3-year university level course leading to a certificate.

Facultad de Musicoterapia
J F Kennedy University, c/o Dr Rolando Benenzon, JF Segui 3816 1 piso, 1425 Buenos Aires, **Argentina**
Postgraduate course for physicians and psychologists.

Faculty of Music
University of Melbourne, Parkville, Victoria 3052, **Australia**
4-year programme leading to BA with additional 26 weeks' clinical training.

Hochschule fur Musik u. Darstellende Kunst
Lothringerstrasse 18, A 1037, Vienna, **Austria**
3-year full-time degree leading to a certificate.

Conservatorio Brasiliero de Musica
Av. Graca Aranha 57-12, Andar Castelo 20.0 30, Rio de Janerio, **Brazil**
4-year conservatory programme leading to a degree.

Universidad Federal de Rio Grande
Avenida Paulo Game, FN, 7 Andar Centro, Porto Allegre, Rio Grande do Sul, CEP 90000,**Brazil**
4-year degree programme at a university level.

Centrum voor Muziektherapie
I. PE. M. EM. Muinkaai 45, 9000 Gent, **Belgium**
Short courses in music therapy.

Capilano College
Music Therapy Dept., 2055 Purcell Way, North Vancouver, BC V7J 3H5, **Canada**
2-year course leading to a diploma.

University of Montreal
PO Box 6128, Station A, Montreal 83T 3J7, **Canada**

Aalborg Universitet Center Musikterapi
Fibigerstraede 5, DK 9220 Aalborg Ost, **Denmark**
3-year university programme.

University of Jyvaskyla
Music Therapy Programme, Seminaarimkatu 15, 40100 Jyvaskyla, **Finland**
5-year degree programme in music therapy.

Paul Valerie University
Musicotherapie, c/o J. M. Guiraud-Caladou, 190 Allée du Nouveau Monde, 3400 Montpellier, **France**

Université de Montpellier
UER IX 'Les Chènes Verts', Mas Prunet, Route de Laverune, 3400 Montpellier, **France**
2-year full-time course leading to university certificate in music therapy.

Université de Paris VI
UER de Musicologie, 4 Jussieu, 75230 Paris, **France**

Université de Paris VII
UER des Sciences Humaines Cliniques, Institut de Formation Permanente, 13 Rue de Santeuil, 75005 Paris, **France**
1-month full-time intensive course open to foreign therapists, taught in French and English.

Université de Paris VII
UER des Sciences Humaines Cliniques, 13 Rue de Santeuil, 75005 Paris, **France**
2-year course leading to a certificate.

Université de Saint Etienne
UER De Musicologie, 63 rue Désire Claude, 42100 St Etienne, **France**
Full-time course especially for hospital staff working in psycho-musical techniques.

Musiktherapeutische Arbeitsstatte
Arno Holzstrasse 16, 1000 Berlin 41, **Germany FRG**
4-year training course in anthroposophically oriented music.

Stattliche Hochschule fur Musik u. Darstellende Kunst
Harvestehuder Weg 12, 2000 Hamburg 13, **Germany FRG**
3-year part-time service training in musical psychology.

Universitat Witten/Herdecke
Insititute for Music Therapy, Faculty of Medicine, Beckweg 4, D-5804 Herdecke, **Germany FRG**
2-year postgraduate course. For students with completed full-time music training.

University of Cape Town
Faculty of Music, University Private Bag, Rondebosch 7700, **South Africa**
2-year course leading to the Advanced Diploma in Remedial Music. For BA holders. Offers grants.

Ecole Sociale de Musique
Musicotherpie, Saunerie 8a, 2013 Clombier, **Switzerland**
3-year one-day-a-week course based on theory and practice.

The City University Diploma Course
Nordoff-Robins Music Therapy Centre, 3 Leighton Place, London NW5 2QL, **UK**
1-year full-time course leading to diploma. Emphasis on practical work.

Dartington College of Arts
Totnes, Devon TQ9 6EJ, **UK**
Full-time course for teachers in special education.

Guildhall School of Music and Drama
Barbican, London EC2Y 8DT, **UK**
1-year postgraduate course leading to a diploma in music therapy.

Roehampton Institute of Higher Education
Roehampton Lane, London SW15 5PJ, **UK**
1-year full-time course leading to a diploma in music therapy.

Centro Para Las Artes
Fco. Solano Antuna 2923, Montevideo, **Uruguay**
3-year course leading to a title of teacher specialising in musical education or music therapy technique.

ORGANISATIONS FOR INFORMATION ON MUSIC THERAPY TRAINING

Asociacion Argentina de Musicoterapia
Cangallo 1558 1 piso, 1037 Buenos Aires, **Argentina**

Associacion Medico Argentina de Musicoterapia
Sante Fe 3380, 1425 Buenos Aires, **Argentina**

Associacion de Musicoterapeutas
Universitarios de la Republica, Guatemala 4429, 1425 Buenos Aires, **Argentina**

Australian Music Therapy Association
8 Haig Street, Deepdene, Victoria 3103, **Australia**

Australia Music Therapy Association
New South Wales Branch, 83 Bland Street, Ashfield 2131, NSW, **Australia**

Evangelische Akademie
Arnoldstein, 6384 Schmitten 1, **Austria**

Oesterichischer Berufsverbund der Musiktherapeuten
Marc-Aurelstrasse 10/8, 1010 Vienna, **Austria**

Professor A. Schmölz
Hochschule für Musik und Darstellende Kunst, Lehrgang für Musiktherapie, Lothringer Strasse 18, 1037 Vienna, **Austria**

Associcao Brasiliera de Musicoterapia
Av. Graca Aranha 57-12, Andar, Castelo, Rio de Janeiro 20.0 30, **Brazil**

Associacao de Musicoterapia de Parana
R 13 de Maio, 723 Curtiba Parana 80 000, **Brazil**

Associacao Paulista de Musicoterapia
c/o Clementina Nastari, Rua Major Margaliano 457, CEP 04017 Villa Mariana 04017, Sao Paulo, **Brazil**

Assocaicao Sul Brasiliera de Musicoterapia
Rua Senhor dos Passos 248, Porto Allegre, Rio Grande do Sol 90 000, **Brazil**

Centre Belge de Musicotherapie
Ave Paul Deschanel 101, 1030 Brussels, **Belgium**

Canadian Association for Music Therapy
Woodstock, Ontario N4S 8T6, **Canada**

Sociedad Colombiana de Musicoterapia
Carrera 19, no 72-30, Estudio de Musicoterapia, Bogota, **Colombia**

Sociedad Antoquena de Musicoterapia
c/o Dr Alberto Correa, Calle 27, no 79-147, Medellin, **Colombia**

Psychatricia Clinic: Music Therapy
c/o Dr J. Schaniclova Vodnanska Apolinarska 4, 128 00 Prague 2, **Czechoslovakia**
A clinical centre for music therapists. Publishes journals.

Claus Bang
Aalsborgskolen, Statens Specialskole, Kollegievej 1, 9000 Aalborg, **Denmark**

Dansk Forbund for Musikterapi
Kochsvej 28, 1812 Copenhagen V, **Denmark**
Temporary association publishing biannual journal.

Forbundet for Nordoff/Robbins Musikterapi
Hjerndrupvej 95, 6070 Christiansfeld, **Denmark**
Association to advance the work of Nordoff/Robbins.

Associacion Dominicana de Musicoterapia
Gral. Cambiasso Apto 2, A 300 Santo Domingo, **Dominican Republic**

Deutscher Berufsverband der Musikterapeuten
Professor Klaus Finkel-Haus, 2 Hosseringen, 3113 Suderburg, **Germany FRG**

Deutscher Berufsverband der MT
Postfach 810307, D-7000 Stuttgart 81, **Germany FRG**

Deutsche Gesselschaft fur Musikterapie
Postfach 101224, 6900 Heidelberg 1, **Germany FRG**
Association sponsors conferences, publishes journal.

Internationale Gesselschaft fur Musik in der Medizin E.V.
Sportkrankenhaus-Hellersen, D-5580 Ludenscheid, **Germany FRG**

Verein zur Forderung der Nordoff/Robbins Music Therapie
Beckweg 4, 5804 Herdécke, **Germany FRG**
Promotes Nordoff/Robbins therapy and supports training.

Finnish Art Therapy Union
c/o Pekka Halonen, Viialantie 10, 33700 Tampere 70, **Finland**
Association for art therapies.

Finnish Association for Music Therapy
c/o Mr Juha Nummelin, Jokelan Pannkitalo, 05400 Jokela, **Finland**
National association, sponsors conferences, publishes journal.

Association de Recherches et d'Application des Techniques Psychomusicales du Centre International de Musicotherapie
73 rue Curial, Batiment C, 75019 Paris, **France**
Insititute and clinic sponsors group therapy and seminars, publishes reports.

Association Française de Musicotherapie
40 rue de Provence, 75009 Paris, **France**
National association, sponsors world conferences, publishes journal.

Atelier de Musicotherapie de Bordeaux
45 rue de Général de Gaulle, Parempuyre, F 33920 Blanquefort, **France**
Regional association, sponsors conferences.

Societa Italiana di Musicoterapia
Via Capo d'Africa 44, 00184 Rome, **Italy**
National society sponsors conferences and training.

Assoziazione Italiana Studi di Musicoterapia (AISM)
Via Caffaro 21-32, 16129 Genoa, **Italy**

Assoziazione Sportiva-Ontomusic
Via Baldo degli Ubaldi 147a, 00167 Rome, **Italy**
Association devoted to ontopsychology, sponsors conferences, publishes journal.

Japan Society for the Study of Music Therapy
c/o Dr Tadafumi Yamamatsu, Ohtemon Gakuin University, Faculty of Letters, Dept. of Psychology, 1-1-15 Nishi-Ai, Ibaraka City, Osaka Pref., **Japan**

Japanese Association for Music Psychology and Therapy
Musashino Academia Musicae, Hazawa 1-13, Nerima-Ku, Tokyo 176, **Japan**

New Zealand Society for Music Therapy
c/o 167 Wadestown Road, Wellington, **New Zealand**
National association, sponsors annual conference, publishes journal, raises funds for research.

International Society for Music Education
School of Music, University of Canterbury, Private Bag, Christchurch 1, **New Zealand**

International Association for Vibro-Acoustic Therapy
N-9072 Birtavarre, **Norway**

Norsk Forening for Musikterapi
c/o Gladengveien 8-10, Oslo 6, **Norway**
National Association, publishes journal.

Associacao Portugesa de Educao Musical
Rua Rosa Araujo 6-3, 1200 Lisbon, **Portugal**
Music education association, publishes journal.

Asociacion Puertorriquena de Musicoterapia
PO Box 1448, Hato Rey, **Puerto Rico**
Sponsors conferences.

Music Therapy Society of South Africa
PO Box 57, Newlands 7725, **South Africa**

South African Institute of Music Therapy
PO Box 1661, Port Elizabeth 6000, **South Africa**

Associaciao Catalana de Musicoterapia
Av Diagonal 408, 70, 1a, 08037 Barcelona, **Spain**

Svenska Förbundet für Musikterapi
c/o Kungliga Musikaliska Akademien, Blasieholmstorg 8, 111 48 Stockholm, **Sweden;** Djaknetatan 16, S-72215 Vasteras, **Sweden**

Schweizerischer Fachverband fur Musik Therapie (SFMT)
Association Professionelle Suisse de Musicotherapie (ASMT), CH-Marsens VD 1633, **Switzerland**

Association of Professional Music Therapists in Great Britain (APMT)
c/o Music Therapy Dept, Harperbury Hospital, Shenley, Radlett, Herts, **UK**
Sponsors meetings and seminars, publishes quarterly newsletter.

British Society for Music Therapy
Guildhall School of Music & Drama, Barbican, London EC2Y 8DT, **UK**

Orff Society
31 Roedean Crescent, London SW15 5JX, **UK**

Orff-Schulwerk Association of New South Wales
PO Box 225, Strathfield, NSW 2135, **Australia**

Musicierende Jeugd Orff-Association Vlanderen-Belgie
Oude Brüsselsweg 284, B-9219 Gent, **Belgium**

Music for Children, Carl Orff Canada
Faculty of Music, University of Toronto, Edward Johnson Building, Toronto, Ontario M521A1, **Canada**

Association Orff de la Région Parisienne,
2 rue Thiers, F-94500 Campigny sur Marne, **France**

Orff-Schulwerk Association
c/o Polyxene Mathéy, Dimocharous 27, Athens 601, **Greece**

Stichtung Orff-Werkgroep Nederland
Koornmarkt 10, Delft 1, **Holland**

Societa Italiana di Musica Elementare
Via Biondella 1/A, I-37100 Verona, **Italy**

Astrid de nino musical 'Carl Orff'
S. de. R.L., Picacho 103, Pedregalde San Angel, **Mexico**

Orff-Schulwerk Association of Southern Africa
Dawn Drive, Northcliff View, Johannesburg 58, **South Africa**

Orff-Schulwerk Gesellschaft,
Waldheimstrasse 63, CH-6314 Unterägeri, **Switzerland**

Orff-Schulwerk Society of England
31 Roedean Crescent, London SW15 5JX, **UK**

American Orff-Schulwerk Association (AOSA)
Cleveland State University, Department of Music, Cleveland, Ohio 44115, **USA**

American Association for Music Therapy
66 Morris Ave, PO Box 359, Springfield, NJ 07081, **USA**

Certification Board for Music Therapists
1133 15th Street, NW, Suite 1000, Washington, DC 20005, **USA**

National Coalition of Arts Therapy Associations (NCATA)
655 15th Street, NW, Suite 300, Washington, DC 20005, **USA**

National Association for Music Therapy Inc.
505 Eleventh St, SE, Washington, DC 20003, **USA**

Asociacion Uruguaya de Musicoterapia
Libertad 2879/103, Montevideo, **Uruguay**

Association for Promotion of Music Therapy
c/o Dr Darko Breitenfeld, Utjesinoviceva 4a, YU 4100 Zagreb, **Yugoslavia**

EXPORT CONTACTS FOR HANDICRAFTS

ALTERNATIVE TRADING ORGANISATIONS

A number of trading organisations have been set up specifically to sell products from developing countries. They differ generally from profit-maximising commercial importers in the following ways:

They give priority to small producers who find it difficult to undertake export trade without a sympathetic marketing partner.

They are especially interested in the organisational structure of the producer, preferring groups which offer equal remuneration to members, and other benefits such as educational or welfare schemes. They do not usually trade with privately owned companies.

They pay fair prices which allow the producer a reasonable return, and will often give advance payments on orders.

They build their ranges around products made by producers whom they want to support.

They promote their suppliers amongst their customers, giving information about the project, the locality, and the difficulties faced by small producers.

They aim to provide producers with information on overseas market requirements and assist with matters such as design, technology, packaging, labelling and sales promotion.

Action for World Development
112a Gays Arcade, Adelaide, SA 5000, **Australia**
Products imported: foodstuffs. Sales outlets: establishing a cooperative Third World shop.

International Handicrafts
22 Renaissance Arcade, Adelaide, SA 5000, **Australia**
Division of Community Aid Abroad.

Trading Partners (AUST) Ltd
39 Pyrmont Street, Pyrmont 2009, **Australia**
Products imported: handicrafts. Sales outlets: through local groups and representatives; and on wholesale basis. Remarks: non-profit making organisation aiming to support the effort of self-help groups to improve their living conditions by marketing their products.

World Vision International Clubs
161 Stivet Street, Box 339c, Melbourne, **Australia**

Caritas Wien
Wachringergoertel 104, PO Box 63, Vienna 4, **Austria**

EZA (Entwicklungszusammenarbert mit der Dritten Welt Gesellschaft mbH)
Lengfelden 169, PO Box 74, 5101 Bergheim, Salzburg, **Austria**

Les Magasins du Monde Oxfam
rue de la Caserne 74, 1000 Brussels, **Belgium**
Sales outlets: about 40 shops.

Oxfam-Wereldwinkels V zw
National Sekretariat, Burggravenlaan 62, 9000 Gent, **Belgium**
Products imported: foodstuffs. Sales outlets: coordinating office for about 80 'world shops' in the Flemish part of Belgium.

SOS-Wereldhandel
Blijde Inkomstraat 14, B 3000 Leuven, **Belgium**
Subsidiary to SOS Wereldhandel, Holland.

Bridgehead Trading
54 Jackman Avenue, Toronto, Ontario M4K 2X5, **Canada**

Caravan – World Unversity Service of Canada
PO Box 3000, Station C, Ottawa, Ontario, **Canada**
Products imported: handicrafts. Remarks: incorporated as a non-profit organisation.

Self Help Crafts (Canada)
PO Box 869, 175 Waterloo Street, New Hamburg, Ontario NOB 2GO, **Canada**

Oversoeisk
Kurve Import A-S, Nyager 3, 2660 Gloslrup, **Denmark**

The Developing Countries Foundation of 1962
Arjus Statsgymnasium, PO Box 1290, Fenrisvej 33, 8210 Arhus V, **Denmark**
Products imported: handicrafts. Remarks: seeks to promote projects in developing countries by contact with groups in Denmark and distribution of information and educational material.

The Swallows in Denmark
Osterbrogade 49, DK-2100 Copenhagen, **Denmark**
Products imported: handicrafts; foodstuffs.

Aktion Partnerschaft Dritte Welt e.v.
Postfach Neuburgweier, Otto - Worner - Strasse 7, D7512 Rheunstetten 3, **Germany FRG**
Products imported: handicrafts; foodstuffs.

Deutsches Aussatzigen – Hilfswerk e.v.
Aktionszentrale Nord West, Osthofenstrabe 18, Postfach 112, D-4770 Soest, **Germany FRG**
German Leprosy Relief Association.

Deutsche Kalkutta Gruppe
Forderkreis Kalkutta e.v., c/o Karin Nitschke, Solberweg 73, 4600 Dortmund 50,**Germany FRG**
Remarks: market products from craft cooperatives in Calcutta.

Dritte Welt Laden e.v.
PO Box 1661, D-4500 Osnabruck, **Germany FRG**
Products imported: handicrafts; foodstuffs. Sales outlets: publish own mail order catalogue. Own shop at Osnabruck and wholesale through alternative shops, action groups, health food stores. Remarks: longest established AMO in Germany, founded 1970. Profits used for re-investment in Third World development.

DW Shop
Hermannstrasse 63, 5300 Bonn 3, **Germany FRG**
Products imported: handicrafts; foodstuffs.

GEPA mbH
Talstrasse 20, D-5830 Schwelm, **Germany FRG**
Products imported: handicrafts; foodstuffs.

The Swallows of North Finland
Aleksanterink ATU 21, 90100 Oulu 10, **Finland**

Féderation des Artisans du Monde
20 rue Rochechouart, 75009 Paris, **France**
Products imported: handicrafts; foodstuffs. Sales outlets: 27 shops throughout France, which buy independently.

1 3 Stanzoni s.r.l.
Via Cavenaghi 6, 20149 Milan, **Italy**
Products imported: handicrafts.

Help Bangladesh Committee
c/o Waseda houhien, 2-3-1 Nishiwaseda, Shinjuku-ku, Tokyo, **Japan**
Remarks: buys only from Bangladesh.

Refugees International – Japan
c/o Shell Sekiyu KK, CPO Box 1239, **Japan**
Remarks: markets crafts from refugee projects only.

Inter-Church Development Education Foundation
Esdoornlaan 10, Nijkerk, **Netherlands**
Products imported: foodstuffs.

Novib
5-7 Amaliastaat, 2514 J C The Hague, **Netherlands**

SOS Wereldhandel
PO Box 25, Holzstraat 19, 6461 Kerkrade, **Netherlands**
Products imported: handicrafts; foodstuffs. Sales outlets: own shops in four towns in Holland, sells tò other organisations through own branches in Holland and Belgium.. Remarks: established in 1959 as funding agency, and engaged in trade since 1967. Provides information service about products and projects.

Stichting Ideele Import
Keizersgracht 240, 1016 EV Amsterdam, **Netherlands**
Products imported: mainly foodstuffs; a few handicrafts. Sales outlets: wholesale. Remarks: non-profit organisation founded in 1976. Also offers advisory service and arranging supplies of equipment to projects.

Stichting Tear-Craft
Industrieweg Noord 6, 3958 VY Amerongen, **Netherlands**

Tearfund
Postbus 80, 3958 zv Amerongen, **Netherlands**
Products imported: handicrafts.

Trade Aid (NZ) Inc.
PO Box 18620, Christchurch, **New Zealand**
Products imported: handicrafts.

Alternativ Handel
Uranienborgvn 29, Oslo 2, **Norway**

A/S San-Te-Bo Import of Handicrafts
PB 6811, St Olavs Plass, N-Oslo 1, **Norway**

Tanzania Import A/S
Postboks 9564 – Egertorget, Tollbuganten 28, Oslo 1 **Norway**

Afro-Art Foundation
Drottninggatan 12, 11151 Stockholm,**Sweden**
Products imported: handicrafts.

Alternativ Handel AB
C/o U-gruppen, Majorsgatan 3, 41308 Goteberg, **Sweden**
Products imported: handicrafts; foodstuffs.

Handelsfront
Hollandargartan 9A, S-111 36 Stockholm, **Sweden**
Products imported: handicrafts; foodstuffs.

Solidarisk Handel
Kungsstengatan 27, S-113 57 Stockholm, **Sweden**
Products imported: foodstuffs; art and gramophone records (S.R. Vietnam).

Swallows in Sweden
Spolegatan 5, S-22220 Lund, **Sweden**
Sales outlets: own shop; also sell through regional volunteers.

Swedish Free Church Aid
Alvsjo Gardsvag 3, S-125 30 Alvsjo, **Sweden**

Swedish Trust for Trade with Developing Countries
Ostermalmstorg 2, Stockholm, **Sweden**
Products imported: handicrafts.

Tanzania Import Ekonomisk Forening
Box 6022, 580 06 Linkoping, **Sweden**
Products imported: from Tanzania only.

OS 3
rue de la Gare 17, CH-2605 Sonceboz, **Switzerland**
Products imported: handicrafts; foodstuffs. Remarks: offers information and research services.

Zentrallager fur Kunsthandwerkliche Gegenstande aus Eubersee
Basel Mission, Missionstrasse 21, 4003 Basel, **Switzerland**
Products imported: handicrafts.

Schweizerische Caritas
Fairness Shop, Lowenstrasse 3, CH-6002 Luzern, **Switzerland.**
Sales outlets: own retail shops.

One Village
Charlbury, Oxford OX7 3SQ, **UK**
Products imported: handicrafts; foodstuffs. Sales outlets: own shop.

Oxfam Trading
Murdock Road, Bicester OX6 7RF Oxon, **UK**
Products imported: handicrafts; foodstuffs. Sales outlets: own shops plus mail order. Remarks: maintain offices in India, Bangladesh and

Indonesia; offer extensive range of services through producer assistance programme and producer dividend schemes. (See next section.)

Tearcraft Limited
11 Station Road, Teddington, Middlesex, TW11 9AA, **UK**
Products imported: handicrafts. Sales outlets: Mail order catalogue.

Traidcraft
Kingsway, Gateshead NE11 0NE, **UK**
Products imported: handicrafts; foodstuffs. Sales outlets: wholesale, mail order and through regional agents.

Aid to Artisans Inc.
64 Fairgreen Place, Chestnut Hill, Mass 02167,**USA**
Products imported: handicrafts. Sales outlets: specialises in sales through museum shops. Remarks: makes small grants for materials and equipment.

Friends of the Third World Inc.
611 West Wayne Street, Fort Wayne, Indiana 46802, **USA**
Products imported: handicrafts.

International Program for Human Resource Development Inc.
PO Box 30216, Bethesda, Maryland 20014, **USA**
Products imported: handicrafts. Sales outlets: own retail shop.

Self-Help Crafts
21 South 12th Street, Akron, Pennsylvania 17501, **USA**
Products imported: handicrafts. Remarks: programme of the Mennonite Central Committee.

Save the Children Federation
48 Wilton Road, Westport, Connecticut 06880, **USA**

Serrv Self-Help Handicrafts
PO Box 365, New Windsor, Maryland 21776, **USA**
Products imported: handicrafts. Remarks: project of the World Ministries Commission of the Church of the Brethren.

United Nations Association of the United States
345 East 46th Street, New York 10017, **USA**
Remarks: head office of the UNA, which has many regional centres running gift shops.

United Nations Gift Center
UN Headquarters, New York 10017, **USA**
Remarks: markets crafts from member nations at the United Nations.

World Concern/Worldcraft
22314, 70th West no B/5, Mountlake Terrace, WA 98043, **USA**

OXFAM

HOW OXFAM TRADING WORKS

Oxfam Trading's 'Bridge' scheme serves as a link between people in developing countries who have a skill and need a buyer, and customers in more prosperous countries where there is a market for their crafts. Oxfam Trading buys from over 100 producer groups and marketing cooperatives throughout the world. Goods are sold through Oxfam's shops (800 in Great Britain), and mail order catalogues which are issued twice a year. 'Bridge' is a non-profit making scheme; a fair price is paid for products, and the net profits from their sale are returned to the producers as dividends for the improvement of community or welfare facilities. Some of the dividend is also available for expansion of the producer group's operations. As well as buying from producer groups, Oxfam Trading may be able to assist producers to develop sales of their goods to their local markets and to other export markets, and it strongly encourages them not to become reliant on its own purchases.

OXFAM'S BUYING POLICY

Almost all of the products offered for sale by Oxfam have been made by producer cooperatives or community enterprises, some of which Oxfam helped to establish. For example, the brass and woodworkers of India produce lovely goods, practical yet ornamental, and Oxfam has helped them to find a market for their craft. As it is often the women who bear the brunt of poverty; many of the goods – the sikas, baskets, planters etc are made in cooperatives where women can work, receive a living wage and sometimes medical and educational assistance. Items which are the most saleable tend to be utilitarian and functional goods. Most materials are acceptable, but some such as pottery pose problems in shipping successfully. Oxfam's main criterion in accepting goods is the necessity for good quality and design which can compete with the world market.

THE FIRST STEP

The organisation in question should contact Oxfam Trading and request one of its *Producer Contact Forms.* These are available from: The General Manager, Oxfam Trading, Murdock Road, Bicester, Oxfordshire OX6 7RF, Great Britain. They should then complete and return this, giving as many details about themselves, their products and the objectives of the organisation as possible. The more comprehensive the information is, the better will Oxfam Trading understand the producer's circumstances, and be able to help them.

SAMPLES

If Oxfam Trading is able to assist the organisation by purchasing its products, it will ask for samples to be sent to them. All samples should be securely labelled with the name of the producing organisation, the product description, any reference number used by the producer, and the quantity that could be produced per month. The FOB (Free on Board) price of the product should also be sent with the sample. This will include the cost of delivery as far as placing the goods on board a ship in the producer's country. From then on all shipping costs will be met by Oxfam Trading.

PRODUCT SELECTION AND ORDERING

On receipt of samples, Oxfam Trading will acknowledge their arrival. The next stage can be lengthy as the samples then go before a Product Selection Committee, but Oxfam Trading aims to respond to the producer within 8-10 weeks. All products will go to this stage but there is no guarantee that any product will be selected. Oxfam Trading may ask for slight changes to the product, or suggest a different product that could be made by the producer, in which case a new sample will be requested. If a product is selected, the Oxfam Trading will send its official Purchase Order for the quantity required. A copy of this should be completed and returned by the producer as an acknowledgement of the order. Goods can *only* be accepted by Oxfam Trading against its official Purchase Order.

PRICING

Oxfam Trading does not negotiate prices and will only accept or decline the price offered by the producer. If the price of a product has changed between the time of submitting the sample and receiving an order, the producer should advise Oxfam Trading when acknowledging the order and wait for their acceptance of the new price before proceeding with it.

DEADLINES

Oxfam Trading tries to give producers as long as possible to supply goods. However, deadlines are particularly important if the product is required for the Christmas season (September-December) or for the mail order catalogues. If the required delivery date shown on the order cannot be met, Oxfam Trading should be advised immediately.

TRADE PROMOTION OFFICES

Many countries have a government office which can provide information and further contact for marketing in their country. They are not themselves trading organisations, and do not necessarily give special priority to non-private producer groups. They can provide useful assistance especially regarding the straightforward commercial market. A list is printed at the end of this section.

SOME OF THE COUNTRIES WHERE OXFAM TRADING IS ACTIVE

Bangladesh; Brazil; Burma; Ecuador; Grenada; Haiti; India; Indonesia; Jamaica; Kenya; Madagascar; Mexico; Pakistan; Peru; Philippines; Rwanda; Singapore; Sri Lanka; Tanzania; Upper Volta; Thailand; Vietnam; Zimbabwe.

TRADE PROMOTION OFFICES

Australia
Trade Relations & Markets Division, Department of Trade & Resources, Edmund Barton Office, King's Avenue, Canberra ACT 2600.

Austria
Foreign Trade Promotions, Federal Chamber of Commerce & Industry, Stubenring 12, A-1010 Vienna.

Belgium
Belgian Office for Foreign Trade, 162 Blvd Emile Jacqmain, B-1000, Brussels.

Canada
Trade Facilitation Office (CESO), 200 Promenade du portage, Hull, Quebec K1A 0G4.

Finland
Development Corporation Programme, Helsinki School of Economics, Lapuankatu 4, SF-00100 Helsinki 10.
The Finnish Foreign Trade Association, Information Centre, PO Box 908, SF-0010 Helsinki 10.

France
Office of Foreign Exports, Centre Français du Commerce, Exterieur (CFCE), 10 Avenue d'Iena, F-75783 Paris Cedex 16

Germany DRG
Chamber of Foreign Trade, Schadowstrasse 1, PO Box 12729, DDR-1080 Berlin.

Germany FRG
Federal Foreign Trade Information Office, Blauback 13, PO Box 108007, D-5000 Cologne 1

Hungary
Hungarian Chamber of Commerce, Kossuth Ter 6-8, PO Box 106, H-1389 Budapest

Israel
Israel Centre for Trade Chamber of Commerce, 84 Hachasmonaim Street, PO Box 20027, 61200 Tel-Aviv

Italy
CROI, National Institute for Foreign Trade, Via Liszt 21, PO Box 10057, I-10010 Rome-EUR

Japan
JETRO, 2-5-Toranomon 2-chome, Minato-ku, Tokyo 105

Netherlands
CBI, Coolsingel 58, PO Box 30009, NL-3001 DA Rotterdam.

New Zealand
Developing Countries Liaison Unit, Department of Trade and Industry, Bowen State Building, Bowen Street, Wellington.

Norway

Norwegian Import Promotion Office for Products from Developing Countries, Klingenberggaten 4, PO Box 8147 Dep, N-Oslo 1.

Sweden

IMPOD, Norrmalmstorg 1, PO Box 7508, S-10392 Stockholm.

Switzerland

OSEC, Avenue de 1 Avantposte, CH-1001 Lausanne

USSR

Foreign Relations Department, USSR Chamber of Commerce and Industry, 6 Kuibysheva, PO Box 103.684, 103012 Moscow

United Kingdom

UK Trade Agency, c/o London Chamber of Commerce & Industry, 69 Cannon Street, London, EC4N 5AB

About the Contributors

Dick Allwood began his professional career in 1960 as a teacher of music and drama in schools. He quickly became head of a creative arts department in a comprehensive school and during this period was very active in the theatre in a semi-professional capacity, as an actor, musician and director. He gave up teaching eventually to concentrate full time on bringing theatre to young people by becoming a member of a professional Theatre in Education company. In the last ten years he has worked as an actor, musical director and workshop director in addition to running his own professional touring theatre company for four years. He is presently working as a music and drama workshop organiser in various hospitals, day centres, prisons, and other centres where people do not normally have the chance to join in a creative activity.

Gerard Benson was born in London in 1931. He dropped out of university and spent several years as an actor before training at the Central School of Speech and Drama as a teacher. He taught drama for a while in schools and then became a full-time lecturer at the Central School. Concurrently with all this he persistently wrote poetry – and over the years has had much poetry published, and some prose. In 1960 he joined the Barrow Poets, with which troupe of clown-poet-minstrels he has performed extensively, in Great Britain and Ireland, in Germany and Holland, in Canada and the United States. He is an experienced broadcaster of both drama and poetry, also as a singer. Over the past eight years he has run many writers' workshops with groups of all kinds.

Pat Brennan was trained as teacher of young children, specialising in art and craft. In 1973 she was the first woman and first primary school teacher to graduate as Member of the College of Craft Education. She is a freelance, full-time teacher of puppetry at all levels from pre-school to university, working with associations for disadvantaged people. She is a member of UNIMA, BMTPG and Puppeteers of America.

Liz Faunce was born in Plymouth in 1957 and educated there. She trained in Fine Art at Manchester Polytechnic and in 1978, after several mural projects, joined Hospital Arts – Manchester as an artist. She has worked with and coordinated projects with all age groups. In 1983/4 she was involved in art work for one year in Greece and India and has recently run an Interlink 'Arts Ideas' project in Sri Lanka. She also plays the saxophone and her projects with patients often combine art and music.

Peter Senior is Senior Lecturer in Art and Design at Manchester Polytechnic and Director of Manchester Hospitals Arts. Originator of the project in 1973, he is now director of a team of some twelve people who work within the three District Health Authorities of Manchester. The project seeks ways of using the arts in all forms to complement health care. He was a member of the Attenborough Committee, which reported on the Arts and Disabled People, and the subsequent Carnegie Council; he is Director of Partnership Environmental Art Company, a trustee of North West Shape, and Arts Consultant to the DHSS for the arts provision in the Isle of Wight Health Authority.

Geoff Stow has worked in community video for the past nine years. Over that period he has been involved in making tapes with a wide range of community groups. His interest has always been to work closely with groups who would not normally be given access to equipment and expertise to make programmes on issues that are of concern to them.

Photographic Acknowledgements

pp.26-7 Format Photographers; Leon Morris; pp. 110-111 The City Lit; pp.120-1 Jack Sutton; p.154 K. Heatherley; pp.155, 154 (Stec) K. Fusmanek. Otherwise courtesy of Contributors/Interlink.